Paralegal Employment
Facts and Strategies for the 1990s
Second Edition

Paralegal Employment
Facts and Strategies for the 1990s
Second Edition

William P. Statsky

West Publishing Company

Minneapolis/St. Paul ■ New York ■ Los Angeles ■ San Francisco

Text Design: Rosyln Stendahl, Dapper Design

Composition: Parkwood Composition

Cover: Patricia Boman

WEST'S COMMITMENT TO THE ENVIRONMENT

In 1906, West Publishing Company began recycling materials
left over from the production of books. This began a tradition
of efficient and responsible use of resources. Today, up to 95
percent of our legal books and 70 percent of our college texts
are printed on recycled, acid-free stock. West also recycles
nearly 22 million pounds of scrap paper annually—the equivalent of 181,717 trees. Since the 1960s, West has devised ways
to capture and recycle waste inks, solvents, oils, and vapors
created in the printing process. We also recycle plastics of all
kinds, wood, glass, corrugated cardboard, and batteries, and
have eliminated the use of styrofoam book packaging. We at
West are proud of the longevity and the scope of our commitment to our environment.

Product, Prepress, Printing and Binding by West Publishing
Company.

Library of Congress Cataloging-In-Publication Data

Statsky, William P.
    Paralegal employment : facts and strategies for the 1990s /
William P. Statsky—2nd ed.
        p.   cm.
    Includes index.
    ISBN 0-314-01208-7 (soft)
    1. Legal assistance—Employment—United States.   I. Title.
KF320.L4S74   1993
340'.023'73—dc20   92-18131
                                                        CIP ∞

■ Also by William P. Statsky

Case Analysis and Fundamentals of Legal Writing, 3d ed. St.Paul: West Publishing Company, 1989 (with J. Wernet)

Essentials of Paralegalism, 2d ed. St. Paul: West Publishing Company, 1993

Family Law, 3d ed. St. Paul: West Publishing Company, 1991

Inmate Involvement in Prison Legal Services: Roles and Training Options for the Inmate as Paralegal. American Bar Association, Commission on Correctional Facilities and Services, 1974

Introduction to Paralegalism: Problems, Perspectives and Skills, 4th ed. St. Paul: West Publishing Company, 1992

Legal Desk Reference. St. Paul: West Publishing Co., 1991 (with B. Hussey, M. Diamond & R. Nakamura)

The Legal Paraprofessional as Advocate and Assistant: Roles, Training Concepts and Materials. Center on Social Welfare Policy and Law, 1971 (with P. Lang)

Legal Research and Writing: Some Starting Points, 4th ed. St. Paul: West Publishing Company, 1993

Legal Thesaurus/Dictionary: A Resource for the Writer and Computer Researcher. St. Paul: West Publishing Company, 1985

Legislative Analysis and Drafting, 2d ed. St. Paul: West Publishing Company, 1984

Paralegal Ethics and Regulation, 2d ed. St. Paul: West Publishing Company, 1993

Torts: Personal Injury Litigation, 2d ed. St. Paul: West Publishing Company, 1990

Rights of the Imprisoned: Cases, Materials and Directions. Indianapolis: Bobbs-Merrill Company, 1974 (with R. Singer)

What Have Paralegals Done? A Dictionary of Functions. National Paralegal Institute, 1973

For Jessica

■ Contents

▪ Preface

A paralegal is a person with legal skills who works under the supervision of an attorney or who is otherwise authorized to use those skills; this person performs tasks that do not require all the skills of an attorney and that most legal secretaries are not trained to perform. It is an exciting time to be entering this field. While competition for good jobs is keen, the potential for fulfillment in this still-developing new career makes the effort worthwhile.

Changes in the Second Edition:

- Updated statistics on employment in the private sector and in government
- Expanded data on paralegal specialties
- Quotations from paralegals on what life is like in different specialties
- Excerpts from want ads indicating what employers are looking for in a competitive market
- A glossary

Acknowledgments

Valuable guidance and suggestions were made by a very talented team in the College Division of West Publishing Company: Elizabeth Hannan, acquisitions editor; Sandy Gangelhoff, production editor; and Carrie Kish, promotion manager. In addition, the contributions of the adopters and reviewers of the first edition are gratefully acknowledged.

CHAPTER 1

Where Paralegals Work

■ Chapter Outline

 ## Section A. The Job Market

For many paralegals seeking their first job, these are difficult times. Even many attorneys are having a hard time obtaining their first job. Most employers are inundated with job applications. According to one expert, for every $10,000 in salary you hope to earn as a paralegal, you will need to set aside one month of search time. "So if you want $25,000 per year, your search should take about two and one-half months. But do not be disappointed if it takes longer."[1]

Competition for paralegal jobs is likely to come from several sources:

- Other recent graduates from paralegal training programs
- Secretaries and clerks now working in law offices who want to be promoted into paralegal positions
- Paralegals with a year or more of experience who are seeking a job change
- People with no legal training or experience who walk into an office "cold" seeking a job
- People with no legal training or experience but who have connections (a friend of an important client, a relative of a partner)
- Frustrated attorneys applying for paralegal jobs!

---

[1]Wagner, *Tips & Traps for the New Paralegal*, 8 Legal Assistant Today 78 (March/April 1991).

FIGURE 1.1   Where Do Paralegals Work and in What Percentages?

I. Traditional private law firms
   A. Small firm—1–10 lawyers (26%)
   B. Medium firm—11–50 lawyers (15%)
   C. Large firm—over 50 lawyers (30%)

II. Untraditional private law firms (3%)

III. Government
   A. Federal government (4%)
   B. State government (2%)
   C. Local government (1%)

IV. Legal Service/Legal Aid Offices (Civil Law) (3%)

V. Law departments of corporations, banks, insurance companies, and other businesses (8%)

VI. Special interest groups or associations (1%)

VII. Criminal law offices
   A. Prosecution (1%)
   B. Defense (1%)

VIII. Freelance or independent paralegals (1%)

IX. Service companies/consulting firms (1%)

X. Related fields (3%)
   A. Law librarian
   B. Paralegal teacher
   C. Paralegal supervisor/office administrator
   D. Miscellaneous

Fortunately, the last category is relatively small, but such attorneys exist.[2] Recently, for example, a paralegal job announcement drew more than 100 responses from paralegals, plus "four from attorneys."[3]

In this environment, the two keys to success are *information* about the employment scene and *techniques* to market yourself. With these objectives in mind, we turn now to the following themes:

■ Places where paralegals work

■ Paralegal specialties

■ Effective job-finding strategies

■ Alternative career options

---

[2]There are even some unemployed attorneys who are angry at bar associations for promoting the hiring of paralegals. "In the current market, a young attorney might well work for the same salary as a paralegal." After all, "bar associations represent lawyers, not paralegals. It must be pointed out that paralegals steal jobs from lawyers recently admitted to the bar." Anonymous, *Buddy, Can You Spare a Job,* 46 The Shingle 25 (Philadelphia Bar Ass'n, Fall 1983).
[3]Zavalney, *The Price of Success,* 6 Texas Lawyer 10 (January 21, 1991).

Section B. The Major Employers

There are ten major locations where paralegals work. They are summarized in Figure 1.1, along with the approximate percentage of paralegals working in each location.

1. Traditional Private Law Firms

Most paralegals today work for *private law firms*. While the need for paralegals may be just as great in the other categories, it is the traditional private law firms that have been doing most of the hiring. A "private" law firm is simply one that generates its income primarily from the fees of individual clients.

There are a number of characteristics of paralegals working for traditional private law firms, particularly the larger ones:

- They are among the highest paid paralegals.
- They tend to experience more law office management and personnel problems than other paralegals.
- They tend to specialize more and hence have less variety in their work assignments.
- They have been the most politically active paralegals in forming associations and in dealing with the bar associations.
- They are predominantly women.

Figure 1.2 presents a survey of the employment of paralegals in many of the largest law firms in the country.

2. Untraditional Private Law Firms

Since the mid-1970s a new kind of private law firm (sometimes called a *legal clinic*) has come into existence. It also receives its income from fees, but it differs from the traditional law firm in a number of respects:

- It tends to charge lower fees.
- It tends to serve the middle class.
- It has branch offices that are storefront in character (as opposed to a single downtown office in a plush suite on the 11th floor).
- It tends to have a higher proportion of paralegals (there are more paralegals per attorney than in the traditional private law firm).
- It is more likely to advertise and to use such devices as credit-card payment.

Such law firms have been controversial in the past. The traditional bar generally does not like these firms. The charge is that they are not dignified enough for the professional image that the bar wishes to project. In fact, during the early days, the bar went to court to try to force such firms out of existence. The bar lost, particularly over the issue of whether attorneys were allowed to advertise.

(continued on page 27)

FIGURE 1.2 Employment in Selected Large Law Firms*

Generally, a law firm is more likely to hire paralegals if it has hired them in the past, if it has a paralegal manager, and if it has many attorneys in the firm. This table tries to provide as much of this information as possible for selected—not all—large law firms in the country. Many law firms have branch offices. When you find two numbers separated by a slash, for example, 94/70, the first number is the total number in all offices of the firm (including headquarters), and the second number is the number in the city listed.

Law Firm (Number of Attorneys)	Title of Paralegal Manager	Number of Paralegals
Alabama *Birmingham*		
Balch & Bingham (66)		19
Bradley, Arant, Rose (97)		23
Burr & Forman (67)		12
Sirote & Permutt (94/70)		32
Alaska *Anchorage*		
Guess & Rudd (28)		6
Perkins Coie (336/19)		85/5
Arizona *Phoenix*		
Beus, Gilbert & Morrill (38)		15
Brown & Bain (125/79)	Paralegal Coordinator	48/24
Bryan, Cave, McPheeters (367/20)		76/8
Fennemore Craig (131/100)		15
Jennings, Strouss & Salmon (106)		17
Lewis & Roca (135/124)	Associate & Paralegal Coordinator	38
Mariscal, Weeks & McIntyre (33)		8
Meyer, Hendricks, Victor (56)		18
O'Connor, Cavanagh, Anderson (129/123)	Legal Administrator	24
Snell & Wilmer (238/171)	Paralegal Administrator	50/39
Squire, Sanders & Dempsey (430/29)		80/7
Streich, Lang, Weeks (140/125)		50/37
California *Century City*		
Irell & Manella (204/140)	Director of Legal Assistants	41
O'Melveny & Myers (560/64)		105/7
Costa Mesa		
Latham & Watkins (54)	Administrative Paralegal	13
Paul, Hastings, Janofsky (43)		9
Rutan & Tucker (106)		11

FIGURE 1.2   Employment in Selected Large Law Firms*—*Continued*

Law Firm (Number of Attorneys)	Title of Paralegal Manager	Number of Paralegals
California *Los Angeles*		
Adams, Duque & Hazeltine (89)		20
Alschuler, Grossman & Pines (41)	Paralegal Coordinator	7
Baker & Hostetler (503/85)		78/24
Baker & McKenzie (1580/70)	Paralegal Coordinator	11
Bottum & Feliton	Paralegal Manager	
Bryan, Cave, McPheeters (367/38)	Administrator	76/19
Buchalter, Nemer, Fields (179/124)	Paralegal Coordinator; General Litigation Paralegal Supervisor	55
Cox, Castle & Nicholson (95)		11
Dewey, Ballantine (394/39)	Senior Paralegal	81/8
Fadem, Berger & Norton	Paralegal Supervisor	
Finnegan, Henderson, Farabow	Director, Legal Assistant Services	
Frandzel & Share	Litigation Manager	
Gendel, Raskoff, Shapiro (49)	Paralegal Director	9
Gibson, Dunn & Crutcher (725/202)		145/60
Graham & James (385/104)		83/19
Hufstedler, Miller, Kaus	Paralegal Coordinator	10
Iwasaki, Thomas & Sheffield	Paralegal Coordinator	
Jones, Day, Reavis (1259/123)	Litigation Group/Administrative Assistant	21
Kindel & Anderson		11
Latham & Watkins (570/257)	Senior Legal Assistant	115/45
Lewis, D'Amato, Brisbois (197/104)		33/25
Loeb & Loeb (189/89)	Paralegal Administrator	26
Lyon & Lyon (50)	Paralegal & Data Processing Manager	14
Manatt, Phelps, Rothenberg (105)		15
McCutchen, Black, Verleger (95)		15
McKenna, Conner & Cuneo (197/43)	Paralegal Coordinator	12
Milbank, Tweed, Hadley (504/81)		12
Mitchell, Silberberg & Knupp (155/153)		22
Morgan, Lewis & Bockius (672/125)		113/21
Morrison & Foerster (588/118)		210/15
Munger, Tolles & Olson (83)		35
Musick, Peeler & Garrett (117)		20
O'Melveny & Myers (560/270)	Supervisor of Litigation Paralegal Services	136/80
Paul, Hastings, Janofsky (388/150)	Legal Assistant Administrator	55/31

FIGURE 1.2 Employment in Selected Large Law Firms*—*Continued*

Law Firm (Number of Attorneys)	Title of Paralegal Manager	Number of Paralegals
California		
Los Angeles		
Pillsbury, Madison, Sutro (625/46)		162/50
Pretty, Schroeder, Brueggemann	Paralegal Supervisor	
Rosen & Winston	Paralegal Coordinator	
Sheppard, Mullin, Richter (249/146)		21/18
Sidley & Austin (707/93)	Legal Assistant Coordinator	25
Skadden, Arps, Slate (1133/132)	Administrative Supervisor	77
Tuttle & Taylor (61)		16
Wyman, Bautzer, Kuchel (131/118)	Legal Assistant Manager	22
Newport Beach		
Gibson, Dunn & Crutcher (725/93)		165/15
O'Melveny & Myers (533/52)		136/10
Oakland		
Crosby, Heafey, Roach (192/225)		37
Donahue, Gallagher, Thomas	Paralegal Administrator	
King, Shapiro, Mittleman	Legal Assistant Coordinator	
Lempres & Wulfsberg	Legal Assistant Coordinator	
Palo Alto		
Brown & Bain (125/33)		48/20
Cooley, Godward, Castro (174/64)	Legal Assistant Manager	20
Brobeck, Phleger & Harrison (414/53)		136/12
Fenwick & West		30
Ware & Freidenrich (89)		14
Wilson, Sonsini, Goodrich (214)	Legal Assistant Coordinator	63
Riverside		
Best, Best & Krieger (114/74)		27
Sacramento		
Kronick, Moskovitz, Tiedemann (60)		12
Downey, Brand, Seymour (63)		10
San Diego		
Baker & McKensie (1580/27)	Paralegal Manager	16
Gray, Cary, Ames (183/170)	Paralegal Coordinator	28
Jennings, Engstrand & Henrickson (57)		13

FIGURE 1.2   Employment in Selected Large Law Firms*—*Continued*

Law Firm (Number of Attorneys)	Title of Paralegal Manager	Number of Paralegals
California *San Diego*		
Latham & Watkins (570/64)		174/16
Luce, Forward, Hamilton (146/134)		22
Schall, Boudreau & Gore	Legal Assistant Supervisor	
Seltzer, Caplan, Wilkins (53)	Paralegal Administrator	24
Solomon, Ward, Seidenwurm	Paralegal Coordinator	
Stutz, Gallagher & Artiano	Paralegal Coordinator	
San Francisco		
Brobeck, Phleger & Harrison (414/224)	Legal Assistant Manager	136/62
Bronson, Bronson & McKinnon (169/115)	Legal Assistant Administrator	64/25
Cooley, Godward, Castro (174/93)	Legal Assistant Administrator	36
Farella, Braun & Martel (75)	Director, Human Resources & Legal Support; Litigation Coordinator	39
Graham & James (385/133)		83/36
Handcock, Rothert & Bunshof (53)		43
Heller, Ehrman, White (355/193)	Legal Assistant Coordinator	143/55
Howard, Rice, Nemerovski (100)	Legal Assistant Administrator(s)	41
Jackson, Tufts, Cole (52)		24
Jeffer, Mangels, Butler (90/74)	Legal Assistant Coordinator	15
Landels, Ripley & Diamond (82)	Legal Assistant Manager	21
Long & Levit	Legal Assistant Manager	26
McCutchen, Doyle, Brown (274/198)	Paralegal Manager	59/52
Morrison & Foerster (588/245)	Legal Assistant Coordinator	175/125
Orrick, Herrington (258/167)	Legal Assistant Manager	62/34
Pettit & Martin (249/148)	Legal Assistant Manager	37/20
Pillsbury, Madison, Sutro (625/321)	Director, Legal Assistant & Computer Litigation Support Departments	116/58
Sedgwick, Detert, Moran (167/92)		39
Shartsis, Friese & Ginsburg (32)	Legal Assistant Supervisor	15
Thelen, Marrin, Johnson (361/168)	Legal Assistant Manager	86/62
San Jose		
Gibson, Dunn & Crutcher (738/19)		165/15
Hopkins & Carley (44)		11
Pillsbury, Madison, Sutro (625/44)	Information Resources Coordinator	162/14

FIGURE 1.2 Employment in Selected Large Law Firms*—*Continued*

Law Firm (Number of Attorneys)	Title of Paralegal Manager	Number of Paralegals
California Santa Monica		
Haight, Brown & Bonesteel (150/140)	Paralegal Training & Development Coordinator	44/41
Colorado Denver		
Coghill & Goodspeed	Paralegal Manager	
Davis, Graham & Stubbs (189/155)	Paralegal Coordinator	35/30
Gorsuch, Kirgis, Campbell (63)	Legal Assistant Coordinator	19
Hall & Evans (101)		43
Holland & Hart (229/144)	Legal Assistant Coordinator	37/22
Holme, Roberts & Owen (199/139)		54/40
Hopper, Kanouff, Smith	Legal Assistant/Manager	
Kirkland & Ellis (425/45)	Legal Assistant Supervisor	13
Rothgerber, Appel, Powers		15
Sherman & Howard (171/124)	Litigation Paralegal Supervisor	30/23
Tilly & Graves	Senior Legal Assistant	
Connecticut Hartford		
Cummings & Lockwood (159/28)		13
Day, Berry & Howard (220/151)	Legal Assistant Supervisor	50/39
Murtha, Cullina, Richter (92)		16
Robinson & Cole (141/120)		29
Schatz & Schatz (75)		11
Shipman & Goodwin (80)		23
Tyler, Cooper & Alcorn (84)		14
Updike, Kelly & Spellacy	Manager, Litigation Paralegals	12
Stamford		
Cummings & Lockwood (159/100)		25/13
Kelly, Drye & Warren (409/30)		47/10
Waterbury		
Carmody & Torrance (37)		12
Gager & Henry (34)		12
Delaware Wilmington		
Bayard, Handelman & Murdoc (28)		12
Elzufor, Austin & Drexler	Paralegal Supervisor	

FIGURE 1.2   Employment in Selected Large Law Firms*—*Continued*

Law Firm (Number of Attorneys)	Title of Paralegal Manager	Number of Paralegals
Delaware		
Wilmington		
Morris, James, Hitchens (38)		16
Morris, Nichols, Arscht (47)		14
Potter, Anderson & Corroon (51)		9
Prickett, Jones, Elliott (44)		11
Richards, Layton & Finger (76)	Paralegal Administrator	14
Young, Conaway, Stargatt (42)	Paralegal Supervisor	14
District of Columbia		
Akin, Gump, Strauss (485/233)	Legal Assistant Staff Manager	68
Anderson, Kill, Orlick (28)		16
Arent, Fox, Kintner (251/218)	Legal Assistant Administrator	40
Arnold & Porter (341/294)	Coordinator, Legal Assistant Programs	96
Baker & Hostetler (503/96)	Paralegal Coordinator	78/15
Beverage & Diamond (59)		16
Brownstein, Zeidman & Schomer (69)		26
Bryan, Cave, McPheeters (367/49)		76/13
Cadwalader, Wickersham & Taft (295/62)	Coordinator of Legal Assistants	11
Covington & Burling (282/273)		76
Crowell & Moring (182)	Coordinator, Legal Assistants	45
Davis, Polk & Wardwell (433/36)	Legal Assistant Coordinator	123/20
Dewey, Ballantine (394/66)		81/24
Dickstein, Shapiro & Morin (160/135)		58/32
Dow, Lohnes & Albertson (224/166)	Transaction Coordinator; Manager of Information Services	47/31
Dunnells, Duvall, Bennett (65)	Paralegal Coordinator	12
Finnegan, Henderson, Farabow (103)	Director, Legal Assistant Services	30
Fried, Frank, Harris (397/126)		143/34
Fulbright & Jaworski (685/72)		160/14
Gibson, Dunn & Crutcher (725/101)		165/20
Heron, Burchette, Ruckert		28
Hogan & Hartson (334/289)	Legal Assistant Administrator	43/35
Howrey & Simon (174)	Legal Assistant Administrator	61
Hunton & Williams (471/63)		146/16
Jones, Day, Reavis (1259/123)	Litigation Group/Administrative Assistant	221/46
Kaplan, Russin & Vecchi (138)		19
Keller & Heckman (43)		14

FIGURE 1.2   Employment in Selected Large Law Firms*—*Continued*

Law Firm (Number of Attorneys)	Title of Paralegal Manager	Number of Paralegals
District of Columbia		
Kirkland & Ellis (425/81)	Legal Assistant Supervisor	110/26
Kirkpatrick & Lockhart (315/84)		72/17
Melrod, Redman & Gartlan (66)	Paralegal Coordinator	13
McDermott, Will & Emery (520/71)	Paralegal Coordinator	
McKenna, Conner & Cuneo (197/122)	Paralegal Coordinator	36/28
Morgan, Lewis & Bockius (672/169)	Personnel Administrator	130/25
Newman & Holtzinger (69)	Senior Paralegal	22
Patton, Boggs & Blow (173/143)		23/13
Piper & Marbury (269/71)	Legal Assistant Administrator	10
Powell, Goldstein, Frazer (241/44)	Legal Assistant Coordinator	
Reed, Smith, Shaw (387/105)		85/18
Shaw, Pittman, Potts (248/231)	Director of Legal Assistants	52/46
Sidley & Austin (707/124)	Legal Assistant Administrator	27
Skadden, Arps, Slate (1133/164)	Paralegal Supervisor	
Squire, Sanders & Dempsey (430/82)		80/14
Steptoe & Johnson (232/220)	Director of Practice Support	42
Sutherland, Asbill & Brennan (244/134)	Chairman, Legal Assistant Committee	51/32
Swidler & Berlin (86)	Paralegal Coordinator	45
Venable, Baetjer & Howard (295/67)		42/15
Weil, Gotshal & Manges (552/46)	Paralegal Coordinator	13
Wiley, Rein & Fielding (105)	Legal Assistant Administrator	21
Williams & Connolly (126)		20
Willkie, Farr & Gallagher (350/46)	Legal Assistant Supervisor	17
Wilmer, Cutler & Pickering (200)	Practice Area Manager	99
Florida *Fort Lauderdale*		
Fleming, O'Bryan & Fleming (34)		10
Holland & Knight (284/27)		39/9
Ruden, Barnett, McClosky (103)		33
Miami		
Anderson, Moss, Parks	Legal Assistant Coordinator	
Floyd, Pearson, Richman (31)		8
Fowler, White, Burnett (54)		14
Greenberg, Traurig, Hoffman (134)	Paralegal Manager	38
Mershon, Sawyer, Johnson (93)		12
McDermott, Will & Emery (520/30)		90/8

FIGURE 1.2   Employment in Selected Large Law Firms*—*Continued*

Law Firm (Number of Attorneys)	Title of Paralegal Manager	Number of Paralegals
Florida		
Miami		
Mershon, Sayer, Johnston (77)		11
Shutts & Bowen (83)	Paralegal Supervisor	25
Steel, Hector & Davis (143/111)		18/12
Valdes-Fauli, Cobb, Petrey	Paralegal Supervisor	
Orlando		
Akerman, Senterfitt & Eidson (42)		9
Baker & Hostetler (503/35)		78/15
Gray, Harris & Robinson (32)		10
Lowndes, Drosdick, Doster (48)		9
McGuire, Voorhis & Wells (59)		22
Rumberger, Kirk, Caldwell	Legal Assistant Coordinator	
Tampa		
Carlton, Fields, Ward (150/107)		35/22
Fowler, White, Gillen (77)	Director of Personnel and Recruiting	21
Holland & Knight (284/74)	Legal Assistant Coordinator	39/16
Rudnick & Wolfe (246/17)	Personnel Manager	37/8
Shackleford, Farrior, Stallings (58)		10
Trenam, Simmons, Kemker (75)		16
Georgia		
Atlanta		
Alston & Bird (221/179)	Legal Assistant Coordinator	36
Arnall, Golden & Gregory (62)	Senior Litigation Paralegal	21
Hurt, Richardson, Garner (89)	Paralegal Coordinator	16
Hyatt & Rhoads (49)		17
Jones, Day, Reavis (1259/102)		221/17
Kilpatrick & Cody (172/124)		35
King & Spalding (270/230)	Paralegal Coordinator	73
Long, Aldridge & Norman (90)	Human Resources Manager	22
Neely & Player (42)		14
Parker, Johnson, Cook	Coodinator, Paralegal Program	
Powell, Goldstein, Frazer (241/197)	Paralegal Manager	53
Schwall, Ruff & Goodman	Director of Administration	
Smith, Gambrell & Russell (90)	Paralegal Coordinator	10
Stokes, Shapiro, Fussell	Senior Legal Assistant	
Sutherland, Asbill & Brennan (244/110)	Paralegal Specialist	51/29

FIGURE 1.2 Employment in Selected Large Law Firms*—*Continued*

Law Firm (Number of Attorneys)	Title of Paralegal Manager	Number of Paralegals
Georgia *Atlanta*		
Troutman, Sanders, Lockerman (165)		28
Hawaii		
Cades, Schutte, Fleming (74)		16
Goodsill, Anderson, Quinn (81)		20
Illinois *Chicago*		
Altheimer & Gray (179)	Director, Corporate Support Group	27
Baker & McKenzie (1580/174)	Paralegal Coordinator	20
Bell, Boyd & Lloyd (206/165)		27/23
Cassiday, Schade & Gloor	Paralegal Director	
Chapman & Cutler (257/241)		18/16
Clausen, Miller, Gorman (121)		18
Coffield, Ungaretti, Harris (90)		17
Gardner, Carton & Douglas (204/163)		28/23
Hinshaw, Culbertson, Moelmann (279/155)	Paralegal Coordinator	32/16
Hopkins & Sutter (287/182)	Paralegal Coordinator	31/19
Jenner & Block (289/248)	Paralegal Manager	101/91
Jones, Day, Reavis (1259/83)		221/13
Katten, Muchin & Zavis (341/283)		42
Keck, Mahin & Cate (351/212)	Legal Assistant Coordinator	39/29
Kirkland & Ellis (425/259)	Manager of Legal Assistants; Legal Assistant Coordinator	110/77
Latham & Watkins (570/67)		174/12
Levin & Funkhouser (18)		14
Lord, Bissel & Brook (275/227)		41/33
Mayer, Brown & Platt (566/381)	Paralegal Coordinator	113/91
McDermott, Will & Emery (520/309)		90/57
Peterson, Ross, Schloerb (163/147)		35
Phelan, Pope & John (74)		18
Pretzel & Stouffer	Supervisor of Litigation Paralegals	
Ross & Hardies (166/128)		15
Rudnick & Wolfe (246/219)	Personnel Manager	37/31
Sachnoff & Weaver (103)		23
Schiff, Hardin & Waite (213/198)		31

FIGURE 1.2   Employment in Selected Large Law Firms*—*Continued*

Law Firm (Number of Attorneys)	Title of Paralegal Manager	Number of Paralegals
Illinois		
Chicago		
'Seyfarth, Shaw, Fairweather (318/176)		29/14
Sidley & Austin (707/414)	Paralegal Recruiting Coordinator	174/89
Skadden, Arps, Slate (1133/106)	Legal Assistant Supervisor	
Sonnenschein, Nath (300/207)	Paralegal Administrator	24
Vedder, Price, Kaufman (155/138)		17
Wildman, Harrold, Allen (194/191)	Paralegal Coordinator	24
Winston & Strawn (404/298)	Paralegal Manager; Legal Assistant Supervisor	33
Indiana		
Indianapolis		
Baker & Daniels (182/139)		33
Barnes & Thornburg (202/118)		27/18
Bingham, Summers, Welsh (54)	Legal Assistant Supervisor	12
Bose, McKinney & Evans (48)		13
Ice, Miller, Donadio (165)	Chief Operating Officer	19
Kentucky		
Lexington		
Greenebaum, Doll & McDonald	Paralegal Coordinator	
Stoll, Keenon & Park (63)		14
Wyatt, Tarrant & Combs (162/35)		
Louisville		
Brown, Todd & Heyburn (131/100)	Paralegal Coordinator	22
Greenebaum, Doll & McDonald (67)	Administrative Paralegal Coordinator	11
Stites & Harbison (100)	Paralegal Administrator	
Wyatt, Tarrant & Combs (162/89)	Professional Personnel Administrator	28
Louisiana		
New Orleans		
Adams & Reese (86)		50
Chaffe, McCall, Phillips	Paralegal Coordinator	
Carmouche, Gray, Hoffman (55)		13
Deutsch, Kerrigan & Stiles	Senior Paralegal	
Jones, Walker, Waechter (161/153)	Paralegal Manager, General Litigation Section	41
McGlinchey, Stafford, Cellini (137/123)		58

FIGURE 1.2   Employment in Selected Large Law Firms*—*Continued*

Law Firm (Number of Attorneys)	Title of Paralegal Manager	Number of Paralegals
Louisiana *New Orleans*		
Milling, Benson, Woodward (71)		22
Phelps, Dunbar, Marks (161/95)		36/25
Stone, Pigman, Walther (62)		13
Maine *Bangor*		
Eaton, Peabody, Bradford (30)		14
Portland		
Bernstein, Shur, Sawyer (50)		17
Drummond, Woodsum, Plimpton (41)		8
Poerce, Atwood, Scribner (83)		18
Verrill & Dana (70)		16
Maryland *Baltimore*		
Frank, Bernstein, Conaway (200/133)	Assistant Director of Recruitment	35/25
Gordon Feinblatt, Rothman (72)		16
Melnicove, Kaufman, Weiner (78)		8
Miles & Stockbridge (192/107)		39/25
Montedonico & Mason (52)		10
Ober, Kalor, Grimes (107)		21
Piper & Marbury (269/195)	Recruiting Administrator	44/36
Semmes, Bowen & Semmes (165/144)		44
Smith, Somerville & Case (89)		18
Tydings & Rosenberg (32)	Paralegal Supervisor	12
Venable, Baetjer & Howard (295/167)		53
Weinberg & Green (146/134)		18
Whiteford, Taylor & Preston (138)		41
Massachusetts *Boston*		
Bingham, Dana & Gould (236/225)		41
Brown, Rudnick, Freed (114)	Corporate Paralegal Coordinator; Litigation Paralegal Supervisor	23
Burns & Levinson (103)		34
Campbell & Associates (31)		12
Choate, Hall & Stewart (165)		23
Fish & Richardson (38)		21

FIGURE 1.2   Employment in Selected Large Law Firms*—*Continued*

Law Firm (Number of Attorneys)	Title of Paralegal Manager	Number of Paralegals
Massachusetts *Boston*		
Foley, Hoag & Eliot (149/138)		28/25
Gaston & Snow (272/174)	Paralegal Coordinator	55/30
Goodwin, Proctor & Hoar (288)	Director of Administration & Human Resources	39
Goulston & Storrs (91)		16
Hale & Dorr (324/293)	Manager of Paralegal Services	63
Hill & Barlow (93)		22
Hutchins & Wheeler (83)		13
Mintz, Levin, Cohn (188/167)		36
Nutter, McClennen & Fish (168/160)	Paralegal Coordinator	20
Palmer & Dodge (144)	Legal Assistant Coordinator	22
Rackemann, Sawyer & Brewster (60)	Paralegal Administrator	17
Ropes & Gray (312/289)	Director of Paralegal Services; Senior Legal Assistant Coordinator	47/44
Sullivan & Worcester (133/114)	Paralegal Manager	28/23
Testa, Hurwitz & Thiebeault (82)	Paralegal Manager	13
Warner & Stackpole (49)	Executive Director	10
Widett, Slater & Goldman (83)	Director of Personnel	15
Worcester		
Bowditch & Dewey (59)	Paralegal Administrator	16
Fletcher, Tilton & Whipple	Paralegal Manager	
Michigan *Detroit*		
Butzel, Long, Gust (85)	Legal Assistant Coordinator	16
Clark, Klein & Beaumont (86)		10
Dickinson, Wright, Moon (213/138)		37
Dykema Gossett (312/162)		37
Honigman, Miller, Schwartz (236/182)	Manager of Legal Assistants	55/40
Kitch, Saurbier, Drutchas (90)		23
Miller, Canfield, Paddock (239/123)		43
Plunkett & Cooney (150/105)		25
Vandeveer, Garzia, Tonkin (48)		28
Grand Rapids		
Miller, Johnson, Snell (77)		13
Varnum, Riddering, Schmidt (119)		18
Warner, Norcross & Judd (96)	Director of Administration	16

FIGURE 1.2   Employment in Selected Large Law Firms*—*Continued*

Law Firm (Number of Attorneys)	Title of Paralegal Manager	Number of Paralegals
Minnesota *Minneapolis*		
Bowman & Brooke (23)		19
Dorsey & Whitney (352/269)	Senior Legal Assistant Supervisor	70/45
Faegre & Benson (233/184)		47/39
Fredrikson & Byron (100)		22
Gray, Plant, Mooty (86)		19
Larkin, Hoffman, Daly (84)		22
Leonard, Street & Deinar (89)		17
Lindquist, Vennum (94)	Human Resources Manager	15
Mackall, Crounse & Moore (49)		11
Maslon, Edelman, Borman (43)		20
Oppenheimer, Wolff & Donnelly (251/178)	Legal Assistant Manager	36/27
Popham, Haik, Schnobrich (175/129)	Legal Assistant Manager	39/33
Robins, Kaplan, Miller (190/117)	Legal Assistant Manager	60/52
St. Paul		
Briggs & Morgan (143/76)	Paralegal Coordinator	24
Doherty, Rumble & Butler (77)		13
Mississippi *Jackson*		
McDavid, Noblin & West (8)		8
Thomas, Price, Alston (27)		15
Watkins, Ludlam & Stennis (50)	Legal Assistant Coordinator	18
Missouri *Kansas City*		
Blackwell, Sanders, Matheny (72)		12
Polsinelli, White, Vardeman	Legal Assistant Coordinator	
Shook, Hardy & Bacon (151/127)	Paralegal Supervisor	44
Shughart, Thomson & Kilroy	Paralegal Coordinator	
Stinson, Mag & Fizzell (146/133)	Litigation Paralegal Coordinator	23
St. Louis		
Armstrong, Teasdale, Schlafly (162/118)		22
Bryan, Cave, McPheeters (367/181)		76/37
Coburn, Croft & Putzell (70)		14
Greensfelder, Hemker & Gale (81)		11
Husch, Eppenberger, Donohue (74)		10

FIGURE 1.2   Employment in Selected Large Law Firms*—*Continued*

Law Firm (Number of Attorneys)	Title of Paralegal Manager	Number of Paralegals
Missouri *St. Louis*		
Lewis, Rice & Fingersh (141/90)		18
Peper, Martin, Jensen (80)		14
Sandberg, Phoenix & von Gontard (37)		10
Stolar Partnership (44)		12
Thompson & Mitchell (176/124)		20/16
Nebraska *Omaha*		
Fraser, Stryker, Vaughn (31)		7
Kutak, Rock & Campbell (205/90)	Manager of Litigation Support Services	44/14
Nevada *Las Vegas*		
Lionel, Sawyer & Collins (52)		12
Reno		
Hill, Cassas, deLipkau (135)		23
New Hampshire *Concord*		
Sullivan, Hollis & Soden (40)		26
Manchester		
Devine, Millimet, Stahl (48)		16
McLane, Graf, Raulerson (50)		16
Sheehan, Phinney, Bass (52)		19
New Jersey *Morristown*		
Pitney, Hardin, Kipp (155)	Administrator of Litigation Paralegals	15
Porzio, Bromberg & Newman (30)	Paralegal Coordinator	40
Riker, Danzig, Scherer (116)	Paralegal Manager	20
Stanely & Fisher (116)	Paralegal Manager, Litigation	32
Newark		
Carpenter, Bennett & Morrissey (78)		13
Crummy, Del Deo, Dolan (105)	Paralegal Administrator	25
McCarter & English (182/159)	Paralegal Coordinator	48/34

FIGURE 1.2   Employment in Selected Large Law Firms*—*Continued*

Law Firm (Number of Attorneys)	Title of Paralegal Manager	Number of Paralegals
New Jersey *Newark*		
Sills, Cummis, Zuckerman (138/128)	Paralegal Coordinator	40
Roseland		
Hannoch Weisman (150/128)	Director of Paralegal Service	33
Lowenstein, Sandler, Kohl (132/115)	Corporate Supervisor; Litigation Paralegal Supervisor	27
Woodbridge		
Greenbaum, Rowe, Smith (81)	Legal Assistant Coordinator	21
Wilentz, Goldman & Spitzer (138/122)	Paralegal Manager	34/28
New Mexico *Albuquerque*		
Eaves, Darling & Porter	Supervising Paralegal	
Modrall, Sperling, Roehl (68)	Legal Assistant Coordinator	21
Poor Law Firm (37)		10
New York *Buffalo*		
Damon & Morey (55)		17
Hodgson, Russ, Andrews (135/108)		34
Jaeckle, Fleischmann & Mugel (81)		17
Moot & Sprague (61)		15
Phillips, Lytle, Hitchcock (136/98)		52/34
Saperston & Day (80)		17
New York City		
Anderson, Kill, Olick (182/150)		100
Battle, Fowler (127)		21
Bower & Gardner (218/212)		54
Breed, Abbott & Morgan (117)	Legal Personnel Coordinator	20
Brown & Wood (242/195)	Legal Assistant Supervisor	49
Cadwalader, Wickersham & Taft (295/208)	Director of Legal Assistants	40/36
Cahill, Gordon & Reindel (287/273)	Legal Assistant Coordinator	76/68
Carter, Ledyard & Milburn (76)	Paralegal Supervisor	27
Chadbourne & Parke (276/220)	Legal Assistant Manager	55
Cleary, Gottlieb, Steen (429/270)	Coordinator of Paralegal Services	66
Coudert Brothers (360/172)	Legal Personnel Manager	61/33
Cravath, Swaine & Moore (309/301)	Manager of Legal Assistants	117

FIGURE 1.2   Employment in Selected Large Law Firms*—*Continued*

Law Firm (Number of Attorneys)	Title of Paralegal Manager	Number of Paralegals
New York *New York City*		
Davis, Polk & Wardwell (433/378)	Manager, Corporate Assistants; Manager, Litigation Assistants	123/114
Debevoise & Plimpton (349/288)	Manager, Legal Assistant Department	81
Dewey, Ballantine (394/287)	Legal Assistant Administrator	81/53
Dilworth, Paxson, Kalish (145)	Paralegal Supervisor	20
Dreyer & Traub (95)		37
Fish & Neave (102)		35
Fitzpatrick, Cella, Harper (49)		27
Fried, Frank, Harris (397/250)	Legal Assistant Manager	143/75
Hughes, Hubbard & Reed (244/179)		35/27
Kaye, Scholer, Fierman (399/305)	Manager of Legal Assistants	88/65
Kramer, Levin, Nessen (140)	Paralegal Coordinator	33
LeBoeuf, Lamb, Leiby (405/218)	Paralegal Supervisor	110/80
Lord, Day, Lord (205/193)		45
Milbank, Tweed, Hadley (504/350)		116/91
Milgram, Thomajan & Lee (85)		21
Morgan & Finnegan (76)	Paralegal Coordinator	34
Mudge, Rose, Guthrie (304/237)		72/52
Patterson, Belknap, Webb (144/138)	Paralegal Manager	40/35
Parker, Chapin, Flattau (130)		21
Paul, Weiss, Rifkind (411/382)	Paralegal Supervisor	116
Proskauer, Rose, Goetz (425/350)	Corporate Paralegal Supervisor	90/84
Reid & Priest (203/159)		28/20
Rogers & Wells (337/255)	Litigation Legal Assistant Supervisor; Corporate Legal Assistant Coordinator; Real Estate Legal Assistant Coordinator	40
Rosenman & Colin (229/223)	Paralegal Coordinator	40
Rubin, Baum, Levin (54)		24
Schulte, Roth & Zabel (162/161)	Litigation Legal Assistant/Supervisor	34
Shey & Gould (292/252)	Legal Assistant Manager; Corporate Paralegal Supervisor	82/69
Shearman & Sterling (624/478)	Legal Assistant Manager	112/105
Sidley & Austin (707/66)	Paralegal Manager	174/20
Simpson, Thacher & Bartlett (442/431)	Paralegal Coordinator	128
Skadden, Arps, Slate (1133/583)	Director of Legal Assistant Services	433

FIGURE 1.2   Employment in Selected Large Law Firms*—*Continued*

Law Firm (Number of Attorneys)	Title of Paralegal Manager	Number of Paralegals
New York		
New York City		
Stroock, Stroock & Lavan (339/250)	Litigation Paralegal Supervisor	74/29
Sullivan & Cromwell (366/303)	Director of Paralegal Services	73/60
Weil, Gotshall & Manges (552/392)	Legal Assistant Manager	137/108
White & Case (462/311)	Manager of Legal Assistants; Coordinator of Evening Legal Assistants	64
Whitman & Ransom (255/149)		34/24
Willkie, Farr & Gallagher (350/281)	Corporate Supervisor; Director of Litigation Services	74/58
Wilson, Elser, Moskowitz (379/222)	Legal Assistant Supervisor	30
Winthrop, Stimson, Putnam (289/222)	Legal Assistant Manager	42/29
Winston & Strawn (404/91)	Legal Assistant Manager	62
Rochester		
Chamberlain, D'Amanda, Oppenheimer (31)		13
Harter, Secrest & Emery (93)		30
Harris, Beach, Wilcox (96)		15
Nixon, Hargrave, Devans (259/142)	Manager of Paralegal Services	46
Phillips, Lytle, Hitchcock (136/24)		52/10
Woods, Oviatt, Gilman (40)		11
Syracuse		
Bond, Schoeneck & King (143/98)		29/19
Hiscock & Barclay (95)		26/11
North Carolina		
Charlotte		
Kennedy, Covington, Lobdell (74/68)		17/13
Moore & Van Allen (62)	Legal Assistant Coordinator	18
Robinson, Bradshaw & Hinson (66)		14
Smith, Helms, Mulliss (147/64)		60/19
Greensboro		
Smith, Helms, Mulliss (147/69)		60/41
Raleigh		
Hunton & Williams (471/33)		142/10
Maupin, Taylor, Ellis (59)		12
Moore & Van Allen	Legal Assistant Coordinator	
Poyner & Spruill (106/70)		28/17

FIGURE 1.2   Employment in Selected Large Law Firms*—*Continued*

Law Firm (Number of Attorneys)	Title of Paralegal Manager	Number of Paralegals
North Carolina *Winston-Salem*		
Petree, Stockton & Robinson (70)		10
Womble, Carlyle, Sandridge (182/125)		48
Ohio *Cincinnati*		
Dinsmore & Shohl (133/122)	Paralegal Administrator	38
Frost & Jacobs (167/141)		49
Graydon, Heed & Ritchey (63)		12
Keating, Muething & Klekamp (61)		15
Taft, Stettinius & Hollister (154/133)	Administrator	26
Thompson, Hine & Flory (348/65)		61/20
Cleveland		
Arter & Hadden (337/126)	Paralegal Coordinator	77/20
Baker & Hostetler (503/173)	Paralegal Manager	78/29
Benesch, Friedlander, Coplan (174/127)		28/19
Calfee, Halater & Griswold (150/147)		24
Hahn, Laeser & Parks (73)		16
Jones, Day & Reavis (1259/228)	Administrative Assistant	221/41
McDonald, Hopkins, Burke (62)		18
Squire, Sanders & Dempsey (430/185)	Chairman, Legal Assistant Personnel Committee	80/33
Thompson, Hine & Flory (348/166)	Legal Assistant Manager	61/29
Columbus		
Arter & Hadden (337/61)		77/10
Baker & Hostetler (503/84)		78/10
Bricker & Eckler (82)		22
Carlile, Patchen, Murphy (33)		9
Emens, Hurd, Kegler (63)		11
Porter, Wright, Morris (214/134)	Paralegal Administrator	40
Schottenstein, Zox & Dunn (79)		10
Schwartz, Kelm, Warren (39)	Director, Paralegal Services	12
Squire, Sanders & Dempsey (430/87)		80/18
Thompson, Hine & Flory (348/36)		61/13
Vorys, Sater, Seymour (255/203)	Paralegal Administrator	56

FIGURE 1.2 Employment in Selected Large Law Firms*—*Continued*

Law Firm (Number of Attorneys)	Title of Paralegal Manager	Number of Paralegals
Ohio *Toledo*		
Fuller & Henry (53)		10
Nathan & Roberts	Paralegal Administrator	
Schumaker, Loap & Kendrick (69)		7
Oklahoma *Oklahoma City*		
Crowe & Dunlevy (91)		22
Tulsa		
Conner & Winters (45)		9
Gable & Gotwals (46)		7
Hall, Estill, Hardwick (79)		32
Oregon *Portland*		
Bullivant, Houser (61)	Paralegal Manager	14
Davis, Wright, Tremaine (238/60)		22/9
Miller, Nash, Wiener (104)	Coordinator, Litigation Legal Assistants	15
Schwabe, Williamson & Wyatt (151/125)		21
Sears, Lubersky, Bledsoe (86)		15
Stoel, Rives, Boley (220/153)	Legal Assistant Manager	40/11
Pennsylvania *Philadelphia*		
Ballard, Spahr, Andrews (218/158) ·	Senior Legal Assistant	51/32
Blank, Rome, Comisky (227/204)		35
Clark, Ladner, Fortenbaugh (51)		17
Cohen, Shapiro, Polisher (83)		14
Cozen & O'Connor (136/106)		46
Dechert, Price & Rhoades (384/254)	Paralegal Coordinator	82/58
Dilworth, Paxson, Kalish (155/116)	Paralegal Supervisor, Litigation Department	27/20
Drinker, Biddle & Reath (217/178)	Senior Legal Assistant	56/36
Duane, Morris, Heckscher (223/167)		56/42
Fox, Rothchild, O'Brien (118)		25
Hoyle, Morris & Kerr (60)	Legal Assistant Administrator	36
Mesirov, Gelman, Jaffe (102)		33
Montgomery, McCracken, Walker (160/146)	Paralegal Coordinator	35/32

FIGURE 1.2   Employment in Selected Large Law Firms*—*Continued*

Law Firm (Number of Attorneys)	Title of Paralegal Manager	Number of Paralegals
Pennsylvania *Philadelphia*		
Morgan, Lewis & Bockius (672/173)		113/50
Pechner, Dorfman, Wolffe (62)		11
Pepper, Hamilton & Scheetz (355/177)	Legal Assistant Administrator	73/39
Rawle & Henderson (72)		19
Reed, Smith, Shaw (387/61)	Paralegal Coordinator	24
Saul, Ewing, Remick (183/152)	Litigation Support Manager	42
Schnader, Harrison, Segal (245/199)	Supervisor of Legal Assistants	45
Stradley, Ronon, Stevens (80)		19
White & Williams (101)		42
Wolf, Block, Schorr (244/221)		40/38
Pittsburgh		
Buchanan Ingersoll (190/174)	Legal Assistant Coordinator	33
Eckert, Seamans, Cherin (201/155)	Paralegal Coordinator	27/24
Kirkpatrick & Lockhart (315/190)	Legal Assistant Coordinator	83
Klett, Lieber, Rooney (63)	Director of Paralegal Services	13
Reed, Smith, Shaw (387/201)	Paralegal Manager	85/37
Wilkes-Barre		
Rosenn, Jenkins & Greenwald (46)		18
Rhode Island *Providence*		
Edwards & Angell (170/93)		34
Hinckley, Allen, Snuder (78)		22
Gamma Law Associates	Paralegal Manager	
Roberts, Carroll, Feldstein	Paralegal Manager	
Tillinghast, Collins & Graham (51)		14
South Carolina *Charleston*		
Sinkler & Boyd (50/19)	Legal Assistant Coordinator	15/9
Young, Clement, Rivers	Paralegal Coordinator	
Columbia		
Nelson, Mullins, Riley (86)	Legal Assistant Coordinator	35
Greenville		
Leatherwood, Walker, Todd (40)		13
Wyche, Burgess, Freeman (22)		8

FIGURE 1.2   Employment in Selected Large Law Firms*—*Continued*

Law Firm (Number of Attorneys)	Title of Paralegal Manager	Number of Paralegals
Tennessee		
Nashville		
Baker, Worthington, Crossley (94/34)		16
Bass, Berry & Sims (80/77)		25
Boult, Cummings, Conners (33)	Administrator/Paralegal Coordinator	13
Farris, Warfield, Kanaday (46)		13
Hartwell, Martin & Stegall (24)		10
Manier, Herod, Hollabaugh (41)		11
Texas		
Austin		
Brown, Maroney, Oaks (81)	Legal Assistant Coordinator	32
Clark, Thomas, Winters (74)		17
Graves, Dougherty, Hearon (71)		13
Fulbright & Jaworski (685/33)		160/12
Johnson & Gibbs (312/32)		40/13
Small, Craig, Werkenthin (63)		25
Vinson & Elkins (503/33)		174/21
Dallas		
Akin, Gump, Strauss (485/167)	Legal Assistant Staff Manager	109/32
Arter & Hadden (337/61)	Paralegal Coordinator	24
Baker & Botts (407/76)	Legal Assistant Coordinator	13
Baker, Mills, Glast (88)		22
Carrington, Coleman, Sloman (81)	Legal Assistant Administrator	18
Cowles & Thompson (69)		25
Fulbright & Jaworski (685/66)		160/16
Gardere & Wynne (200)		46
Gibson, Dunn & Crutcher (738/33)		165/11
Goodwin, Carlton & Maxwell (100)		20
Haynes & Boone (246/161)	Legal Assistant Coordinator; Litigation Support Coordinator	47
Hughes & Luce (156/133)		30/26
Jackson & Walker (216/144)	Legal Assistant Manager	35/25
Jenkins & Gilchrist (199/148)		32/24
Johnson & Gibbs (312/230)		40
Jones, Day, Reavis (1259/162)	Administrative Assistant	221/40
Locke, Purnell, Rain (190/183)		33
Page & Addison (28/24)		16/14
Riddle & Brown (50)		20

FIGURE 1.2   Employment in Selected Large Law Firms*—*Continued*

Law Firm (Number of Attorneys)	Title of Paralegal Manager	Number of Paralegals
Texas		
Dallas		
Shank, Irwin, Conant	Paralegal Coordinator	
Strasburger & Price (183/169)	Legal Assistant Coordinator	51
Thompson & Knight (213/198)	Legal Assistant Coordinator	46
Vial, Hamilton, Koch (85)		29
Wendel Turley (21)		24
Winstead, McGuire, Sechrest (180/128)	Paralegal Coordinator	41/37
El Paso		
Grambling & Mounce (37)		11
Kemp, Smith, Duncan (82)		18
Scott, Hulse, Marshall (40)		15
Fort Worth		
Cantey & Hanger (75)		16
Kelly, Hart & Hallman (76)		14
Houston		
Andrews & Kurth (287/202)	Legal Assistant Coordinator for Litigation	93/27
Arnold, White & Durkee (67)	Paralegal Coordinator	27
Baker & Botts (407/259)	Legal Assistant Manager	95/62
Baker, Brown, Sharman (60)	Legal Assistant Coordinator	15
Beirne, Maynard & Parsons (21)		12
Bracewell & Patterson (207/155)		40/36
Butler & Binion (171/140)	Legal Assistant Coordinator	45/28
Davis & McFall (33)	Paralegal Coordinator	20
Fulbright & Jaworski (685/337)	Coordinator, Legal Assistants	160/68
Hutcheson & Grundy (66)	Legal Assistant Coordinator	14
Jackson & Walker (216/54)		35/13
Liddell, Sapp, Zivley (178/130)		35/27
Lorance & Thompson (33)		11
Mayer, Day, Caldwell (70)		16
Porter & Clements (47)		11
Sewell & Riggs (53)		11
Sheinfeld, Maley & Key (71)		17
Vinson & Elkins (495/387)	Legal Assistant Manager; Legal Assistant Recruiter	174/146
Weil, Gotshal & Manges (552/60)	Legal Assistant Coordinator	22

FIGURE 1.2 Employment in Selected Large Law Firms*—*Continued*

Law Firm (Number of Attorneys)	Title of Paralegal Manager	Number of Paralegals
Texas *San Antonio*		
Cox & Smith (82)		19
Fulbright & Jaworski (685/48)		160/12
Groce, Locke & Hebdon (82)	Personnel Administrator	27
Matthews & Branscomb (82)	Legal Assistant Supervisor	19
Utah *Salt Lake City*		
Ray, Quinney & Nebeker (73)		11
Van Cott, Bagley, Cornwall (78)		11
Virginia *Fairfax*		
Hazel & Thomas (166/61)		32
Wilkes, Artis, Hedrick (40)		13
McLean		
McGuire, Woods, Battle (336/67)		94/19
Watt, Tieder, Killian (46)		13
Richmond		
Browder & Russell (44)	Paralegal Manager	17
Hunton & Williams (471/241)	Legal Services Manager; Human Resources Administrator	146/77
Mays & Valentine (131/111)		29
McGuire, Woods, Battle (336/180)	Legal Assistant Administrator	111/58
Sands, Anderson, Marks (42)		12
Williams, Mullen, Christian (58)	Personnel Manager	18
Washington *Seattle*		
Betts, Patterson & Mines (51)	Paralegal Coordinator	15
Bogle & Gates (235/159)		78/53
Davis, Wright, Tremaine (238/125)	Legal Assistant Coordinator	20
Foster, Pepper & Shefelman (138/105)		21
Gibson, Dunn & Crutcher		18
Helsell, Fetterman, Martin (49)		13
Lane, Powell, Spears (241/133)	Paralegal Manager	43/37
Oles, Morrison & Rinker (32)		10
Perkins Coie (336/178)	Legal Assistant Coordinator	85/47

FIGURE 1.2   Employment in Selected Large Law Firms*—*Continued*

Law Firm (Number of Attorneys)	Title of Paralegal Manager	Number of Paralegals
Washington *Seattle*		
Preston, Thorgrimson, Shidler (207/125)	Coordinator/Litigation Legal Assistants and Clerks	41/25
Reed, McClure, Moceri (46)		18
Riddall, Williams, Bullitt (73)	Personnel Manager	14
Stoel, Rives, Boley (220/60)		40/11
Williams, Kastner & Gibbs (80)	Paralegal Coordinator	18
Wilson, Smith, Cochran		18
West Virginia *Charleston*		
Bowles, Rice, McDavid (66/47)		17/12
Huntington		
Jenkins, Fenstermaker, Krieger (16)		5
Wisconsin *Milwaukee*		
Foley & Lardner (410/210)		56/25
Geofrey & Kahn (88)		23
Quarles & Brady (207/162)		27/22
Whythe & Hirschboeck (60)		10

*Sources: West's Legal Directory; National Association of Legal Placement Directory; National Law Journal (September 26, 1988; September 18, 1989; September 24, 1990); PIC's National Law Network; California Lawyer (November 1990); Legal Assistants Management Association Directory (1990); and independent checking.

(continued from page 3)
The number of untraditional law firms is relatively small, but they are growing. The fear of losing business has caused many small traditional firms to begin imitating some of the characteristics of the more aggressive new breed.

3. Government

The civil service departments of federal, state, and local governments have established standards and classifications for many different kinds of government paralegals. These paralegals work in four main areas of government:

- In the office of the chief government attorney, e.g., attorney general, corporation counsel
- In the general counsel's office of individual agencies
- In other departments of individual agencies, e.g., enforcement department, civil rights division

▪ In the office of individual legislators, legislative committees, legislative counsel, or the legislative drafting office of the legislature

Federal Government

Thousands of paralegals work for the federal government in the capital (Washington, D.C.) and the main regional cities of the federal government (Boston, New York, Philadelphia, Atlanta, Chicago, Kansas City, Dallas, Denver, Seattle, and San Francisco). The most important job classification for this position is the *Paralegal Specialist* (GS-950).[4] This position is described in the following excerpt from the *Office of Personnel Management Handbook, X-118.* Note the extensive responsibility that these individuals have. The ending of this description is quite remarkable: paralegals perform "duties requiring discretion and independent judgment" which "may or may not be performed under the direction of a lawyer." There is no doubt that government paralegals have a range of responsibility that is broader than paralegals working anywhere else in the country.

Description of Work

Paralegal specialist positions involve such activities as (a) legal research, analyzing legal decisions, opinions, rulings, memoranda, and other legal material, selecting principles of law, and preparing digests of the points of law involved; (b) selecting, assembling, summarizing and compiling substantive information on statutes, treaties, contracts, other legal instruments, and specific legal subjects; (c) case preparation for civil litigation, criminal law proceedings or agency hearings, including the collection, analysis and evaluation of evidence, e.g., as to fraud and fraudulent and other irregular activities or violations of laws; (d) analyzing facts and legal questions presented by personnel administering specific Federal laws, answering the questions where they have been settled by interpretations of applicable legal provisions, regulations, precedents, and agency policy, and in some instances preparing informative and instructional material for general use; (e) adjudicating applications or cases on the basis of pertinent laws, regulations, policies and precedent decisions; or (f) performing other paralegal duties requiring discretion and independent judgment in the application of specialized knowledge of particular laws, regulations, precedents, or agency practices based thereon. These duties may or may not be performed under the direction of a lawyer.

The largest numbers of Paralegal Specialists are employed in the following units of the federal government:[5]

> U.S. Department of Health & Human Services
> U.S. Department of Justice
> U.S. Court System
> U.S. Department of Treasury

---

[4]GS stands for *General Schedule,* which is the main pay-scale system used by the federal government. The number 950 is the occupational code for the Paralegal Specialist.

[5]J. Harris, *The Paralegal's Guide to U.S. Government Jobs,* 3 (Federal Reports, 1986).

U.S. Department of Transportation
U.S. Department of the Army
U.S. Department of the Interior
U.S. Equal Employment Opportunity Commission
U.S. General Services Administration
U.S. Department of Energy
U.S. Department of State
U.S. Department of Labor

Paralegal Specialists are not the only individuals using special legal skills in the federal government. The following law-related occupations, filled mainly by nonattorneys, should be considered:

Legal Clerk
Legal Technician
Immigration Specialist
Foreign Affairs Analyst/Officer
Civil Rights Analyst
Social Services Representative
Equal Employment Opportunity
   Specialist
Hearings and Appeals Officer
Legal Instruments Examiner
Public Utilities Specialist
Tax Law Specialist
Patent Advisor
Patent Examiner
Patent Technician
Intelligence Analyst
Internal Revenue Officer
Import Specialist
Environmental Protection Specialist
Security Specialist
Freedom of Information Act
   Specialist

Contract Specialist
Contract Representative
Labor Relations Specialist
Employee Relations Specialist
Wage & Hour Compliance Specialist
Mediation Specialist
Investigator
Regulatory Analyst
Legislative Analyst
Land Law Examiner
Copyright Examiner
Copyright Technician
Railroad Retirement Claims
   Examiner
Estate Tax Examiner
Workers Compensation Claims
   Examiner
Unemployment Compensation
   Claims Examiner

When there is an opening for a Paralegal Specialist or for one of the positions listed above, the individual agency with this opening may do its own recruiting or may recruit through the Office of Personnel Management[6] (formerly called the Civil Service Commission), which oversees hiring procedures throughout the federal government. For a list of job information centers in your area where you can inquire about paralegal and other law-related positions in the federal government, see Appendix B.

State Government

When looking for work as a paralegal in the *state* government, find out if your state has established civil service classification standards for paralegal po-

---

[6]1900 E. St. NW, Wash. D.C. 20415 (202-606-1800).

sitions. See Figure 1.3 for some of this data. In addition, locate a directory of agencies, commissions, boards, or departments for your state, county, and city governments. You want to find a list of all (or most of the major) government offices. Many local public libraries will have a government directory. Alternatively, check the offices of state and local politicians, such as governor, mayor, commissioner, alderman, representative, or senator. They will probably have such a directory. Finally, check your local phone book for the sections on government offices. Contact as many of them as you can to find out whether they employ paralegals. If you have difficulty obtaining an answer to this question, find out where their attorneys are located. Sections or departments that employ attorneys will probably be able to tell you about paralegal employment opportunities. In your search, include a list of all the courts in the state. Judges and court clerks may have legal positions open for nonattorneys.

In addition to the statewide personnel departments listed in Figure 1.3, many government offices have their own personnel department that will list employment openings. Also, whenever possible, talk with attorneys and paralegals who already work in these offices. They may know of opportunities that you can pursue.

Do not limit your search to paralegal or legal assistant positions. Legal jobs for nonattorneys may be listed under other headings, such as research assistant, legal analyst, administrative aide, administrative officer, executive assistant, examiner, clerk, and investigator. As we have seen, this is also true for employment in the federal government.

4. Legal Service/Legal Aid Offices (Civil)

Community or neighborhood legal service offices and legal aid offices exist throughout the country. (See *Directory of Legal Aid & Defender Offices,* published by the National Legal Aid & Defender Association.) They obtain most of their funds from the government, often in the form of yearly grants to provide legal services to the poor. The clients do not pay fees. These offices make extensive use of paralegals with titles such as:

Administrative Benefits
   Representative
Administrative Hearing
   Representative
AFDC Specialist (Aid to Families
   with Dependent Children)
Bankruptcy Law Specialist
Case Advocate
Case Specialist
Community Law Specialist
Disability Law Specialist
Domestic Relations Specialist

Employment Law Specialist
Food Stamp Specialist
Generalist Paralegal
Health Law Specialist
Housing/Tenant Law Specialist
Immigration Paralegal
Information and Referral Specialist
Legal Assistant
Legal Research Specialist
Legislative Advocate
Paralegal

(continued on page 49)

FIGURE 1.3 Summary Chart—Survey of State Government Job Classifications for Paralegals

GOVERNMENT	POSITION	RESPONSIBILITIES	QUALIFICATIONS	SALARY
Alabama Personnel Dept. 64 N. Union St., Rm. 402 Montgomery, AL 36130-2301 205-261-3389	Legal Assistant 10/22/82 (11503)	■ Perform legal research ■ Draft pleadings ■ Interview witnesses in preparation for trial ■ Conduct routine investigations ■ Prepare and interpret legal documents in noncomplex cases ■ Prepare summaries of documents ■ Perform office administrative duties	Graduation from an accredited legal assistant program <u>OR</u> possession of a legal assistant certificate	$15,366–$23,369 per year
Other positions to check in Alabama: Docket Clerk (11501); Legal Opinions Clerk (11505); Contract Clerk (119.267-018); Legal Investigator (119.267-022); Title Examiner (119.287-010); Appeals Referee (119.267-014).				
Alaska Dept. of Administration Division of Personnel Pouch C Juneau, AK 99811 907-465-4430	Paralegal Assistant I 4/1/84 (7105-13)	■ Interview clients ■ Obtain statements and affidavits ■ Conduct investigations ■ Perform legal research ■ Coordinate witness scheduling ■ Represent clients at hearings	Certificate from a state paralegal training program <u>OR</u> Associate of Arts program with a major in paralegal, criminal justice, or law studies <u>OR</u> 3 years of experience as legal secretary, court clerk, etc.	$26,460–$36,048 per year
Other positions to check in Alaska: Legal Assistant II (7106); Investigator II (7767); Latent Fingerprint Examiner (7756).				
American Samoa Dept. of Human Resources American Samoa Government	Legal Assistant I (E2-09-7524)	■ Conduct routine investigations ■ Perform legal research ■ Review citations for traffic court cases	A bachelor's degree with a major in police science, corrections, or a related field	$9,317–$15,167 per year

Continued

FIGURE 1.3 Summary Chart—Survey of State Government Job Classifications for Paralegals—*Continued*

GOVERNMENT	POSITION	RESPONSIBILITIES	QUALIFICATIONS	SALARY
Pago Pago, AS 96799 684-633-4489		■ Interview witnesses ■ Present traffic cases in court ■ Prepare orders to show cause		
Other positions to check in American Samoa: Legal Assistant II (E2-10-7525); Legal Assistant III (E2-11-7526); Paralegal (12-13-7552).				
Arizona Dept. of Administration Personnel Division 1831 West Jefferson St. Phoenix, AZ 85007 602-542-5482	Legal Assistant 1/11/77 (74510)	■ Perform legal research ■ Help prepare briefs and pleadings ■ Take statements and depositions ■ Interview complainants ■ Index laws ■ Serve papers ■ Help answer court calendars	2 years of college study in relevant courses (experience involving legal terminology and legal research procedures can substitute for the education requirement)	$16,618–$23,937 per year
Other positions to check in Arizona: Legal Assistant I, Legal Assistant II (Child Support Enforcement Administration)				
Arkansas Office of Personnel Management P.O. Box 3278, 1509 West 7th St. Little Rock, AR 72203 501-682-1507	Legal Assistant 7/1/77 7/1/79-R (R177)	■ Receive legal questions from agency attorneys ■ Collect and evaluate information on the questions ■ Provide reports (orally or in memo form) to attorneys ■ File pleadings and briefs ■ Maintain law library	The education equivalent of completion of 1 year of law school, including a course in legal bibliography	$14,118 per year

California State Personnel Board 801 Capitol Mall P.O. Box 944201 Sacramento, CA 94244-2010 916-445-5291 ALSO: Dept. of Personnel Administration 1115 11th St., 1st Fl. Sacramento, CA 95814-3860 916-322-5193	Legal Assistant 3/13/75 9/20/78 (CW55, 1820)	▪ Assist in reviewing legal documents to determine if they comply with the law ▪ Analyze proposed legislation ▪ Digest and index opinions, testimony, depositions, and other trial documents ▪ Perform research of legislative history ▪ Assist in drafting complaints and other pleadings ▪ Perform routine legal research	2 years of legal clerical experience in California government OR 3 years in a law office	$2,009–$2,418 per month
	Legal Analyst 7/2/81 (LE18, 5237)	▪ Investigate and analyze facts ▪ Coordinate witnesses ▪ Draft interrogatories ▪ Draft pleadings ▪ Summarize discovery documents ▪ Supervise other staff	1 year as a state Legal Assistant OR 2 years in another paralegal job and 15 semester hours or 22 quarter units in a paralegal curriculum or equivalent to graduation from college	$2,278–$2,700 per month
Colorado Dept. of Personnel State Centennial Bldg. 1313 Sherman St Denver, CO 80203 303-866-2321	Legal Assistant 6/23/82 ("A" 77500) ("B" 77501)	▪ Provide discovery and investigation assistance ▪ Digest and index legal documents ▪ Check legal citations ▪ Take notes during deposition ▪ Prepare simple pleadings and briefs ▪ Maintain case files ▪ Prepare statistical reports ▪ Perform legal research	Bachelor's degree and approved paralegal studies program (experience can substitute for general education)	Legal Assistant A $2,025–$2,713 per month Legal Assistant B $2,344–$3,141 per month

Continued

FIGURE 1.3 Summary Chart—Survey of State Government Job Classifications for Paralegals—*Continued*

GOVERNMENT	POSITION	RESPONSIBILITIES	QUALIFICATIONS	SALARY
Connecticut Personnel Div. Dept. of Administration Services 165 Capital Ave. Hartford, CT 06106-1630 203-566-3081	Paralegal Specialist I 10/1/87 (6140)(NL16)	▪ Act as liaison between legal and clerical staff ▪ Perform legal research ▪ Assist in drafting legal documents ▪ Maintain tickler systems ▪ Present written and oral argument at administrative hearings ▪ Maintain records	2 years of experience working for a lawyer <u>OR</u> A designated number of college courses in law or paralegal studies (Note: substitutions are allowed)	$970–$1,168 biweekly
Other positions to check in Connecticut: Paralegal Specialist II (6141, NL 20); Legal Office Administrator (5373, 9389c, MP 18).				
Delaware State Personnel Office Townsend Bldg. P.O. Box 1401 Dover, DE 19901 302-736-4195	Legal Assistant 8/75 (12846)	▪ Review documents to assess consistency with law ▪ Summarize cases ▪ Draft pleadings, deeds, and other documents ▪ Interview clients and witnesses ▪ Assist in investigations ▪ File documents in court	Enough education and/or experience to demonstrate competence in research, drafting, filing, interviewing, record keeping, and communication (oral and written)	$17,400 per year
Other positions to check in Delaware: License Investigator (Dept. of Administrative Services); Clerk of Court I (Family Court) (12311); Law Library Assistant.				
District of Columbia D.C. Personnel Office 613 G St. NW, Rm 306 Wash. D.C. 20001-3798 202-727-6406	Paralegal Specialist	Similar to Paralegal Specialist positions in the federal government. (See page 28)		

Florida Dept. of Administration Division of Personnel Management Services 330 Carlton Bldg. Tallahassee, FL 32399 904-488-5823	Paralegal Specialist 1/1/84 (7703) (0807)	▪ Take affidavits from victims and witnesses ▪ Perform legal research under supervision ▪ Maintain case files and tickler system ▪ Perform notary functions ▪ Prepare case summaries ▪ Draft pleadings	Completion of legal assistant training course <u>OR</u> Bachelor's degree with major in allied legal services <u>OR</u> 4 years of experience as a paralegal or legal secretary	$1,220–$1,975 per month
Other positions to check in Florida: Appeals Coordinator/Clerk (Public Employees Relations Commission) (7704) Legal Trainee (7706)				
Georgia State Merit System of Personnel Administration 200 Piedmont Ave. Atlanta, GA 30334-5100 404-656-2705	Legal Assistant 1/1/81 (44330)	▪ Perform legal research ▪ Review litigation documents ▪ Summarize law ▪ Develop forms and procedures	2 years of legal experience involving legal research, interpreting laws, or relevant administrative responsibilities	$20,310–$32,052 per year
Other positions to check in Georgia: Law Clerk (44340)—requires a law degree <u>OR</u> two years of legal assistant experience; Para-Legal (nonmerit position in State Law Department); Research Assistant (nonmerit position in State Law Department).				
Guam Civil Service Commission Kumision I Setbision Sibit P.O. Box 3156 Agana, GU 96910 011-671-649-NORM Dept. of Administration Division of Personnel P.O. Box 3156	Paralegal I 12/83 (2.810)	▪ Perform legal research ▪ Index public laws ▪ Prepare updates to administrative laws ▪ Draft bills and simple pleadings ▪ Compile laws by subject matter ▪ Interview clients and witnesses	3 years of experience working with laws and procedures <u>OR</u> A bachelor's degree <u>OR</u> Completion of a course leading to certification as a paralegal <u>OR</u> Equivalent experience and training	$13,930–$18,610 per year

Continued

FIGURE 1.3 Summary Chart—Survey of State Government Job Classifications for Paralegals—*Continued*

GOVERNMENT	POSITION	RESPONSIBILITIES	QUALIFICATIONS	SALARY
Guam Agana, GU 96910 011-671-472-8194				
Other position to check in Guam: Legal Clerk I (2.805).				
Hawaii Dept. of Personnel Services 830 Punchbowl St. Honolulu, HI 96813 808-548-7405	Legal Assistant II 4/15/83 (2.141)	■ Act as conduit between attorneys and client, e.g., provide legal information ■ Perform legal research ■ Summarize laws ■ Collect and evaluate evidence for trial ■ Perform cite checks ■ Index depositions	4 years of legal experience OR Graduation from an accredited legal assistant training program	$1,690–$2,326 per month
Idaho Personnel Commission 700 West State Boise, ID 83720 208-334-2263	Idaho currently does not have any job classifications for paralegal work. The Legal Assistant position (05916) was phased out. The Office of the Attorney General does, however, employ a paralegal in its Consumer Protection Unit and in its Natural Resource Division.			
Illinois Dept. of Central Management Services Bureau of Personnel 505 Stratton Office Bldg. Springfield, IL 62706 217-782-2141 312-917-2141 (Chicago)	Paralegal Assistant 11/17/83 (1887, 30860) (RC-062-12)	■ Write legal memoranda and other documents for attorneys ■ Analyze hearing transcripts ■ Excerpt data from transcripts ■ Prepare statistical reports ■ Edit, index, and proofread decisions ■ Perform legal research	Knowledge and skill equivalent to four years of college and knowledge and skills relevant to job responsibilities	$1,643–$2,102 per month

Illinois
Other position to check in Illinois: Legal Research Assistant (1888) (23350) (MC-02) (RC-028-13).

State / Contact	Job Title	Duties	Requirements	Salary
Indiana State Personnel Dept. Rm. 513, State Office Bldg. 100 North Senate Ave. Indianapolis, IN 46204 317-232-3056		The state has no special classifications for paralegals working in the state government. In the Offices of Attorney General, however, the Consumer Protection Division now has Complaint Analyst positions that have been filled with paralegals. Complaint Analysts act as a mediator between the consumer and the business against which the consumer has a complaint. Each Complaint Analyst handles at least 200 cases.		
Iowa Dept. of Personnel Grimes State Office Bldg. E. 14th St. & Grand Ave. Des Moines, IA 50319 515-281-3351	Paralegal (Office of Attorney General) (45004)	■ Represent the state at revocation hearings ■ Write administrative appeal briefs ■ Resolve appeals not needing a hearing ■ Initiate suggestions to improve hearing procedures	2-year paralegal degree	$787–$1,024 biweekly

Other position to check in Iowa: Administrative Assistant I (00708).

State / Contact	Job Title	Duties	Requirements	Salary
Kansas Dept. of Administration Div. of Personnel Services Landon State Office Bldg. 900 SW Jackson St. Topeka, KS 66612-1251 913-296-4278	Legal Assistant 6/83 (D3 1961)	■ Perform legal research ■ Draft pleadings ■ Compile administrative transcript ■ Conduct investigations	Completion of a Legal Assistant training program of at least 60 semester hours.	$1,630–$2,254 per month
Kentucky Dept. of Personnel Capitol Annex, Rm. 373 Frankfort, KY 40601 502-564-4460	Paralegal 12/1/85 (9856)	■ Conduct analytical research ■ Investigate cases ■ Interview complainants and witnesses ■ Draft documents	Bachelor's degree in paralegal science OR Post-baccalaureate certificate in paralegal studies	$1,139–$1,826 per month

Continued

FIGURE 1.3 Summary Chart—Survey of State Government Job Classifications for Paralegals—*Continued*

GOVERNMENT	POSITION	RESPONSIBILITIES	QUALIFICATIONS	SALARY
Kentucky		▪ Provide general assistance to attorneys in litigation	OR Completion of a 2-year program in paralegal studies (Note: paralegal experience can be substituted)	
Other positions to check in Kentucky: Paralegal Senior (9857); Law Clerk (9801).				
Louisiana Dept. of Civil Service P.O. Box 94111 Capitol Station Baton Rouge, LA 70804-9111 504-342-8083	Paralegal Assistant 6/3/86 (113470) (C1 PA)	▪ Perform legal research ▪ Draft pleadings ▪ Interview potential trial witnesses ▪ Compose briefs and memoranda ▪ Collect delinquent payments ▪ Index legal opinions ▪ Maintain law library	1 year of law school OR Paralegal certification OR A baccalaureate degree and 30 semester hours of paralegal courses OR 2 years of paralegal school with 30 semester hours of paralegal courses	$1,180–$1,770 per month
Other position to check in Louisiana: Legal Research Assistant (70490).				
Maine Bureau of Human Resources State Office Bldg. State House Station 4 Augusta, ME 04333 207-289-3761	Paralegal Assistant (0016/U336)	▪ Assist attorney in title search ▪ Perform legal research ▪ Assist attorney at hearings ▪ Conduct investigations	4 years of college and 1 year of paralegal experience OR Graduation from an approved paralegal course	$21,507–$28,787 per year

Maine
Other positions to check in Maine: Legal Researcher (0018, 02045, 0979, 20E); Law Clerk (secretarial position with paralegal duties)(0061, 41255, 202.362-014, 0380, 0880, 18R); Workers Compensation Assistant (036900).

Agency	Title	Duties	Salary
Maryland Dept. of Personnel State Office Bldg. #1 301 W. Preston St. Baltimore, MD 21201 301-225-4715 800-492-7845	Legal Assistant I (10/31/47) (9/3/68) 0589	• Perform legal research • Conduct investigations • File pleadings • Prepare affidavits • Maintain docket file • Coordinate employee activities	High school diploma or certificate and 4 years of experience as a clerk or secretary in a law office (Note: One year of paralegal education can substitute for two years of experience)	$17,261–$22,609 per year

Other positions to check in Maryland: Legal Assistant (209, 13); Legal Assistant II (1292); Para-Legal I (e.g., Howard County Office of State's Attorney).

Agency	Title	Duties	Requirements	Salary
Massachusetts Dept. of Personnel Administration One Ashburton Pl. Boston, MA 02108 617-727-3555	Paralegal Specialist 5/11/88 (10-R39) (Group 31)	• Perform legal research • Analyze statutes • Digest the law • Prepare briefs and answers to interrogatories • Interview parties • Evaluate evidence • Develop case tracking systems • Schedule appointments	2 years of experience in legal research or legal assistant work (Note: An associate's degree or a higher degree with a major in paralegal studies can be substituted for the required experience)	$24,490–$32,691 per year
Michigan Dept. of Civil Service Capitol Commons Center 400 South Pine St. P.O. Box 30002 Lansing, M 48909 517-373-3020	Paralegal III 5/81 (8020403, BA, 7)	• Perform legal research • Conduct investigations • Draft legal documents • Prepare interrogatories • Digest and index laws • Serve and file legal papers	Associate degree in a paralegal program OR Equivalent combination of experience and education to perform the job	$10.43–$12.78 per hour

Continued

FIGURE 1.3 Summary Chart—Survey of State Government Job Classifications for Paralegals—*Continued*

GOVERNMENT	POSITION	RESPONSIBILITIES	QUALIFICATIONS	SALARY
Other positions to check in Michigan: Paralegal IV (8020404, BA, 7); Paralegal VB (8020405, BA, 7); Paralegal VI (8031106, BA, 7). Note: The Legal Assistant I position requires a law degree.				
Minnesota Dept. of Employee Relations 520 LaFayette Rd. St. Paul, MN 55101 612-296-8366	Legal Technician 2/75 3/76 (17526C)	▪ Perform legal research ▪ Prepare legal documents ▪ Collect documents for attorney	Completion of paralegal training program OR 2 years of varied paralegal experience OR 1 year of law school	$20,609–$25,829 per year
Other positions to check in Minnesota: Legal Technician-Farm Real Estate (Dept. of Agriculture); Legal Text Edit Specialist (001936, 206).				
Mississippi State Personnel Board 301 N. Lamar St. Jackson, MS 39201 601-359-1406	Paralegal Specialist 7/83 (1848-PR 188-269, D)	▪ Interpret and explain laws to staff ▪ Assist in preparing legal documents ▪ Review reports ▪ Assist in referring cases for prosecution ▪ Train and supervise staff in research ▪ Perform research	Bachelor's degree in paralegal studies or a related field and 1 year of experience	$17,323 per year
Other position to check in Mississippi: Legal Clerk I (1962-PR 081-162, B) (clerical position with paralegal duties).				
Missouri Office of Administration Division of Personnel P.O. Box 388 Jefferson City, MO 65102 314-751-4162	Paralegal or legal assistant positions are not found under the Missouri Merit System. Individual agencies not covered by the Merit System, however, may have such positions.			

Montana
Dept. of Administration
Personnel Division
Mitchell Bldg., Rm. 130
205 Roberts St.
Helena, MT 59620
406-444-3871
	Paralegal Assistant I
	1/80
	(119004)
		■ Perform legal research
		■ Compile citations and references;
		  check cites
		■ Assemble exhibits
		■ Explain laws
		■ Arrange interviews and
		  depositions
		■ File pleadings
		■ Supervise clerical staff
			Completion of paralegal training
			program
			<u>OR</u>
			Education and experience equivalent
			to a bachelor's degree with courses
			in business, economics, law, etc.
				Grade 11
				$16,092–$22,236
				per year

Other positions to check in Montana: Paralegal Assistant II (119005); Agency Legal Services Investigator (163155).

Nebraska Dept. of Personnel Box 94905 Lincoln, NE 68509-4905 402-471-2075	Legal Aide I 5/1/78 C318131	■ Perform legal research ■ Proofread legal material ■ Help draft regulations ■ Help maintain hearing room tapes and films	Any combination of training and/or experience that will enable the appli- cant to possess the required knowl- edge, ability, and skills	$13,054 per year

Other position to check in Nebraska: Legal Aide II (C318132).

Nevada Dept. of Personnel 209 E. Musser St. Capitol Complex Carson City, NV 89710 702-885-4050 800-992-0900	Legal Assistant 7/1/89 (2.155)	■ Digest information in files ■ Explain status of case to clients or to the public ■ Offer advice on procedures ■ Interview clients and witnesses ■ Schedule depositions ■ Organize and prepare exhibits	Completion of 1-year or 2-year para- legal course <u>AND</u> Legal secretarial experience or training <u>OR</u> Any combination of education and experience to demonstrate entry level knowledge, skills, and abilities	$18,803–$25,136 per year

Other positions to check in Nevada: Legal Assistant II (2.159); Legal Research Assistant (7.750).

Continued

FIGURE 1.3 Summary Chart—Survey of State Government Job Classifications for Paralegals—*Continued*

GOVERNMENT	POSITION	RESPONSIBILITIES	QUALIFICATIONS	SALARY
New Hampshire Division of Personnel State House Annex 25 Capitol St., Rm. 1 Concord, NH 03301 603-271-3261	Paralegal I 2/4/76 1/27/87 (6793-15)	▪ Evaluate complaints of violations of state law ▪ Interview business owners and consumers ▪ Perform legal research ▪ Examine contracts, agreements, and related legal documents to insure they comply with the law	4 years of college with 9 semester credits in law topics related to paralegal studies and 6 months of experience in research or investigation	$19,110–$22,542 per year

Other positions to check in New Hampshire: Paralegal II (6792-18); Legal Coordinator and Contracts Monitor (5668-22); Legal Research Assistant (5676-23); Legal Research Aide I (5670-16); Legal Research Aide II (5671-18); Legal Aide (5660-14).

GOVERNMENT	POSITION	RESPONSIBILITIES	QUALIFICATIONS	SALARY
New Jersey Dept. of Personnel Front & Montgomery Sts. CN 317 Trenton, NJ 08625 609-292-4144	Paralegal Technician Assistant 2/4/87 (A13-30459)	▪ Perform legal research under close supervision ▪ Help draft noncomplex memoranda ▪ Help prepare correspondence ▪ Help prepare pleadings ▪ Perform cite checks ▪ Proofread legal documents	Completion of an approved course of paralegal training	$25,535–$35,266 per year

Other positions to check in New Jersey: Legal Services Assistant I (A18-72743); Paralegal Technician, Law and Public Safety (A17-30461); Paralegal Technician, Casino Control Commission (X17-98648); Research Analyst (A18-03171); Research Analyst–Civil Service (A18-03171); Supervising Research Analyst–Div. of Youth and Fam. Services (A28-03184B).

GOVERNMENT	POSITION	RESPONSIBILITIES	QUALIFICATIONS	SALARY
New Mexico State Personnel Office 810 W. San Mateo Rd. Santa Fe, NM 87503 505-827-8190	Legal Assistant I 8/29/79 (1330)	▪ Provide help in legal research ▪ Prepare affidavits and exhibits ▪ Serve legal papers ▪ Prepare and maintain records ▪ Handle routine legal correspondence	Education and legal experience equaling 4 years. The experience can be gained as a paralegal. An Associate's Degree in paralegal studies can substitute for 3 years of experience.	$14,891–$24,760 per year

New Mexico
Other position to check in New Mexico: Legal Assistant II (1331).

		Duties	Requirements	Salary
New York Dept. of Civil Service One Harriman State Office Bldg. Albany, NY 12239 518-457-3701	Legal Assistant I 2/10/84 (26-880)	■ Compile and organize documents ■ Help prepare legal documents and forms ■ Respond to inquiries and complaints ■ Maintain files ■ Monitor legislation ■ Perform legal research	Associate's degree in paralegal studies <u>OR</u> Completion of general practice legal specialty training <u>AND</u> Passing a test on law and procedure	$25,786 per year

Other positions to check in New York: Legal Assistant Trainee I (00-107); Legal Assistant II (26-881).

North Carolina Office of State Personnel 116 West Jones St. Raleigh, NC 27603-8004 919-733-7108	Paralegal I 6/82 (NC 1422) (INCAC 8G.0402)	■ Draft legal instruments ■ Prepare routine opinions ■ Handle complaints and inquiries from the public ■ Administer the law office ■ Perform legal research	Graduation from a certified paralegal school and 1 year of paralegal experience	$19,783–$31,428 per year
North Dakota Central Personnel Division Office of Management & Budget State Capitol, 14th Fl. Bismarck, ND 58505 701-224-3290	Legal Assistant I 4/87 (0701)	■ Perform legal research ■ Maintain case files ■ Maintain law library ■ Assist attorneys in litigation ■ Perform general secretarial duties	The equivalent of 2 years of college in a curriculum appropriate to prelaw and 2 years of related experience.	$1,219–$1,882 per month

Other position to check in North Dakota: Legal Assistant II (0702).

Continued

FIGURE 1.3 Summary Chart—Survey of State Government Job Classifications for Paralegals—*Continued*

GOVERNMENT	POSITION	RESPONSIBILITIES	QUALIFICATIONS	SALARY
Ohio Dept. of Administrative Services Div. of Personnel 30 E. Broad Street Columbus, OH 43266 614-466-3455	Legal Aide 8/84 (63810)	■ Perform legal research ■ Conduct investigations ■ Draft legal documents ■ Draft responses to legal questions ■ Assist attorneys at hearings ■ File legal papers ■ Maintain legal records	Completion of certification program for paralegals <u>OR</u> Completion of designated courses, e.g., legal research, case analysis, legal analysis, civil procedure	$9.01–$10.58 per hour
Other positions to check in Ohio: Hearing Assistant (63821); Hearing Officer (63831).				
Oklahoma Office of Personnel Management 2101 N. Lincoln Blvd. Oklahoma City, OK 73105 405-521-2171 800-522-8122	Legal Research Assistant 7/1/81 (K101 FC: K10)	■ Perform legal research ■ Conduct investigations ■ Assist attorneys in litigation ■ File pleadings ■ Maintain law library	Completion of approved legal research assistant program <u>OR</u> Completion of 18 semester hours of law school	$1,691–$2,256 per month
Other positions to check in Oklahoma: Legal Assistant I; Legal Assistant II (Office of the Municipal Counselor, Oklahoma City).				
Oregon Executive Dept. Personnel & Labor Relations Div. 155 Cottage St. N.E. Salem, OR 97310-0310 503-378-3020	Paralegal Specialist (1526)	■ Organize complex facts ■ Communicate with experts ■ Analyze cases ■ Assist attorneys in litigation ■ Arrange for case settlements ■ Answer interrogatories	Experience and training that demonstrate the knowledge and skills required for the position	$2,140–$2,845 per month
Other positions to check in Oregon: Paralegal I (1523); Paralegal II (1524); Paralegal III (1525); Investigator (C1031); Special Investigator (X 1032); Legal Assistant (C0680).				

Pennsylvania Office of Administration Bureau of Personnel 517 Finance Bldg. Harrisburg, PA 17105 717-787-5545	Legal Assistant I 6/89 (0701)	■ Review work of field personnel for possible legal implications ■ Summarize cases ■ Prepare reports	1 year of experience as legal assistant trainee OR 4 years of experience in clerical work, investigation, or enforcement	$16,919–$26,171 per year

Other positions to check in Pennsylvania: Legal Assistant II (07020); Legal Assistant Supervisor (07030); Legal Assistant Manager (07040).

Rhode Island Office of Personnel Administration 289 Promenade St. Providence, RI 02908 401-277-2160	Paralegal Aide 11/24/35 (0246-300)	■ Perform legal research ■ Conduct investigations ■ Answer questions by interpreting laws ■ Assist in litigation ■ Maintain files	Completion of an approved paralegal training program OR Paraprofessional experience in an extensive legal service program	$18,380–$19,965 per year
South Carolina Budget and Control Board Division of Human Resource Management 1201 Main St. P.O. Box 12547 Columbia, SC 29211 803-737-0900	Paralegal Assistant I 4/84 (2066)	■ Obtain and assemble witness statements, reports, and exhibits ■ Draft and proofread pleadings ■ Maintain tickler system ■ Assist in document control	Certification from an approved paralegal program OR High school diploma and 1 year of experience with a South Carolina attorney	$17,821–$26,731 per year

Other positions to check in South Carolina: Paralegal Assistant II (2067); Legal Aide (2065).

South Dakota Bureau of Personnel 500 E. Capitol Pierre, SD 57501-5070 605-773-3148	South Dakota does not have positions within state government specifically titled paralegal, legal assistant, legal technician, or legal aide. Individuals performing these functions are usually classified as administrative assistants, secretaries, or exempt professionals.			

Continued

FIGURE 1.3 Summary Chart—Survey of State Government Job Classifications for Paralegals—*Continued*

GOVERNMENT	POSITION	RESPONSIBILITIES	QUALIFICATIONS	SALARY
Tennessee Dept. of Personnel 505 Deaderick St. Nashville, TN 37243-0635 615-741-2958	Legal Assistant 7/1/84 (02350)	■ Perform legal research e.g., cite checking ■ Draft regulations ■ Maintain law library ■ Answer routine inquiries on laws and regulations	Completion of an approved curriculum in paralegal studies	$1,128–$1,677 per month
Texas State Auditor's Office P.O. Box 12067 419 Reagan State Office Bldg. Austin, TX 78711-2067 512-463-5788	Legal Assistant I 9/1/89 (3570)	■ Perform legal research ■ Compile citations and references ■ Research land titles ■ Assemble exhibits ■ Help prepare legal documents ■ File pleadings in court	Completion of a paralegal training program OR The equivalent in experience	$20,772–$26,160 per year
Other positions to check in Texas: Legal Assistant II (3572); Legal Assistant III (3574); Administrative Technician II (Office of Attorney General).				
Utah Department of Human Resource Management 2229 State Office Bldg. Salt Lake City, UT 84114 801-538-3025	Paralegal 9/30/89 (18750)	■ Digest pretrial data ■ Maintain calendar/docket systems ■ Draft subpoenas, motions, etc. ■ Assist at depositions and hearings ■ Interview witnesses	Certificate of paralegal studies, plus 2 years work experience, preferably in a legal field	$18,325–$27,165 per year
Other position to check in Utah: Paralegal (18751).				
Vermont Agency of Administration Dept. of Personnel 110 State St.	Paralegal Technician 8/11/89 (081800)	■ Assist attorneys in litigation ■ Conduct investigations ■ Interview parties ■ Perform legal research	1 year of experience in investigatory, analytical, research or paralegal duties; plus 3 years of additional experience at or above a senior clerical	$20,072–$30,305 per year

Vermont Montpelier, VT 05602 802-828-3497	(P.G. 18)	■ Audit records ■ Interpret laws ■ Draft briefs and legal documents	or technical level (Note: 30 college credits in legal or paralegal studies can substitute for the 3 years of additional experience.)	
Other position to check in Vermont: State Investigator—Civil Rights.				
Virginia Office of Compensation Management Dept. of Personnel and Training 101 N. 14th St. Richmond, VA 23219-3657 804-225-2131	Legal Assistant 11/1/83 (21521)	■ Help supervise clerical staff ■ Monitor compliance requirements ■ Draft briefs and fact narratives ■ Perform legal research ■ Prepare witnesses and exhibits ■ Manage law library	Paralegal course work or training preferred, plus experience in judicial and quasi-judicial systems and in the application of legal principles	$18,723–$25,572 per year
Washington D.C. (See District of Columbia)				
Washington State Dept. of Personnel 600 S. Franklin P.O. Box 1789 Olympia, WA 98504 206-586-0194	Legal Examiner I 9/14/89 (4661)	■ Assist in litigation ■ Assist in investigations ■ Perform legal research ■ Collect and organize economic data ■ Help organize large volume of documents	2 years of experience as a legal assistant OR Completion of approved 2 year paralegal or legal assistant course OR 4-year college degree and either completion of a 10-month legal assistant program or 1-year of experience as paralegal or legal assistant	$1,647–$2,081 per month
Other positions to check in Washington: Legal Examiner II (4662); Legal Examiner III (4663).				

Continued

FIGURE 1.3 Summary Chart—Survey of State Government Job Classifications for Paralegals—*Continued*

GOVERNMENT	POSITION	RESPONSIBILITIES	QUALIFICATIONS	SALARY
West Virginia Civil Service System 1900 Washington St. East, Rm. B-456 Charleston, WV 25305 304-348-3950	Para-Legal Assistant 10/7/74 10/21/80 (0550)	■ Perform legal research ■ Write abstracts of evidence ■ Supervise clerical staff ■ Maintain case records ■ Summarize legal literature ■ Maintain statistical records ■ Monitor pending legislation ■ Prepare legal documents	Completion of approved Para-Legal Assistant program OR 2 years of relevant legal experience under the supervision of an attorney	$1,064–$1,920 per month
Other position to check in West Virginia: Child Advocate Para-Legal (8098).				
Wisconsin Dept. of Employment Relations 149 East Wilson St. P.O. Box 7855 Madison, WI 53707 608-266-9820	Legal Assistant I 4/79 (PR2-08)	■ Abridge transcripts of testimony ■ Prepare appendices for appellate briefs ■ Paginate appeal records ■ Collect and organize facts for trial preparation ■ Draft routine pleadings ■ Conduct elementary research	There must be reasonable assurance that the applicant has the skills and knowledge to perform the tasks. "Under current civil service statutes, the state of Wisconsin does not require specific credentials unless it can be established that the position needs professional licensing."	$10.03–$14.02 per hour
Other positions to check in Wisconsin: Legal Assistant II (PR2-09); Legal Assistant I—Confidential (PR1-08) (Dept. of Justice, Attorney General); Administrative Assistant IV (PR1-13).				
Wyoming Personnel Division Department of Administration and Fiscal Control 2001 Capitol Ave. Cheyenne, WY 82002 307-777-6713	There are no paralegal or legal assistant classifications in Wyoming state government. The closest may be the positions of Executive Secretary and Legal Investigator (LE52).			

(continued from page 30)

Paralegal Coordinator	Social Security Specialist
Paralegal Supervisor	Tribal Court Representative
Public Entitlement Specialist	Veterans Law Specialist
Senior Citizen Specialist	Wills Procedures Specialist

Many administrative agencies permit nonattorneys to represent citizens at hearings before those agencies. Legal service and legal aid offices take advantage of this authorization. Their paralegals undertake extensive agency representation. (See Figure 1.4 for a sample job announcement that lists paralegal duties, including work at hearings, on behalf of clients.) The distinction between attorneys and paralegals in such offices is less pronounced than in any other setting. Unfortunately, however, such paralegals are among the lowest paid because of the limited resources of the offices where they work.

Another way in which legal services are provided to poor people (sometimes referred to as *indigents*) is through *judicare*. This is a system of paying private attorneys for legal services to the poor on a case-by-case basis. Instead of receiving a government grant to open up an office that will serve only the poor, the Judicare attorney maintains a private office and bills the government whenever legal services are delivered to the poor. These attorneys often employ paralegals.

Further variations on methods by which paralegals are used to deliver legal services to the poor include:

- Paralegals who work in special institutions such as mental health hospitals or prisons
- Paralegals who are senior citizens providing legal services to senior citizens at nursing homes, neighborhood centers, and similar locations

5. Law Departments of Corporations, Banks, Insurance Companies, and Other Businesses

Not every corporation or business in the country uses a law firm to handle all of its legal problems. Many have their own in-house law department under the direction of an attorney who is often called the *general counsel* or *corporate counsel*.[7] The attorneys in this department have only one client—the corporation or business itself. Examples include manufacturers, retailers, transportation companies, publishers, general insurance companies, real estate and title insurance companies, estate and trust departments of large banks, hospitals, universities, etc. In increasing numbers, paralegals are being hired in these settings. The average corporate law department employs seventeen attorneys, two paralegals, two nonattorney professionals, and fourteen legal support personnel.[8] Paralegal salaries are relatively high because the employer (like the large traditional private law office) can afford to pay good wages.

---

[7]Even if a corporation has its own law department, however, it may still occasionally hire an outside law firm in special situations such as complex litigation.

[8]Stanton, *Stepping Up to the Bar,* 35 Occupational Outlook Quarterly 3, 7 (Spring 1991).

FIGURE 1.4 Sample Job Description for Paralegal in Legal
Service Office

Gulf Coast Legal Foundation

Positions Open for Paralegals Experienced in Welfare

The Gulf Coast Legal Foundation, formerly the Houston Legal Foundation, has three
positions open for paralegals with experience in welfare law. However, if experienced persons do not apply, we will seriously consider applicants with no more educational qualifications than a GED. We are discouraging law students and law graduates from applying.
Our program has five neighborhood offices in Houston and Galveston and will expand to
Fort Bend and Brazoria Counties. Our paralegals are assigned to specialty units. These
positions are for the welfare unit where the goal is to increase the number of AFDC (Aid to
Families with Dependent Children) families by 12,000 in the county and the number of SSI
(Supplemental Social Security Income) recipients by 1,500 in the county, and to increase
the level of benefits. The welfare unit represents the local welfare rights organization, which
has ten years of history, parent councils of Title XX day care centers, and in cooperation
with another unit, groups of handicapped people. The paralegal would maintain a direct
service caseload of state welfare appeals and SSI hearings as well as some unemployment,
health claims and other administrative matters. Each paralegal will be expected to handle
six pending hearings and perform one research task each month after a training period of
half a year. And do their own typing. The paralegal would also maintain a library of state
manuals and social security materials. The paralegal would also be expected to participate
in saturation leafleting, to attend some group meetings, and to perform minor educational
services. The supervising attorney of the welfare unit would supervise the paralegal. The
unit will have a total of five lawyers and six paralegals.

Because of inadequate public transportation, the paralegal would be responsible for
transporting clients to welfare centers and maintaining a personal automobile.

Applicants should furnish their scores on the SAT or GRE exam, a writing sample, and
detailed information concerning any prior legal services experience. We will weigh math-
ematical skills over writing skills. Our program will give preference to experienced paralegals who intend to continue a career as a paralegal. Our program also has an affirmative
action policy for the hiring of women and members of minority groups. Our program serves
a substantial Mexican-American population and must give an additional preference to applicants who speak Spanish fluently.

The salary range can go up to the equivalent of a moderately experienced attorney.

6. Special Interest Groups or Associations

Many special interest groups exist in our society: unions, business associations, environmental protection groups, taxpayer associations, consumer protection groups, trade associations, citizen action groups, etc. The larger groups
have their own offices, libraries, and legal staff, including paralegals. The legal
work often involves monitoring legislation, lobbying, preparing studies, etc. Direct legal services to individual members of the groups are usually not provided.
The legal work relates to the needs (or a cause) of the organization as a whole.
Occasionally, however, the legal staff will litigate test cases of individual members that have broad impact on the organization's membership.

A different concept in the use of attorneys and paralegals by such groups is
group legal services. Members of unions or groups of college students, for example, pay a monthly fee to the organization for which they are entitled to
designated legal services, such as preparation of a will or divorce representation.
The members pay *before* the legal problems arise. Group legal service systems

are a form of legal insurance. The group legal service office will usually employ paralegals.

7. Criminal Law Offices

Criminal cases are brought by government attorneys who are called prosecutors, district attorneys, or attorneys general. Defendants are represented by private attorneys if they can afford the fees. If they are indigent, they are assigned private counsel whose fees are paid by the government, or they are represented by public defenders who work in a special office set up by government funds to represent the poor. The use of paralegals in the practice of criminal law is increasing, particularly due to the encouragement of organizations such as the National District Attorneys Association and the National Legal Aid & Defender Association.

8. Freelance Paralegals

Most *freelance paralegals* are self-employed individuals who sell their services to attorneys. They are also called independent paralegals and contract paralegals. They perform their services in their own office or in the offices of the attorneys who hire them for special projects. Often they advertise in publications read by attorneys, such as legal newspapers and bar association journals. Such an ad might look something like this:

> **Improve the quality and**
> ******cost-effectiveness******
> **of your practice with the help of:**
> **Lawyer's Assistant, Inc.**

In addition, these paralegals will usually have a flyer or brochure that describes their services. Here is an excerpt from such a flyer:

> Our staff consists of individuals with formal paralegal training and an average of five years of experience in such areas as estates and trusts, litigation, real estate, tax, and corporate law. Whether you require a real estate paralegal for one day or four litigation paralegals for one month, we can provide you with reliable qualified paralegals to meet your specific needs.

The attorneys in a law firm may be convinced of the value of paralegals but not have enough business to justify hiring a full-time paralegal employee. A freelance paralegal may be an alternative.

For an overview on how to start a freelance business, see Appendix A.

There are also self-employed paralegals who sell their services directly to the public. They, too, are sometimes called freelance paralegals, although the terms legal technician and independent paralegal are more common. Relatively few paralegals are engaged in this kind of business. This may change, however, as a number of states seriously consider a form of limited licensing to authorize what they do.

9. Service Companies/Consulting Firms

Service companies and consulting firms also sell services to attorneys, but usually on a broader and more sophisticated scale than the freelance paralegal does. Examples include:

- Selecting a computer system for a law office
- Designing and managing a computer-assisted document control system for a large case
- Digesting discovery documents
- Helping a law firm establish a branch office
- Designing a filing or financial system for the office
- Incorporating a new company in all fifty states
- Conducting a trademark search
- Undertaking a UCC (Uniform Commercial Code) search and filing in all fifty states

In order to accomplish such tasks, these service companies and consulting firms recruit highly specialized staffs of management experts, accountants, economists, former administrators, etc. More and more paralegals are joining these staffs, particularly paralegals with prior law office experience.

10. Related Fields

Experienced paralegals have also been using their training and experience in a number of nonpractice legal fields. Many are becoming law librarians at firms. Paralegal schools often hire paralegals to teach courses and to work in administration, in such areas as admissions, internship coordination, placement, etc. Law offices with large numbers of paralegals have hired paralegal administrators or supervisors to help recruit, train, and manage the paralegals. Some paralegals have become legal administrators or office managers with administrative responsibilities throughout the firm. It is clear that we have not seen the end of the development of new roles for paralegals within the law firm or in related areas of the law. At the end of Chapter 3, a more extensive list of such roles will be provided. (See Figure 3.11.)

Key Terms

private law firm
legal clinic
paralegal manager
paralegal specialist
general schedule (GS)
Office of Personnel
   Management

neighborhood legal
   service office
judicare
indigents
corporate counsel
special interest groups
group legal services

assigned counsel
legal insurance
public defender
freelance paralegal
service company
consulting firm

What Paralegals Do

■ Chapter Outline

We now examine forty-five areas of specialty work throughout the ten categories of paralegal employment just discussed. Paralegals often work in more than one of these specialties, and there is considerable overlap in the functions performed. The trend, however, is for paralegals to specialize. This follows the pattern of most attorneys.

"The question so often asked of us is, 'What exactly do you do?' "
Douglas Parker, Paralegal, Pasadena, California, 1989.

1. Administrative Law

I. Government Employment

Many paralegals work for specific administrative agencies. (See also Figure 2.3 for a list of paralegal functions in state agencies.) They might:

A. Handle questions and complaints from citizens.

B. Draft proposed regulations for the agency.

C. Perform legal research.

D. Provide litigation assistance in the agency and in court.

E. Represent the government at administrative hearings where authorized.

F. Manage the law office.

G. Train and supervise other nonattorney personnel.

II. Representation of Citizens

Some administrative agencies authorize nonattorneys to represent citizens at hearings and other agency proceedings. (See also *immigration law, pro bono work, public sector, social security law,* and *welfare law.*)

A. Interview client.

B. Conduct investigation.

C. Perform legal research.

D. Engage in informal advocacy at the agency.

E. Represent the client at agency hearing.

F. Draft documents for submission at hearing.

G. Monitor activities of the agency—for example, attend rule-making hearings to take notes on matters relevant to particular clients.

H. Prepare witnesses, reports, and exhibits designed to influence the drafting of regulations at the agency.

▪ Comment on Paralegal Work in this Area:

We "have a great deal of autonomy and an opportunity to develop expertise in particular areas." We have our "own caseloads, interview clients and then represent those clients at administrative hearings." Georgia Ass'n of Legal Assistants, *Sallye Jenkins Sapp, Atlanta Legal Aid; Sharon Mahaffey Hill, Georgia Legal Services,* 10 ParaGraph 5 (1987).

When I got my first case at a hearing before the State Department of Mental Health, I was "scared to death!" But the attorneys in the office were very supportive. "They advised me to make a good record, noting objections for the transcript, in case of future appeal. Making the right objections was scary." Milano, *New Responsibilities Being Given to Paralegals,* 8 Legal Assistant Today 27, 28 (November/December 1990).

2. Admiralty Law

This area of the law, also referred to as maritime law, covers accidents, injuries, and death connected with vessels on navigable waters. Special legislation exists in this area, such as the Jones Act. (See also *international law, litigation,* and *tort law.*)

I. Investigation

A. Obtain the facts of the event involved.

B. Arrange to board the vessel to photograph the scene of the accident.

C. Collect facts relevant to the seaworthiness of the vessel.

D. Take statements from witnesses.

II. Legal Research

A. Research liability under the applicable statutes.

B. Research special procedures to obtain compensation.

III. Subrogation

A. Handle small cargo subrogation files.

B. Prepare status reports for clients.

IV. Litigation

A. Draft complaints and other pleadings.

B. Respond to discovery requests.

C. Monitor maritime files to keep track of discovery deadlines.

D. Coordinate projects by expert witnesses.

E. Provide general trial assistance.

■ Comment on Paralegal Work in this Area:

Jimmie Muvern, CLA (Certified Legal Assistant), works for a sole practitioner in Baton Rouge, Louisiana who specializes in maritime litigation: "If there is a doubt regarding the plaintiff's status as a Jones Act seaman, this issue is generally raised by a motion for summary judgment filed well in advance of trial, and it is good practice for the legal assistant who may be gathering facts regarding the client's accident to also gather facts from the client and from other sources which might assist the attorney in opposing summary judgment on the issue of the client's status as a Jones Act seaman." J. deGravelles & J. Murvin, *Who Is a Jones Act Seaman?* 12 Facts & Findings 34 (NALA, April 1986).

3. Advertising Law

(See also *administrative law* and *intellectual property law*.)

I. Compliance Work

A. *Advertising:* Review advertising of company products in order to identify possible claims made in the advertising about the product. Collect data needed to support the accuracy of claims made in advertising pursuant to regulations of the Federal Trade Commission and company guidelines.

B. *Labels:* Review labels of company products to insure compliance with the regulations on deception of the Federal Trade Commission. Insure compliance with the Food & Drug Administration and company policy on:

1. Product identity,
2. New weight statement,
3. Ingredient list,

4. Name and address of manufacturer/distributor,
5. Nutrition information.

C. *Product promotions:* Review promotions for company products (coupons, sweepstakes, bonus packs, etc.) to insure compliance with Federal Trade Commission guidelines, state laws, and company policy.

II. Inquiries and Complaints

A. Keep up-to-date on government regulations on advertising.

B. Help company attorney respond to inquiries and complaints from the public, a competitor, the Federal Trade Commission, the Food & Drug Administration, the state's attorney general, etc.

■ Comment on Paralegal Work in this Area:

"On the surface, my job certainly does not fit the 'traditional' paralegal role. If a fortune teller had ever read my coffee grounds, I might have learned that my paralegal career would include being part of the production of commercials and labels for household products I had grown up with. . . . My employer, the Proctor & Gamble Company, is one of the largest consumer product companies in the United States." Its "Legal Division consists of forty attorneys and nine paralegals. Advertising law is challenging. It requires ingenuity, fast thinking and mastery of tight deadlines." Kothman, *Advertising Paralegal Finds Own Label,* National Paralegal Reporter 12 (NFPA, Spring 1990).

4. Antitrust Law

(See also *administrative law, corporate law, criminal law,* and *litigation*.)

I. Investigation/Analysis

A. Accumulate statistical and other technical data on a company or industry involved in litigation. Check Securities & Exchange Commission

(SEC) filings, annual reports, advertising brochures, etc.

B. Prepare reports on economic data.

C. Obtain data from government bodies.

D. Find and interview potential witnesses.

II. Administrative Agency

A. Monitor the regulations and decisions of the Federal Trade Commission.

B. Prepare drafts of answers to requests for information from the Federal Trade Commission.

III. Litigation

A. Assist in drafting pleadings.

B. Request company witness files in preparation for deposition.

C. Schedule depositions.

D. Draft form interrogatories.

E. Prepare special exhibits.

F. Organize, index, and digest voluminous records and lengthy documents.

G. Prepare trial notebook.

H. Attend trial and take notes on testimony of witnesses.

I. Cite check briefs of attorneys.

J. Provide general trial assistance.

■ Comment on Paralegal Work in this Area:

When Mitchell became a permanent employee at the firm, "he was given three days' worth of files to read in order to familiarize himself with the [antitrust] case. At this point in the case, the firm had already gone through discovery of 27,000 documents. Mitchell analyzed and summarized documents with the other ten paralegals hired to work on the case. With a major case such as this one, paralegals did not have a regular nine to five work day. Mitchell frequently worked seventy hours a week (for which he was paid overtime). In January, Mitchell and his team were sent across the country to take depo-

sitions for the case. His air transportation, accommodations, and meals were all 'first class,' but this was not a vacation; he worked around the clock." R. Berkey, *New Career Opportunities in the Legal Profession,* 47 (Arco, 1983).

5. Banking Law

Paralegals employed by banks often work in the bank trust department. They also work in bank legal departments, where they become involved with litigation, real estate, bankruptcy, consumer affairs, and securities law. In addition to banks, paralegals work for savings and loan institutions and other commercial lenders. Finally, some paralegals are employed in law firms that specialize in banking law. The following overview of duties is limited to the paralegal working for the legal department of a bank. (See also *administrative law, corporate law, estates law,* and *municipal finance law.*)

I. Claims

Assist legal staff in assessing bank liability for various claims, such as negligence and collection abuse.

II. Compliance Analysis

Determine whether the bank is complying with the regulations and statutes that regulate the banking industry.

III. Monitoring

Keep track of the activities of the various banking regulatory agencies and of the legislative committees with jurisdiction over banks.

IV. Litigation

Assist attorneys litigating claims.

V. Miscellaneous

A. Draft and/or review loan applications and accompanying credit documents.

B. Perform document analysis on
   1. Financial statements,
   2. Mortgages,

3. Assignments,
4. Security agreements.

C. Conduct UCC (Uniform Commercial Code) searches.

D. Assemble closing documents.

E. Arrange for and attend loan closings.

F. Prepare notarization of documents.

G. Monitor recordation.

H. Act as liaison among supervising attorney at the bank, the loan officer, and the customer.

I. Perform routine legal research and analysis for the Compliance Department.

■ Comment on Paralegal Work in this Area:

Ruth Sendecki is "the first legal assistant" at Merchants National Bank, one of the Midwest's largest bank holding companies. Most paralegals employed at banks today work in the trust department; Ruth, however, works with "general banking" at Merchants. Before this job, she worked at a bank, but not in a legal capacity. "You don't have to limit yourself to a law firm. You can combine being a legal assistant with other interests." Her "primary responsibility is in the commercial loan department. . . . She also serves the mortgage loan, correspondent banking and the international banking departments." According to her supervisor at the bank, "She is readily accessible for the benefit of the attorney, the loan officer and the customer to facilitate completion of the arrangements for both sides." Furthermore, she "is expanding her knowledge base, and other departments are drawing on her knowledge." Kane, *A Banker with the Soul of a Legal Assistant,* 5 Legal Assistant Today 65 (July/August 1988).

6. Bankruptcy Law

Paralegals in this area of law may be employed by a law firm that represents the debtor (e.g., an individual, a business); a creditor (e.g., a bank-mortgagee); or the trustee in bankruptcy. (A trustee in bankruptcy does not have to be a lawyer. Some

paralegals with bankruptcy experience have in fact become trustees.) A few paralegals work directly for a bankruptcy judge as a clerk or deputy in Bankruptcy Court. The following overview assumes the paralegal works for a firm that represents the debtor. (See also *banking law, collections law, contract law,* and *litigation.*)

I. Interviewing/Data Collection

A. Help client fill out an extensive questionnaire on assets and liabilities. May visit client's place of business to determine the kinds of records kept there.

B. Help client assemble documents:
1. Loan agreements,
2. Deeds of trust,
3. Security agreements,
4. Creditor lists,
5. Payables lists,
6. Employment contracts,
7. Financial statements,
8. Leases, etc.

II. Investigation

A. Confirm amounts of indebtedness.

B. Identify secured and unsecured claims of creditors.

C. Check UCC (Uniform Commercial Code) filings at the secretary of state's office and at county clerk's office.

D. Check real property records in the clerk's office of the county where the property is located.

E. Verify taxes owed; identify tax liens.

F. Identify exempt property.

III. Asset Control

A. Open bankruptcy file.

B. Prepare inventories of assets and liabilities.

C. Arrange for valuation of assets.

IV. Creditor Contact

A. Answer inquiries of creditors on the status of the case.

B. Request documentation from creditors on claims.

V. Drafting

A. Original bankruptcy petition.

B. Schedule of liabilities.

C. Statement of affairs.

D. Status reports.

E. Final account.

VI. Coordination

A. Serve as liaison with trustee in bankruptcy.

B. Coordinate meeting of creditors.

C. Prepare calendar of filing and other deadlines.

■ *Comment on Paralegal Work in this Area:*

"As a legal assistant, you can play a major role in the representation of a Chapter 11 debtor. From prefiling activities through confirmation of the plan of reorganization, there are numerous duties which you can perform to assist in the successful reorganization of the debtor." Morzak, *Organizing Reorganization,* 5 Legal Assistant Today 33 (January/February).

"Bankruptcy work is unusual in a number of ways—extremely short statutes of limitation, for example. . . . The field is one in which there's lots of opportunity for paralegals. The paralegal does everything except sign the papers. . . . Most attorneys do not like bankruptcy, but if you do all the legwork for them, you can make a lot of money for them." Johnson, *The Role of the Paralegal/Legal Assistant in Bankruptcy and Foreclosure,* AALA News 7 (Alaska Ass'n of Legal Assistants, March 1987).

7. Civil Rights Law

(See also *labor and employment law, pro bono work,* and *public sector.*)

I. Government Paralegal

A. Help identify and resolve discrimination complaints (based on sex, race, age, etc.) made by government employees against the government.

B. Help government attorneys litigate discrimination complaints (based on sex, race, age, etc.) brought by citizens against the government, against other citizens, or against companies.

II. Representation of Citizens

Assist law firms representing citizens in their discrimination complaints against the government, other citizens, or companies:

A. In court.

B. In special agencies created to hear discrimination cases, such as the Equal Employment Opportunity Commission or the Human Rights Commission.

■ *Comment on Paralegal Work in this Area:*

"One aspect that Matthews likes is that each case is a different story, a different set of facts. 'There is a lot of interaction with people in the courts and with the public. We do a great deal of civil rights litigation, everything from excessive police force to wrongful termination. Sometimes there are as many as 60 witnesses. The lawyers depend on me to separate the witnesses out and advise them which ones would do best in the courtroom. A lot of times the lawyer does not know the witness and has not seen the witness until the person is in the courtroom testifying.' For one case, Matthews reviewed more than 1,000 slides taken in a nightclub, looking for examples of unusual or rowdy behavior. The slides included everything from male strippers to people flashing. Autopsy and horrible injury photographs are also part of the job." *Broadening into the Paralegal Field,* 39 The Docket 7 (NALS, January/February 1991).

8. Collections Law[1]

(See also *banking law, bankruptcy law, contract law,* and *litigation.*)

I. Acceptance of Claims

A. Open file.

B. Prepare index of parties.

C. Prepare inventory of debts of debtor.

II. Investigation

A. Conduct asset check.

B. Verify address.

C. Verify filings at secretary of state's office and county clerk's office (e.g., UCC filings).

D. Contact credit bureau.

E. Verify information in probate court, registry of deeds, etc.

III. Litigation Assistant (Civil Court, Small Claims Court)

A. Draft pleadings.

B. Arrange for witnesses.

C. File documents in court.

D. Assist in settlement/negotiation of claim.

E. Assist in enforcement work, such as:

1. Wage attachment (prejudgment attachment),

2. Supplementary process,

3. Execution,

4. Seizure of personal property.

■ *Comment on Paralegal Work in this Area:*

"O.K.—So, it [collections work] is not the nicest job in the world, but somebody has to do it, right? If the attorney you work for does not want to do it, there are plenty more in town who will. For a paralegal working in this area, there is always something new to learn. . . . It is sometimes difficult to see the results of your la-

bor right away in this kind of work, as very few files are paid in full and closed in a short period of time. It is disheartening to go through many steps and possibly spend a great deal of time just trying to get someone served or to locate someone, and then end up with nothing. I will admit that collections can be very frustrating, but boring they are not!" Wexel, *Collections: Persistence Pay$ Off,* The Paraview (Metrolina Paralegal Ass'n, April 1987).

"I currently have responsibility for some 400 collection cases. My days are spent on the phone talking to debtors, drafting the necessary pleadings, executing forms, and hopefully depositing the money collected. The exciting part of collection is executing on a judgment. We were successful in garnishing an insurance company's account for some $80,000 when they refused to pay a judgment that had been taken against them. We have also gone with the Sheriff to a beer distributorship two days before St. Patrick's Day to change the locks on the building housing gallons and gallons of green beer. The debtor suddenly found a large sum of money to pay us so that we would release the beer in time for St. Patrick's day." R. Swoagerm, *Collections Paralegal,* The Citator 9 (Legal Assistants of Central Ohio, August 1990).

9. Communications Law

(See also *administrative law* and *entertainment law.*)

I. Government Paralegal

Assist attorneys at the Federal Communications Commission (FCC) in regulating the communications industry—for example, help with rule-making, license applications, hearings.

II. Representation of Citizens or Companies

A. Draft application for licenses.

B. Prepare compliance reports.

---

[1]See Commercial Law League of America, Seminar, *A Paralegal Approach to the Practice of Commercial Law* (11/14/75).

C. Prepare exemption applications.

D. Prepare statistical analyses.

E. Monitor activities of the FCC.

F. Assist in litigation.
   1. Within the FCC,
   2. In court.

■ *Comment on Paralegal Work in this Area:*

The current specialty of Carol Woods is the regulation of television and radio. "I am able to do work that is important and substantive, and am able to work independently. I have an awful lot of contact with clients, with paralegals at the client's office, and with government agencies. One of the liabilities of private practice for both attorneys and paralegals is that there is so much repetition and you can get bored. A lot of times as a paralegal you can't call the shots or know everything that goes into the planning of a project. However, when you can participate in all facets of a project, it's great!" A. Fins, *Opportunities in Paralegal Careers,* 84 (Nat'l Textbook Co., 1979).

10. Construction Law

(See also *contract law, litigation,* and *tort law.*)

I. Claims Assistance

A. Work with engineering consultants in the preparation of claims.

II. Data Collection

A. Daily manpower hours,

B. Amount of concrete poured,

C. Change of orders.

III. Document Preparation

A. Prepare graphs.

B. Prepare special studies—for example, compare planned with actual progress on construction project.

C. Prepare documents for negotiation/settlement.

D. Help draft arbitration claim forms.

IV. Assist in litigation.

■ *Comment on Paralegal Work in this Area:*

"Because of the complex factual issues that arise with construction disputes, legal assistants are critical in identifying, organizing, preparing, and analyzing the extensive relevant factual information. In many cases, whether a party wins or loses depends on how effectively facts are developed from documents, depositions, interviews, and site inspections. Thus, a successful construction litigation team will generally include a legal assistant skilled in organization and management of complex and voluminous facts. . . . Construction litigation also provides legal assistants with a very distinctive area for expertise and specialization." M. Gowen, *A Guide for Legal Assistants* 229 (Practicing Law Institute, 1986).

11. Contract Law

The law of contracts is involved in a number of different paralegal specialties. (See also *advertising law, antitrust law, banking law, bankruptcy law, collections law, construction law, corporate law, employee benefits law, entertainment law, family law, government contract law, insurance law, intellectual property law, international law, labor and employment law, landlord-tenant law, municipal finance law, oil and gas law, real estate law,* and *tax law.*)

I. Contract Review

A. Review contracts to determine compliance with terms.

B. Investigate facts involving alleged breach of contract.

C. Do legal research on the law of contracts in a particular specialty.

II. Litigation Assistance

III. Preparation of Contract Forms

A. Separation agreements,

B. Employment contracts,

C. Contracts for sale, etc.

■ *Comment on Paralegal Work in this Area:*

"The . . . paralegal also assists two attorneys in drafting reviewing, researching, revising and finalizing a variety of contracts, including Entertainment, Participant and Operational Agreements. Much of the . . . paralegal's time is spent studying existing contracts looking for provisions that may answer any inquiries or disputes. With hundreds of agreements presently active, researching, reviewing, amending, terminating, revising and executing contracts is an everyday activity for [the] . . . Legal Department." Miquel, *Walt Disney World Company's Legal Assistants: Their Role in the Show,* 16 Facts and Findings 29, 30 (NALA, January 1990).

"Initially, my primary job was to review contracts, and act as Plan Administrator for the 401(k). I was also involved in the negotiation and development of a distributor agreement to market SPSS software to the Soviet Union. Most contract amendments were to software license agreements. The pace picked up when I was promoted to Manager of Human Services, while retaining all of my previous responsibilities." Illinois Paralegal Ass'n, *Spotlight on . . . Laurel Bauer,* 20 Outlook 21 (Winter 1991).

12. Corporate Law

Paralegals involved in corporate law mainly work in one of two settings: law firms that represent corporations, and legal departments of corporations. Corporate legal departments often are run by an attorney called the general counsel. (See also *banking law, employee benefits law, insurance law, labor and employment law, real estate law,* and *tax law.*)

I. Incorporation and General Corporate Work

A. Preincorporation.

1. Check availability of proposed corporate name and, if available, reserve it.
2. Draft preincorporation subscriptions and consent forms for initial board of directors where required by statute.
3. Record articles of incorporation.
4. Order corporate supplies.

B. Incorporation.

1. Draft and file articles of incorporation with appropriate state agency.
   a. Subchapter S corporation,
   b. Close corporation,
   c. Nonprofit corporation.
2. Draft minutes of initial meetings of incorporators and directors.
3. Draft corporate bylaws.
4. Obtain corporate seal, minute book, and stock certificate book.
5. Prepare necessary documents to open a corporate bank account.

C. Directors meetings.

1. Prepare and send out waivers and notices of meetings.
2. Draft minutes of directors meetings.
3. Draft resolutions to be considered by directors:
   a. Sale of stock,
   b. Increase in capitalization,
   c. Stock splits,
   d. Stock option,
   e. Pension plan,
   f. Dividend distribution,
   g. Election of officers.

D. Shareholders meetings (annual and special).

1. Draft sections of annual report relating to business activity, officers, and directors of company.
2. Draft notice of meeting, proxy materials, and ballots.

3. Prepare agenda and script of meeting.

4. Draft oath and report of judge of elections when required.

5. Maintain all of the corporate minute books and resolutions. ·

E. Draft and prepare general documents:

1. Shareholder agreement,

2. Employment contract,

3. Employee benefit plan,

4. Stock option plan,

5. Trust agreement,

6. Tax return,

7. Closing papers on corporate acquisition.

8. See also drafting tasks listed above in reference to directors and shareholders meetings.

II. Public Sale of Securities

A. Compile information concerning officers and directors for use in Registration Statement.

B. Assist in research of blue sky requirements.

C. Closing:

1. Prepare agenda,

2. Obtain certificates from state agencies with respect to good standing of company and certified corporate documents,

3. Prepare index and organize closing binders.

III. Research

A. Legislative reporting: keep track of pending legislation that may affect office clients.

B. Extract designated information from corporate records and documents.

C. Assemble financial data from records on file at SEC and state securities regulatory agencies.

D. Undertake short- and long-term statistical and financial research on companies.

E. Perform legal research.

IV. General Assistance

A. Maintain tickler system (specifying, for example, next corporate meeting, upcoming trial, appellate court dates, etc.).

B. Monitor the daily law journal or newspaper in order to identify certain cases on calendars of courts, current court decisions, articles, etc. and forward such data in the journal or newspaper to appropriate office attorneys.

C. Act as file managers for certain clients (index, digest, and monitor documents in the file; prepare case profiles; etc.).

D. Maintain corporate forms file.

V. Miscellaneous

A. Prepare documents for qualification to do business in foreign jurisdictions.

B. Prepare filings with regulatory agencies.

C. Assist in processing patent, copyright, and trademark applications.

D. Coordinate escrow transactions.

E. Work on certificates of occupancy.

F. Prepare documents needed to amend bylaws or articles of incorporation.

G. Prepare interrogatories.

H. Digest deposition testimony.

I. Perform cite checks.

■ *Comment on Paralegal Work in this Area:*

"When the majority of people describe a legal assistant or a paralegal, they often think of courtroom battles, million dollar lawsuits and mountains of depositions. For those of us in the corporate area, these sights are replaced with board room battles, million dollar mergers and mountains of prospectus. Some of us have NEVER seen the inside of a courtroom or have never touched a pleading. I guess it can be said that 'we don't do windows, we don't type, and we don't do litigation.' A corporate paralegal is never without a multitude of projects that offer excitement or anxiety. This isn't to say, however, that the corporate field is without its fair share of boredom. . . . The future is only limited by your imagination. Not every paralegal wants the drama of a landmark case. Some of us are quite content seeing a client's company written up in the *Wall Street Journal* for the first time!" D. Zupanovich, *The Forming of a Corporate Paralegal,* 2 California Paralegal 4 (July/September 1990).

"The company I work for is a major worldwide producer of chemicals. . . . I recently had to obtain some technical information about the computer system at a hotel in a foreign country in order to set up documents on a diskette that would be compatible with the computer system in that country before one of the attorneys went there for contract negotiations. . . . One of the most thrilling experiences I have had since working for the company was that of working on the closing of a leveraged buyout of a portion of our business in Delaware. To experience first-hand the intensity of the negotiating table, the numerous last-minute changes to documents, the multitudinous shuffle of papers, and the late, grueling hours was both exhausting and exhilarating." Grove, *Scenes from a Corporate Law Department,* The Paraview 2 (Metrolina Paralegal Ass'n, February 1990).

"Even 'dream jobs' have their moments of chaos. After only two months on the job [at Nestle Foods Corporation] Cheryl had to prepare for a Federal Trade Commission Second Request for Production of Documents relating to an acquisition. She suddenly was thrown into the job of obtaining and organizing over 6,000 documents from around the world, creating a document database and managing up to 10 temporary paralegals at a time. Of course, this preparation included weekends and evenings for a six-week period. Cheryl calls December the 'lost month.' " Scior, *Paralegal Profile: Corporate Paralegal,* Post Script 14 (Manhattan Paralegal Ass'n, April/May 1990).

■ *Quotes from Want Ads:*

Law firm seeks paralegal for corporate work: "Ideal candidate is a self-starter with good communications skills and is willing to work overtime." "Ability to work independently is a must." Paralegal needed to assist corporate secretary: "Analytical, professional attitude essential. Knowledge of state and/or federal regulatory agencies required." "Ability to work under pressure." "All candidates must possess excellent writing and drafting skills." "Ideal candidate is a self-starter with good communication/research skills and is willing to work overtime." "Candidate having less than three years experience in general corporate legal assistance need not apply." Position requires "word processing experience and ability to manage multiple projects." Position requires "intelligent, highly motivated individual who can work with little supervision." "Great opportunity to learn all aspects of corporate business transactions." Position requires "career-minded paralegal with excellent organizational and communications skills, keen analytical ability and meticulous attention to detail." Position requires "an experienced paralegal with a strong blue-sky background particularly in public and private real estate syndication." Applicant must have "excellent academic credentials, be analytical, objective, and dedicated to performing thorough quality work and to displaying a professional attitude to do whatever it takes to get the job done and meet deadlines."

13. Criminal Law[2]

(See also *litigation* and *military law.*)

I. Paralegal Working for Criminal/ Civil Division Prosecutor

A. Log incoming cases.

---

[2]See J. Stein & B. Hoff, *Paralegals and Administrative Assistants for Prosecutors* (Nat'l District Attorneys Ass'n, 1974); and J. Stein, *Paralegals: A Resource for Defenders and Correctional Services* (1976).

B. Help office screen out cases that are inappropriate for arrest, cases that are eligible for diversion, etc.

C. Act as liaison with police department and other law enforcement agencies.

D. Prepare periodic, statistical, caseload reports.

E. Interview citizens seeking the prosecution of alleged wrongdoers; prepare case files.

F. Help the Consumer Fraud Department resolve minor consumer complaints—for instance, contact the business involved to determine whether a settlement of the case is possible without prosecution.

G. Conduct field investigations as assigned.

H. Prepare documents for URESA cases (Uniform Reciprocal Enforcement of Support Act).

I. Monitor status of URESA cases.

J. Help office maintain its case calendar.

K. Act as liaison among the prosecutor, the victim, and witnesses while the case is being prepared for trial and during the trial.

L. Act as general litigation assistant during the trial and the appeal.

II. Paralegal Working for Defense Attorney

A. Interview defendants to determine eligibility for free legal defense (if the paralegal works for a public defender).

B. Conduct comprehensive interview of defendant on matters relevant to the criminal charge(s).

C. Help the defendant gather information relevant to the determination of bail.

D. Help the defendant gather information relevant to eligibility for diversion programs.

E. Conduct field investigations as assigned; interview witnesses.

F. Help obtain discovery, particularly through police reports and search warrants.

G. Act as general litigation assistant during the trial and the appeal.

■ · Comment on Paralegal Work in this Area:

"Ivy speaks with an obvious love for her current job in the State Attorney's office. In fact, she said she would not want to do anything else! She also said there is no such thing as a typical day in her office, which is one of the many aspects of her job she enjoys. She not only helps interview witnesses and prepare them for trial, but she often must locate a witness, requiring some detective work! Ivy assisted in a case involving an elderly woman who was victimized after the death of her husband. The woman was especially vulnerable because of her illiteracy. Through the help of the State Attorney's office, the woman was able to recover her money and get assistance with housing and learning to read. Ivy continues to keep in touch with the woman and feels the experience to be very rewarding." Frazier, *Spotlight on Ivy Hart-Daniel,* JLA News 2 (Jacksonville Legal Assistants, Inc., January 1989).

"Kitty Polito says she and other lawyers at McClure, McClure & Kammen use the firm's sole paralegal not only to do investigations but 'to pick cases apart piece by piece.' Polito credits legal assistant Juliann Klapp with 'cracking the case' of a client who was accused by a co-defendant of hitting the victim on the back of the head. At trial, the pathologist testified that the victim had been hit from left to right. Klapp passed a note to the attorneys pointing out that such a motion would have been a back-handed swing for their right-handed client. Thus it was more likely that the co-defendant, who is left-handed, was the one who hit the victim. The defendant won." Brandt, *Paralegals' Acceptance and Utilization Increasing in Indy's Legal Community,* 1 The Indiana Lawyer 1 (June 20, 1990).

14. Employee Benefits Law[3]

Employee benefits paralegals work in a number of different settings: in law firms, banks, large corporations, insurance companies, or accounting firms. The following overview of tasks covers a paralegal working for a law firm. (See also *contract law, corporate law, labor and employment law, social security law,* and *worker's compensation law.*)

I. Drafting of Employee Plans

A. Work closely with the attorney, the plan sponsor, the plan administrator, and the trustee in preparing and drafting qualified employee plans, such as:
1. Stock bonus plans,
2. Profit sharing plans,
3. Money purchase pensions,
4. Other pension plans,
5. Trust agreements,
6. Individual Retirement Account (IRA) plans,
7. Annuity plans,
8. HR-10 or Keogh plans,
9. Employee stock ownership plans,
10. Life and health insurance plans,
11. Worker's compensation plans,
12. Social security plans.

II. Document Preparation and Program Monitoring

A. Gather information.
B. Determine eligibility for participation and benefits.
C. Notify employees of participation.
D. Complete input forms for document assembly.
E. Assemble elections to participate.
F. Determine beneficiary designations.
G. Record elections to contribute.

H. Allocate annual contributions to individual participant accounts.
I. Prepare annual account statements for participants.
J. Identify any potential discrimination problems in the program.

III. Government Compliance Work Pertaining To:

A. Tax requirements for qualifications, amendment, and termination of plan.
B. Department of Labor reporting and disclosure requirements.
C. Insurance requirements.
D. Welfare and Pension Plans Disclosure Act requirements.
E. ERISA requirements (Employee Retirement Income Security Act).
F. Pension Benefit Guaranty Corporation requirements.

IV. Miscellaneous

A. Help draft summary plan descriptions for distribution to employees.
B. Help prepare and review annual reports of plans.
C. Continue education in current law of the field—for instance, become a Certified Employee Benefit Specialist (CEBS).

■ *Comment on Paralegal Work in this Area:*

"Michael Montchyk was looking to use his undergraduate degree in statistics. . . . He now works for attorneys specializing in employee benefits, where understanding numbers and familiarity with the law are key skills." Lehren, *Paralegal Work Enhancing Careers of Many,* Philadelphia Business Journal 9B (August 6, 1990).

"This area is not for everybody. To succeed, you need considerable detail orientation, solid writing skills, self-motivation, the ability to keep up with a legal landscape that is never the same, and a knack for handling crisis situations which arise when least expected." Ger-

---

[3]Rocky Mountain Legal Assistants Association, *The Use of the Legal Assistant* (1975).

mani, *Opportunities in Employee Benefits,* SJPA Reporter 7 (South Jersey Paralegal Ass'n, January 1989).

15. Entertainment Law

(See also *contract law, corporate law,* and *intellectual property law.*)

I. Types of Client Problem Areas

A. *Copyright and trademark law:* Applying for government protection for intellectual property, such as plays, films, video, music, and novels.

B. *Contract law:* Help negotiate and draft contracts, and ensure their enforcement.

C. *Labor law:* Assist in compliance with the contracts of unions or guilds.

D. *Corporate law:*
   1. Assist in formation of business organizations.
   2. Work on mergers.
   3. Maintain compliance with federal and state reporting laws and regulations.

E. *Tax law:* planning and compliance.
   1. Report passive royalty income, talent advances, residuals, etc.
   2. Allocate expenditures to specific projects.

F. *Family law:* Assist with prenuptial agreements, divorces, child custody, etc.

II. Tasks

A. Register copyrights.

B. Help a client affiliate with his or her guild.

C. Monitor remake and sequel rights to films.

D. Prepare documents to grant a license to use client's music.

E. Check title registrations with the Motion Picture Association of America.

F. Read scripts to determine whether clearances are needed for certain kinds of material and references.

G. Apply for permits and licenses.

H. Calculate costs of property rights.

■ *Comment on Paralegal Work in this Area:*

"I am a paralegal in the field of entertainment law, one of the fastest growing, and, to me, most exciting areas of the paralegal profession, and one whose duties are as varied as the practices of the lawyers for whom we work. . . . I started in a very large Century City firm whose entertainment practice covers everything from songwriters to financing of major motion pictures, and from major recording stars and producers to popular novelists. . . . My specialty (yes, a specialty within a specialty) is music. . . . My husband is also an entertainment paralegal who works for 20th Century Fox. . . . Never, ever a dull moment!" Birkner, *Entertainment Law: A Growing Industry for the Paralegal,* 2 California Paralegal Magazine 7 (April/June 1990).

16. Environmental Law[4]

(See also *legislation, litigation, oil and gas law, real estate law,* and *water law.*)

I. Research

A. Research questions pertaining to the environment, land use, water pollution, and the National Environmental Policy Act.
   1. Locate and study pertinent state and federal statutes, case law, regulations, and law review articles.
   2. Obtain secondary materials (maps, articles, books) useful for broadening the information base.
   3. Contact, when appropriate, government officials or other informants for data or answers.

---

[4]Colorado Bar Association Legal Assistant Committee. These tasks have been approved by the Committee, not by the Board of Governors of the Colorado Bar.

4. Obtain and develop personality profiles of members of Congress, members of relevant bureaucracies, and other political figures.

5. Help prepare memoranda of findings, including citations and supporting documents.

B. Develop research notebooks for future reference. When new topics arise in environmental law, prepare notebooks to facilitate future research on similar topics.

C. Prepare bibliographies on environmental topics.

II. Drafting

A. Draft memoranda regarding new federal and state laws, regulations, or findings of research.

B. Draft memoranda discussing pertinent issues, problems, and possible solutions regarding public policy developments.

C. Draft narrative histories of legislation regarding political impulses, the impact of administrative and court rulings, and substantive and technical differences between drafts of legislation or results of amendments.

D. Draft and edit articles on coastal management programs and problems, conservation, water pollution, and the National Environmental Policy Act.

E. Edit environmental impact statements.

F. Assist in the preparation of briefs.

1. Check citations for pertinence and accuracy.

2. Develop table of contents, list of authorities, and certificate of service.

III. Hearing Participation

A. Locate and schedule witnesses.

B. Gather pertinent research materials (including necessary local documents, maps, and specific subject matter).

IV. Litigation: Provide General Trial Assistance

■ *Comment on Paralegal Work in this Area:*

Mary Peterson's firm has made a specialty of environmental and land use law. In a recent major hazardous waste case, "we will try to prove that the paint companies, dry cleaning stores and even the federal government, which used the property to build aircraft during the war" are responsible. "Some of the toxic waste dumped there were cited by federal agencies even back to 1935." Her job is to investigate the types of hazardous wastes and, with the help of the Freedom of Information Act, gather all available evidence. Then she studies it, duplicates, indexes, and writes summaries, which she distributes to the partners and associates. It's a case that has taken eight months so far and may go on for several years "because you don't know what you will uncover tomorrow. The toxins and pollutants could be different. There is no standard, just a constantly changing picture." Edwards, *The General Practice Paralegal* 8 Legal Assistant Today 49, 55 (March/April 1991).

17. Estates, Trusts, and Probate Law

(See also *banking law, collections law, employee benefits law, family law,* and *social security law.*)

I. Estate Planning

A. Collect data (birth dates, fair market value of assets, current assets and liabilities, etc.).

B. Prepare preliminary drafts of wills or trusts from sample forms.

C. Perform investment analysis in order to provide attorney who is fiduciary of estate with information relevant to investment options.

II. Office Management

A. Maintain tickler system.

B. Maintain attorney's calendar.

C. Open, index, monitor, and keep current all components of the client's trust and estate office file.

D. Operate computer in connection with accounting aspects of trusts and estates administered by the office.

E. Act as office law librarian (keeping loose-leaf texts up-to-date, etc.).

F. Train secretaries and other paralegals in the system used by the office to handle trusts, estates, and probate cases.

G. Selectively discard certain mail and underline significant parts of other mail.

III. Estate of Decedent

A. Assets phase.

1. Collect assets (such as bank accounts, custody accounts, insurance proceeds, social security death benefits, safety deposit box contents, and apartment contents).

2. Assist in the valuation of assets.

3. Maintain records (for example, record and file wills and trusts, vault inventories, powers of attorney, property settlements, fee cards, bill-payment letters).

4. Notify beneficiaries.

5. Prepare profiles of wills and trusts for attorney review.

B. Accounting phase.

1. Prepare preliminary drafts of federal and state death tax returns.

2. Apply the income-principal rules to the estate.

3. Organize data relevant to the tax implications of estates.

4. Prepare accountings: final and accounts current (this involves setting up a petition for a first and final accounting).

C. Termination-distribution phase.

1. Apply for the transfer of securities into the names of the people entitled.

2. Draw checks for the signature of executors.

3. Monitor legacies to charitable clients.

4. File and prepare tax waivers.

5. Assist with the closing documents.

6. Calculate distributable net income.

7. Follow up on collection and delivery.

IV. Litigation

1. Perform legal research.

2. Conduct factual research (investigation)—for instance, track down the names and addresses of all possible claimants and contact them.

3. Prepare sample pleadings.

4. Digest depositions (review, condense, point out inconsistencies, etc.).

5. Prepare drafts of interrogatories.

6. Prepare drafts of answers to interrogatories.

7. Notarize documents.

8. Act as court witness as to decedent's signature and other matters.

9. Assist with litigation.

■ *Comment on Paralegal Work in this Area:*

"What I like best about estate planning is that you work with people on a very individual basis. I don't think that in many other areas of law you get that one-on-one contact with the client. . . . You're working with people while they are thinking about the most important things in their lives—their families, their wealth and how to distribute it, and what they want to happen after they pass on. A lot of the clients contact me directly with their questions for the attorneys. Some of the widows especially are more comfortable calling me with their questions. They seem to think their questions might be 'stupid' and they're embarrassed to ask the attorneys directly. I can take their questions and see that the attorneys respond to them promptly." Bassett, *Top Gun Patricia Adams: Legal Assistant of the Year*, 6 Legal Assistant Today 70, 74 (July/August 1990).

"The position can be very stressful. But it is seldom boring. My typical day involves responding to many telephone inquiries from clients, dictating memos or letters requesting additional information concerning life insurance policies, valuation of assets, or simply sending notice of an upcoming hearing "to all persons entitled," etc. I draft virtually all documents needed in the administration of an estate, beginning with the initial petition for probate. . . . The decedent may have had an interest in a closely-held business, or leave minor or handicapped children, or leave a spouse with no knowledge of the family assets; these all require additional attention. Every case is different. Probate paralegals to some extent must be 'snoopy,' because you do learn a great deal about people, both deceased and living. In most cases your client is facing a difficult time with trepidation and it is your role to provide confidence. The end results are very rewarding." Rose, *Still a Probate Paralegal*, 12 The Journal 5 (Sacramento Ass'n of Legal Assistants, August 1990).

■ *Quotes from Want Ads:*

Law firm seeks someone with "good communication and organizational skills, [who] is self-motivated, relates well with attorneys, clients, and staff, is detail oriented, has a teamwork attitude, a pleasant personality, and is a non-smoker." Bank has opening for "trust tax administrator, with emphasis on personal and trust planning." Paralegal must have "technical understanding of wills and estate plans and terminology. Must be self-starter." "This is a full-time position with extensive responsibility for both court-supervised and noncourt-supervised estates and trusts." Position requires a person who "enjoys writing and proofreading, and who has excellent grammatical skills." Job is "for individual who enjoys the complexity and detail of accounting and bookkeeping in a

legal environment." "Applicants must be prepared to handle tax work."

18. Ethics and Professional Responsibility

Paralegals in this area work in two main settings: (1) in large law firms as a conflicts specialist, helping the firm determine whether conflicts of interest exist and (2) in state disciplinary agencies that investigate complaints against attorneys for unethical behavior.

I. Law Firm (*Conflicts Specialist* or *Conflicts Manager*)

A. Research
   1. Identify all persons or companies related to the prospective client.
   2. Determine whether the firm has ever represented the prospective client and/or any of its related parties.
   3. Determine whether the firm has ever represented an opponent of the prospective client and/or any of its related parties.

B. *Reports:* Notify attorney in charge of professional-responsibility matters of data indicating possible conflicts.

C. *Database work:* update information in client-list database on current and past clients.

II. Disciplinary Agency

A. Screen incoming data on new ethical complaints against attorneys.

B. Help investigate complaints.

C. Provide general litigation assistance to disciplinary attorneys during the proceedings at the agency and in court.

■ *Comment on Paralegal Work in this Area:*

Jane Palmer "does all the research on every prospective client, identifying all the related parties." Her computertized database tells her if the firm has ever represented a party on either side, or been adverse to them. "The most valuable thing has been my experience with the firm, developing somewhat of a corporate memory. The job takes extreme attention to detail. You may not always have all the information you need, so you have to be a detective. Quick response is important; so is making sure to keep things confidential." Sacramento Ass'n of Legal Assistants, *New Responsibilities Given to Paralegals,* The Journal 5 (February 1991).

19. Family Law[5]

(See also *contract law, employee benefits law, estates law, litigation, pro bono work,* and *public sector.*)

I. Telephone Screening of Clients

II. Commencement of Action

A. Interview client to obtain initial information for pleadings.

B. Prepare initial pleadings, including petition, summons and waiver of service, affidavit as to children, and response.

C. Draft correspondence to clients, courts, and other attorneys.

D. Arrange for service of process.

III. Temporary Orders

A. Prepare motions for temporary orders or temporary injunctions.

B. Draft notice and set hearings.

C. Assist in settlement negotiations.

D. Draft stipulations for temporary orders after negotiations.

IV. Financial Affidavits

A. Work with clients to gather and compile financial information.

B. Analyze income and expense information provided by client.

C. Work with accountants, financial advisors, brokers, and other financial experts retained by client.

D. Retain appraisers for real estate, business, and personal property.

E. Prepare financial affidavits.

V. Discovery

A. Prepare discovery requests.

B. Assist clients—gather documents and data to respond to discovery requests.

C. Help prepare responses to discovery requests.

D. Organize, index, and summarize discovered materials.

VI. Settlement Negotiations

A. Assist attorney in analysis of proposed settlements.

B. Research legal questions and assist in drafting briefs and memoranda.

C. Assist in drafting separation agreements.

VII. Hearings

A. Help prepare for final orders hearings.

B. Research legal questions and assist in drafting briefs and memoranda.

C. Assist in the preparation of trial exhibits and trial notebooks.

D. Arrange for expert witnesses and assist in preparing witnesses and clients for trial.

E. Attend hearings.

F. Prepare decree.

VIII. Post-Decree

A. Prepare documents for transfers of assets.

B. Arrange for the filing and recording of all transfer documents.

C. Review bills for tax-deductible fees and help prepare opinion letters to client.

D. Draft pleadings for withdrawal from case.

IX. Special Projects

A. Develop forms for gathering information from client.

---

[5]See footnote 4.

B. Maintain files on the following: separation-agreement provisions, current case law, resource materials for clients, and experts in various fields (e.g., custody, evaluation, and business appraisals).

■ *Comment on Paralegal Work in this Area:*

Karen Dunn, a family law paralegal, "draws considerable satisfaction from a divorce case where the client was a woman in her sixties whose husband had left her, a situation which created predictable distress, notably during discussion of financial aspects. She was able to tell me things she couldn't tell the attorney. I found out she had a thyroid condition, so she was able to get more money in the end. I worked with her on the financial affidavit and drafted temporary orders to provide child support and spousal maintenance until the decree was entered." Edwards, *The General Practice Paralegal* 8 Legal Assistant Today 49, 54 (March/April 1991).

"As the only paralegal in a one-attorney family law practice, my job responsibilities are numerous. I work for an attorney who believes her paralegal should handle nearly all the legal functions she does, with the exception of appearing in court on behalf of clients, taking depositions and giving legal advice. My skills are used to the maximum, as I gather and organize all case information, allowing the attorney to prepare for court and be more cost-effective. I am the liaison person between clients and the attorney. I am able to deal with the human, emotional aspects of our clients, and not just the technical aspects of the law. As each person is different, so is every case, which makes this job a continuing challenge." Lenihan, *Role of the Family Law Paralegal,* 10 Paragraph 6 (Oregon Legal Assistants Ass'n, August 1987).

■ *Quotes from Want Ads:*

Position is "excellent for a highly motivated person with excellent organizational skills and the ability to interface with clients." "Two swamped attorneys need reliable paralegal to work in fully computerized office. Must have excellent research and writing skills." Applicant must be "self-motivated, well-organized person who has initiative and can assume responsibility." Position requires "ability, experience, and attention to detail." "Looking for very professional applicants."

20. Government Contract Law[6]

(See also *administrative law, construction law, contract law, litigation,* and *water law.*)

I. Calendar

A. Maintain calendar for court and appeals board appearances.

B. Record dates briefs are due, etc.

II. Claims

A. Gather, review, summarize, and index client files.

B. Assist in drafting contract claims.

C. Conduct preliminary research on selected legal issues.

III. Appeals

A. Draft and answer interrogatories and requests for production of documents.

B. Summarize and index answers to discovery.

C. Assist in drafting appeal.

D. Prepare questions for witnesses and summarize prior testimony.

E. Maintain documents during hearing.

IV. Post-Hearing Briefs

A. Summarize and index transcripts.

B. Assist with analysis of government's brief.

C. Conduct preliminary research on selected issues.

D. Assist in drafting the post-hearing brief.

---

[6]Berg, C. *Annual Survey* (San Francisco Association of Legal Assistants, Dec. 19, 1973).

21. Immigration Law

(See also *administrative law, family law, international law, labor and employment law,* and *public sector.*)

I. Problem Identification

A. Help individual who has difficulty in obtaining:

    1. Visa,

    2. Permanent residency based on occupation,

    3. Nonimmigrant status,

    4. Citizenship status.

B. Help individuals who are faced with deportation proceedings.

II. Providing Information on

A. Visa process,

B. Permanent residency process,

C. Nonimmigrant status process,

D. Registration process,

E. Citizenship process,

F. Deportation process.

III. Investigation

Assist the individual in obtaining data and documentation on birth, travel, residency, etc.

IV. Referral

Refer individuals to foreign consulates, nationality organizations, government officials, etc., for assistance concerning their immigration status.

V. Applications/Forms

Assist the individual in filling out visa applications, permanent residency applications, etc.

VI. Monitor Consular Processing Procedure

■ *Comment on Paralegal Work in this Area:*

"This is not a specialty for the fainthearted or the misanthrope. The immigration paralegal may deal with much more than the timely filing of paperwork. One distinguishing feature of immigration work is our knowledge of intensely personal aspects of the client's life. We know his criminal record, the success and failure of his personal life, how much money he makes, and his dreams and aspirations. . . . Some clients have a very laissez-faire attitude towards perjury, and may invite the paralegal to participate without a blush. In America, [said one client] you lie *to* your attorney. In my country, you cook up the lie *with* your attorney." Myers & Raman, *Sweet-Talking Clients and Intransigent Bureaucrats,* 15 National Paralegal Reporter 4 (NFPA, Winter 1991).

22. Insurance Law

Paralegals in this area work for law firms that represent insurance companies who are defendants in litigation, often personal injury litigation. They also work for insurance companies themselves. The following overview covers the latter. (See also *corporate law, employee benefits law, litigation, social security law,* and *worker's compensation law.*)

I. Compliance

A. Analyze government regulations on the insurance industry.

B. Prepare applications for new insurance products to obtain approval from Department of Insurance.

II. Claims

A. Assist in processing disputed claims.

B. Provide trial assistance by coordinating activities of company attorneys with outside counsel representing the company.

III. Monitoring and Research

A. Monitor regulations of agencies and statutes of the legislatures that affect the insurance industry, including the committees of the legislature with jurisdiction over the industry.

B. Provide factual and legal research on inquiries that come into the office from agents and brokers.

■ *Comment on Paralegal Work in this Area:*

"Compliance is an insurance industry term which refers to keeping the company and its products in compliance with state and federal law, and procuring licenses for the company in unlicensed states. Compliance is a good field for paralegals because there is opportunity to work autonomously and also to advance within most companies." [I am a] Senior Compliance Analyst [at a life insurance company]. I have met many paralegals who are compliance analysts, compliance specialists, and compliance managers." Maston, *Insurance,* The Citator 8 (Legal Assistants of Central Ohio, August 1990).

23. Intellectual Property Law

(See also *contract law* and *entertainment law*.)

I. Copyrights

A. Application

1. Help client apply for registration of copyright for a novel, play, or other work with the Copyright Office.

2. Collect data, such as nature of the work, date completed, name of creator/author, name of owner of the work, etc., for application.

3. Help identify the classification for the copyright.

4. Examine the certificate of copyright registration for accuracy.

5. File the application.

B. Marketing

1. Identify potential users/licensees of the copyright.

2. Help prepare contracts.

C. Infringement

1. Conduct investigations to determine whether an infringement exists—for example, compare the copyrighted work with the alleged infringing work.

2. Provide general litigation assistance.

II. Patent

A. Application

1. Help the inventor apply for a patent with the U.S. Patent and Trademark Office.

2. Help the inventor describe the invention—for example, assemble designs, diagrams, and notebooks.

3. Conduct a patent search. Check technical libraries to determine the current state of the art.

4. Determine filing fees.

5. Help the client apply for protection in foreign countries.

6. Monitor the responses from government offices.

7. Examine certificate of patent for accuracy.

B. Marketing the invention

1. Help identify licensees. Solicit bids, conduct financial checks, study the market, etc.

2. Help prepare contracts.

C. Infringement

1. Conduct investigation on products that may have violated the patent.

2. Provide general litigation assistance.

III. Trademarks

A. Registration

1. Research trademark files or order search of trademark or trade name preliminary to an application before the U.S. Patent and Trademark Office.

2. Examine indexes and directories.

3. Conduct investigations to determine when the mark was first used, where, on what products, etc.

4. Prepare foreign trademark applications.

5. Respond to official actions taken by government offices.
6. Examine the certificate of trademark for accuracy.
7. Maintain files for renewals.

B. Infringement
   1. Conduct investigations into who else used the mark, when, where, in what market, etc.
   2. Provide general litigation assistance.

■ *Comment on Paralegal Work in this Area:*

"With the right training, trademark paralegals can find richly rewarding experiences waiting for them, whether they remain in paralegal work or go on to build careers in some other facet of trademark law. Trademark work is very dynamic." Wilkinson, *The Case for a Career in Trademark Law,* 7 Legal Professional 29 (November/December 1989).

"Paula Rein was a trademark paralegal before such a job title was even invented. Her career has spanned over 19 years, leading her to some of the biggest corporations and law firms in New York City. Her extensive knowledge of trademark administration has made her one of the most resourceful trademark paralegals in her occupation. In her current 'diversified position,' at a law firm that specializes in intellectual property, she works on the cases of clients in the food and service industries and professional associations. Paula thrives in her current position." Scior, *Paralegal Profile,* Postscript 13 (Manhattan Paralegal Ass'n, December 1989).

24. International Law

Example: a paralegal working on a "dumping" case in international trade.

I. Investigation

A. Examine the normal behavior in the industry/market affected.
B. Do statistical research (cost and price data).

C. Prepare profiles of domestic competitors.

II. Preparation of Documents

A. Help prepare for presentation before the Commerce Department.
B. Help prepare for presentation before the Court of International Trade.

III. Accounting Research

IV. Coordination of Data From:

A. Members of Congress,
B. Foreign embassies,
C. State Department,
D. U.S. Special Trade Representative.

■ *Comment on Paralegal Work in this Area:*

Steven Stark works "40–50 hours a week, specializing in international legal assisting, a hot area, while the Japanese are busy buying up American properties. [Steve became the liaison for the firm's Tokyo branch office. He originally expected to stay at the firm only three years, but found that] the longer you're here, the more they value you. New things still come up. You work with the constant tension of everyone being expected to perform at a very high level, at all times. This is a high-stakes game, with million and billion dollar deals. It's a peaked, emotional atmosphere, with long hours." Milano, *Career Profiles,* 8 Legal Assistant Today 35, 38 (September/October 1990).

25. Judicial Administration

Most courts have clerks to help with the administrative aspects of deciding cases. In addition, a few courts have paralegals that work for the court. They perform some of the functions of the administrative clerks, such as determining whether the parties have been properly notified of trial dates, checking filings and proposed orders from attorneys to determine whether anything appears inappropriate or premature, or obtaining additional information for a judge.

■ *Comment on Paralegal Work in this Area:*

"The Shreveport City Court has employed me as its paralegal in the civil department for the past six years. The Baton Rouge City Court employs several paralegals." We handle many matters such as determining if the legal delays for pleading have expired "before initialing the pleading and passing it on to the clerk or judge for signature. The most important task is the handling of default judgments. I must certify that proper service has been made. Perhaps I could be called a 'nitpicker' about these cases, but the judge acts on my certificate that everything is in order. It is always challenging to stay informed on our constantly changing procedural laws; I must keep a set of the Civil Procedure at my desk." Waterman, *The Court's Paralegal,* 3 NWLPA News 5 (Northwest Louisiana Paralegal Ass'n, November 1990).

26. Labor and Employment Law

(See also *civil rights law, contract law, employee benefits law,* and *worker's compensation law.*)

I. Investigation

Look into:
A. Sexual harassment.
B. Wrongful discharge.
C. Violation of occupational safety and health laws.
D. Violation of labor laws involving collective bargaining, union organization, grievance and arbitration procedures.
E. Violation of Civil Rights Act protecting against discrimination on the basis of race, national origin, sex, or physical handicap.
F. Violation of Age Discrimination in Employment Act.
G. Violation of Americans with Disabilities Act.

II. Compliance

Assist companies in the design and implementation of policies on:
A. Drug and alcohol testing.
B. AIDS in the workplace.
C. Race, sex, and age discrimination.

III. Litigation Assistance

A. Help handle labor disputes before the National Labor Relations Board, State Labor Relations Board, Civil Service Commission, Human Rights Board, and the courts.
B. Perform a variety of tasks:
 1. Maintain the files.
 2. Digest and index data in files.
 3. Arrange for depositions.
 4. Help draft petition and other pleadings.
 5. Maintain tickler system of due dates.
 6. Prepare exhibits.
 7. Prepare statistical data.
 8. Help prepare appeal.

■ *Comment on Paralegal Work in this Area:*

"My experience in the labor and employment area has proven to be both diverse and unique. It is diverse because of the various labor-related issues accessible to me as a paralegal. It is unique because it is an area of specialty which involves very few paralegals in my part of the state." Batke, *Labor and Employment Paralegal,* The Citator 3 (Legal Assistants of Central Ohio, August 1990).

"In the labor law area, I was responsible for doing background research, preparing witnesses and drafting arbitration briefs. I also assisted with the drafting of revised language during contract negotiations with unions." Diebold, *A Paralegal of Another Kind,* 16 Facts and Findings 38 (NALA, March 1990).

27. Landlord and Tenant Law

Paralegals in real estate law firms occasionally become involved in commercial lease cases, such as a dispute over the interpretation of the lease of a supermarket at a large shopping mall. Such landlord-tenant cases, however, are not as common as the cases that arise between landlords and tenants who live in the apartments they rent. For example, a landlord of a small apartment seeks to evict a tenant for nonpayment of rent. Many of these cases are handled by publicly funded legal service or legal aid offices which do not charge fees. (See *public sector, oil and gas law,* and *real estate law.*)

■ *Comment on Paralegal Work in this Area:*

"The Legal Action Center is the largest non-governmental social service agency in the state. As a paralegal, Virginia Farley handles all eviction calls to the landlord-tenant unit. Three afternoons a week are designated intake times. She screens all eviction cases, determines whether the applicant is eligible for free assistance according to the Center's guidelines, recommends a plan once a case is accepted and assists in carrying out the plan under an attorney's supervision. [After arriving in the city], Virginia made a commitment to work directly with the poor and started serving as a volunteer in five organizations until a job opened up for her at the Legal Action Center." Roche, *Paralegal Profile,* 4 Findings and Conclusions 5 (Washington Ass'n of Legal Assistants, November 1987).

28. Law Librarianship

There is a separate degree that a law librarian can obtain. This degree, however, is not a requirement to be a law librarian. There are a number of small or medium-sized law offices that are hiring paralegals to perform library chores exclusively or in combination with paralegal duties on cases. (See also *law office administration* and *litigation.*)

I. Administration

A. ` Order books for law library.
B. File loose-leaf material and pocket parts in appropriate volumes.

C. Pay bills of library vendors.
D. Test and recommend computer equipment, software, and services for the law library.
E. Prepare budget for library.

II. Cite Checking

A. Check the citations in briefs, speeches, articles, opinion letters, and other legal documents to determine the accuracy of quoted material.
B. Check the citations to determine the accuracy of citation format according to the Uniform System of Citation (the Bluebook), local court rules, or other system required by the office.

III. Research

A. Undertake factual research projects as information resource.
B. Perform legal research.

IV. Training

A. Train office staff in traditional legal research techniques.
B. Train office staff in computer research, for example, WESTLAW.
C. Train office staff in cite checking.

■ *Comment on Paralegal Work in this Area:*

"I suppose my entry into the law librarianship profession might be considered unorthodox because I had no formal educational courses in librarianship. My experience was that of working first as a legal secretary and later evolving into a legal assistant. My job in a small general practice firm included taking care of the office library such as filing supplements and pocket parts (because no one else would do it!!); doing the bookkeeping and paying the bills. [I did some legal research] as an extension of legal drafting. ∴ . In all my working years (and they are many) I had the greatest satisfaction from my work as a law librarian because each day I learned new things." Lewek, *The Legal Assistant as Law Librarian,* 17 Facts & Findings 28 (NALA, March 1991).

29. Law Office Administration

Some experienced paralegals move into management positions at a law office. This might involve helping to administer the *entire* office, or *one component* of it, such as the administration of all the legal assistants in the office, the administration of the legal assistants and other support personnel working on a large case, or the administration of the computer operation in the office. There are some smaller law offices that seek paralegals to perform office management duties along with paralegal duties. (See also *law librarianship* and *litigation.*)

■ *Comment on Paralegal Work in this Area:*

In 1984, the partners at the firm decided to upgrade their legal assistant program and needed a nonlawyer to run it. They offered Linda Katz the new position. "The firm is segmented into practice areas, with legal assistants dispersed throughout the areas. They report to supervising attorneys for work assignments each day. I serve as administrative supervisor, assuring consistency in how legal assistants are treated and utilized, and what opportunities they have for benefits and advancement." Milano, *Career Profiles,* 8 Legal Assistant Today 35 (September/October 1990).

"A good paralegal litigation manager [in a large document case] has both strong paralegal skills and strong management skills. Such a manager must be able to analyze the case's organizational needs, develop methods to cope with them effectively, and often must act as paralegal, office manager and computer expert—all in a day's work." Kaufman, *The Litigation Manager,* 6 Legal Professional 55 (July/August 1989).

30. Legislation

I. Monitoring

Keep track of all events, persons, and organizations involved in the passing of legislation relevant to the clients of the firm.

II. Legislative History

Compile the legislative history of a statute.

III. Drafting of Proposed Legislation

IV. Lobbying

A. Prepare reports and studies on the subject of proposed legislation.

B. Arrange for and help prepare witnesses who will testify at legislative hearings.

■ *Comment on Paralegal Work in this Area:*

Margo Horner "is a legislative analyst for the Nat'l Federation of Independent Business (NFIB). With paralegal training and a masters degree in history, her job is research, creating legislative strategy, working with [legislators] and their staffs to produce legislation favorable to [NFIB]. Margo likes the frenetic tempo of her life." Smith, *Margo,* 1 Legal Assistant Today 14 (Summer 1984).

31. Litigation

I. File Monitoring

A. Index all files.

B. Write case profile based on information in the files.

C. Read attorney briefs to check accuracy of the information in the litigation file.

D. Organize and index documents obtained through discovery.

E. Code documents into the computer.

II. Investigation

A. Gather documents:
1. Medical records,
2. Police records,
3. Birth and death records,
4. Marriage records,
5. Adoption and custody records,
6. Incorporation records.

B. Research records. For instance:
1. Prepare a profit history report of a company.

2. Identify corporate structure of a parent company and its subsidiaries.

3. Trace UCC (Uniform Commercial Code) filings.

4. Find out from court dockets if a particular merchant is being sued, has sued before, etc. Does any pattern exist?

5. Identify the "real owner" of an apartment building.

6. Check housing code agency to find out if a landlord has other building code violations against it on record.

C. Gather facts (other than documents). In a wide range of cases (such as real estate, corporate, criminal, divorce, and custody), the investigator substantiates facts, follows leads for possible evidence in connection with litigation, etc.

III. Discovery

A. Draft interrogatories.

B. Draft answers to interrogatories.

C. Draft deposition questions.

D. Prepare witnesses for deposition.

E. Prepare witness books for deposition.

F. Arrange time and place of deposition.

G. Draft requests for admissions.

H. Draft requests for production of documents.

I. Index and digest discovery data.

J. Work with computer programmer in the design of a system to manage discovery documents.

IV. Filings/Serving

In court, at agencies, on parties, on attorneys, etc.

V. General Assistance

A. Arrange for clients and others to be interviewed.

B. Arrange for expert witnesses to appear in court or at depositions.

C. Reconstruct (from a large collection of disparate records and other evidence) what happened at a particular time and place.

D. Assist clients in completing information questionnaire, especially in class-action cases.

E. Help organize the trial notebook containing items the attorney will need during the trial, such as charts and tables to be used as exhibits at trial.

F. Sit at counsel's table at trial to take notes and suggest questions for attorney to ask witnesses.

G. Attend (and report on) hearings in related cases.

H. Supervise document encodation on a computer project related to a case in litigation.

I. Prepare and evaluate prospective jurors from jury book and during voir dire.

J. Help prepare appeal documents—for example, the notice of appeal.

VI. Legal Research

A. Shepardize; perform cite check.

B. Write preliminary memos and briefs.

C. Prepare bibliographies of source materials related to litigation.

VII. Pleadings

Write preliminary draft of pleadings using standard forms and/or adapting other pleadings written by attorneys on similar cases.

VIII. Expert Analysis

Assist in obtaining expert opinions for attorneys on:

A. Taxation.

B. Accounting.

C. Statistics.

D. Economics (for example, calculation of damages).

IX. Court Witness

A. Act as witness as to service of process.

B. Act as witness as to data uncovered or photographed (such as the condition of an apartment building).

■ *Comment on Paralegal Work in this Area:*

"There are boxes and boxes with an infinite number of documents to be indexed. There are depositions to be summarized. There are cases whose cites need checking. There are trips to the courthouse downtown. There is red-lining of documents to determine changes between two documents. There is Bates-stamping of documents. And there are the exciting trips to visit clients." Lasky, *Impressions of a New Paralegal,* 17 Reporter 5 (Los Angeles Paralegal Ass'n, February 1988).

"I organized. I tabbed and tagged, listed and labelled, hoisted and hole-punched, folded and filed, boxed and Bates-stamped, indexed and itemized, sorted and summarized." Klinkseick, *Aim High,* 16 On Point 4 (Nat'l Capital Area Paralegal Ass'n, July/August 1990).

"Initially, it was overwhelming with the number of files and the names to learn and things to remember, but with help, I learned skills and techniques and polished them day after day as each new case brought with it new quirks and new challenges. I've attended depositions, PTO shaft inspections, and pig farm operations. I've calculated medical expenses, reviewed medical records, and been baffled at how salesmen keep time records! But the ultimate of all experiences, I have to admit, are the trials. You prepare and prepare and hope that you haven't missed any of the details. Then before you know it, the jury has been selected and you're off! The trials keep your adrenaline flowing. They frazzle your patience. They show you your limitations. They elevate you when you win. They shake your confidence when you lose." Riske, *In the Limelight,* 7 Red River Review 4 (Red River Valley Legal Assistants, North Dakota, August 1990).

"For almost six years now . . . , I've experienced the variety (and the drudgery) of preparing civil cases for trial. I've spent countless hours photocopying documents never read by any judge or jury, or worst of all, by anyone else. I've tracked down witnesses and encouraged them to talk only to find out that they know nothing about the case. In this business of endless paper where no two cases are alike, I've come to understand . . . that flexibility is essential and a sense of humor is invaluable in dealing with people, be they stressed-out attorneys or reluctant witnesses." Vore, *A Litigation Recipe* 16 On Point 4 (Nat'l Capital Area Paralegal Ass'n, November 1990).

Rebecca McLaughlin tells of a particularly memorable event during her experience as a paralegal. "It was a few minutes after 12:00 noon on Friday, and presiding Judge Barbour always recesses court at precisely 12:30 on Fridays. The Government's star witness was on the stand and denied he had ever seen a certain letter. One of the trial attorneys motioned me to counsel table and asked if we had any proof that the witness had, in fact, seen this letter." Since there were well over 900 defense exhibits, almost 300 Government exhibits, and well over 40 file cabinets filled with supporting documents, Rebecca felt little hope for success in finding out quickly. "She hurried across the street to the office, found the witness' original copy of the letter with his handwritten notes in the margin, and returned to the courtroom with a BIG SMILE. The witness was impeached with his own document minutes before recess. . . . Later, Rebecca received a well-deserved standing ovation from the attorneys, and all the trial team members. It was the highlight of her career." Johnson, *MALA Spotlight: Rebecca McLaughlin,* 8 The Assistant 17 (Mississippi Ass'n of Legal Assistants, July 1989).

■ *Quotes from Want Ads:*

"Excellent writing skills and attention to detail are absolute requirements." "Plaintiff's medical malpractice firm seeks non-smoker with word processing abilities." Position requires "extensive writing, document summarizing, and medical records research." Must have an ability "to work independently in handling cases from inception through trial preparation; familiarity with drafting law motions pleadings essential." High-energy candidate "needs to be assertive and should have an excellent academic background." "Wanted: a sharp, take-charge litigation paralegal." "Knowledge of computerized litigation support is a plus; good communications and organizational skills are a must." "Applicant must possess a thorough working knowledge of all phases of trial work." "Successful candidate will be professional, prompt, pleasant and personable. No egomaniacs or job hoppers, please." "Overtime flexibility required." "Defense litigation paralegal needed. Must be a self-starter with the ability to accept unstructured responsibility." "Applicant must have a thorough knowledge of state and federal court procedures." Position requires an ability "to organize and manage documents in large multi-party litigation." "Applicants must possess strong supervisory, analytic, writing, and investigative skills, and an ability to perform under pressure." "Position requires good analytical and writing skills, and the ability to organize and control several projects simultaneously." "Deposition summarizer needed; work in your own home on your own computer." "Part-time proofreader for deposition summaries needed."

32. Military Law

In the Navy, a nonattorney who assists attorneys in the practice of law is called a *legalman*. Depending upon the assignment, the legalman can work in a large variety of areas of the law—for example, admiralty law, contracts, and military justice. The following job functions, however, are not limited to any particular branch of the armed services.

I. Military Proceedings

A. Assist in processing the following proceedings:
   1. Special court-martial.
   2. General court-martial.
   3. Courts of inquiry.
   4. Line of duty investigations.
   5. Reclassification board proceedings.
B. Prepare all special orders designating membership of special and general court-martial and courts of inquiry.
C. Assure that charges are properly prepared and that specifications are complete and accurate.
D. Make initial determination on jurisdiction of court, status of accused, and subject matter of offenses.
E. Examine completed records of investigations and other records requiring legal review to ensure that they are administratively correct.
F. Prepare all special court-martial orders promulgating sentence.
G. Assure that records of court-martial are correct and complete before disposing of case.
H. Transmit bad-conduct discharge court-martial cases to appropriate officials.

II. Claims Against the Government

A. Conduct examinations.
B. Process claims against the United States—for instance, federal tort claims.
C. Manage claim funds.
D. Undertake research on FLITE (Federal Legal Information Through Electronics).
E. Write briefs.

III. Administrative Duties

A. Maintain control records of all court-martial and claims cases within command.
B. Maintain law library.
C. Examine and distribute incoming correspondence, directives, publications, and other communications.
D. Supervise cataloging and filing of publications, books, periodicals, journals, etc.

E. Maintain records of discipline within command.

F. Administer office budget.

G. Orient new personnel and monitor their training.

IV. Court Reporting

A. Use the steno-mask for recording legal proceedings.

B. Prepare charges to the jury.

C. Mark exhibits as they are entered into evidence.

D. Transcribe and assemble records of the proceeding.

■ *Comment on Paralegal Work in this Area:*

"I have been working for the Office of the Staff Judge Advocate (SJA) at Fort Ord, California. The SJA is the Army's lawyer. We serve a military community of just over 90,000 people. Staff within the SJA consists of a combination of military and civilian attorneys, paralegals, legal clerks and court reporters. I am responsible for claims filed against the federal government under the Federal Tort Claims Act. I am responsible for discovery and investigative efforts, determining legal issues, writing memorandums of law and recommending settlement or denial. Job satisfaction for paralegal professionals is high in the U.S. government. I know that, should I desire to re-enter the civilian work sector, my experience and knowledge of the government legal systems will uniquely qualify me to work for any firm which deals with the government." Richards, *Marching to a Different Drummer: Paralegal Work in the Military,* 2 California Paralegal Magazine 8 (October/December 1990).

33. Municipal Finance Law[7]

(See also *banking law* and *corporate law*.)

I. Document Preparation

A. Basic documents:

1. Prepare first drafts of basic documents, including bonds, indentures of trust, financing agreements, and all other related documents.

2. Attend drafting sessions and note changes required to initial drafts.

3. Prepare second and subsequent drafts by incorporation of revisions and red-line changes.

B. Closing documents:

1. Prepare first drafts of all closing documents.

2. Prepare second and subsequent drafts by incorporation of revisions and red-line changes.

C. Draft official statement/private offering memorandum:

1. Prepare first drafts.

2. Attend drafting sessions.

3. Perform due diligence to verify the information and data contained in the offering document.

4. Prepare second and subsequent drafts by incorporation of revisions and red-line changes.

II. Coordination

A. Establish timetable and list of participants.

B. Distribute documents to participants.

C. Coordinate printing of bonds and offering documents.

D. File all documents as required.

E. Coordinate publication of notices of meetings and elections, ordinances, public hearing notices, etc.

III. Closing

A. Prepare checklist.

B. Arrange and assist in preclosing and closing.

C. File any documents necessary to be filed prior to closing.

D. Secure requisite documents to be prepared or furnished by other participants.

---

[7]See footnote 4.

E. Perform all post-closing procedures:
  1. File all documents or security agreements.
  2. Supervise preparation of closing binders.

IV. Formation of Special Districts

A. Prepare documents necessary to organize the district.
B. File documents with municipality or county and district court.
C. Prepare documents for organizational meeting of district.

V. Elections (Formation of District or for Bond Election)

Draft election documents and obtain all necessary election materials.

VI. Develop and Maintain Research Files

A. IDB procedures for municipalities.
B. Home rule charters.
C. Demographic and economic statistics.
D. Memoranda noting statutory changes.
E. Interoffice research memoranda.
F. Checklists for each type of financing.

34. Oil and Gas Law

Some paralegals who work in the area of oil and gas law are referred to as *land technicians* or *landmen*. (See also *real estate law*.)

I. Collect and analyze data pertaining to land ownership and activities that may affect the procurement of rights to explore, drill for, and produce oil or gas.
II. Help acquire leases and other operating rights from property owners for exploration, drilling, and producing oil, gas, and related substances.
III. Monitor the execution of the leases and other operating agreements by

ensuring that contract obligations are fulfilled (e.g., payment of rent).
IV. Help negotiate agreements with individuals, companies, and government agencies pertaining to the exploration, drilling, and production of oil or gas.
V. Assist in acquiring oil- and gas-producing properties, royalties, and mineral interests.
VI. Process and monitor the termination of leases and other agreements.
VII. Examine land titles.

■ *Comment on Paralegal Work in this Area:*

"As an oil and gas paralegal, my practice encompasses many different areas of law including real estate, litigation, bankruptcy, and securities, as well as contact with various county, state, and federal government agencies. I frequently spend time searching real estate records in counties . . . for information on leases to determine such things as who has been assigned an interest in the lease. I have worked in mechanic's lien foreclosures, partition actions, and bankruptcy cases. While researching such things as regulatory information and oil prices, I have obtained information from the Federal Energy Regulatory Commission offices in Washington. The variety of work requires a working knowledge of several areas of law, and is always challenging and interesting." Hunt, *Oil and Gas,* The Citator (Legal Assistants of Central Ohio, August 1990).

35. Parajudge

In many states, the judge presiding in certain lower courts does not have to be an attorney. Such courts include justice of the peace courts and local magistrates courts.

Administrative agencies often hold hearings conducted by hearing officers, referees, or administrative law judges (ALJ). Frequently, these individuals are not attorneys, particularly at state and local agencies.

36. Pro Bono Work

Pro bono work refers to services provided to another person at no charge. Law firms often give their attorneys time off in order to take pro bono cases—for example, to defend a poor person charged with a crime. Paralegals are also encouraged to do pro bono work. This is done on their own time or on law firm time with the permission of their supervisor. The following are examples of pro bono work performed by paralegals:

I. Abused Women

A. Draft request for protective order.
B. Draft divorce pleadings.

II. AIDS Patients

A. Interview patients and prepare a memorandum of the interview for the pro bono attorney supervising the paralegals.
B. Assist patients with guardianship problems.
C. Draft powers of attorney.

III. Homeless

A. Handle Supplemental Security Income (SSI) claims.
B. Make referrals to shelters and drug programs.

■ *Comment on Paralegal Work in this Area:*

"Asked to share her favorite pro bono experience, Therese Ortega, a litigation paralegal, answered that to choose was too difficult; any time her efforts result in a benefit to the client, 'I get a warm glow.' One occasion she obviously cherishes was the fight on behalf of some low-income kidney dialysis patients whose eligibility for transportation to and from treatment was threatened. 'Perseverance and appeals paid off,' she says. Rides were re-established through the hearing process, then by information conferences. Finally, the cessation notices stopped." *Spotlight on Therese Ortega,* 13 The Journal 3 (Sacramento Ass'n of Legal Assistants, March 1991).

37. Public Sector

A paralegal in the *private sector* works in an office whose funds come from client fees or from the budget of the corporate treasury. Every other setting is generally considered the *public sector.* More specifically, the latter refers to those law offices that provide civil or criminal legal services to the poor for free. Often, the services consist of helping clients obtain government benefits such as public housing, welfare, medical care, etc. Such services are referred to as *public benefits,* and providing such assistance is called practice of public benefits law. Some of the paralegals who are employed by these offices are called Public Benefits Paralegals. The offices operate with government grants, charitable contributions, and the efforts of volunteers. They are called Legal Aid Society, Legal Aid Foundation, Legal Services Office, Office of the Public Defender, etc. (See also *administrative law, bankruptcy law, civil rights law, criminal law, family law, landlord and tenant law, litigation, pro bono work, social security law, welfare law,* and *worker's compensation law.*)

■ *Comment on Paralegal Work in this Area:*

"If someone asked me what I disliked most about my job, I would have to answer: the size of my paycheck. That is the only drawback of working for a nonprofit law firm—[the Community Legal Aid Society which represents elderly and handicapped persons]. Everything else about my job is positive." For example, to "be an integral part of a case where a landlord is forced by the Courts to bring a house up to code and prevent a tenant from being wrongfully evicted is a great feeling." The positive aspects of the job "more than compensate for the size of the paycheck." Hartman, *Job Profile,* Delaware Paralegal Reporter 5 (Delaware Paralegal Ass'n, November 1988).

"Mr. Watnick stressed that the organization doesn't have the luxury of using paralegals as "xeroxers" or errand runners. Staff paralegals have their own caseloads and represent clients before Administrative Law Judges—with a dramatically high rate of success." Shays, *Paralegals in Human Service,* Postscript 16 (Manhattan Paralegal Ass'n, March/April 1990).

38. Real Estate Law

(See also *banking law, contract law,* and *landlord and tenant law.*)

I. General

Assist law firms, corporations, and development companies in transactions involving land, houses, condominiums, shopping malls, office buildings, redevelopment projects, civic centers, etc.

A. Research zoning regulations.

B. Prepare draft of the contract of sale.

C. Title work:
1. If done outside, order title work from the title company; arrange title insurance.
2. If done in-house:
   a. Examine title abstracts for completeness,
   b. Prepare a map based on a master title plat or the current government survey map,
   c. Help construct a chain of title noting defects, encumbrances, liens, easements, breaks in the chain, etc.,
   d. Obtain releases of liens, payoff statements for existing loans, etc.
   e. Help draft a preliminary title opinion.

D. Mortgages:
1. Assist in obtaining financing,
2. Review mortgage application,
3. Assist in recording mortgage.

E. Closing:
1. Arrange for a closing time with buyer, seller, brokers, and lender. Obtain letter confirming date of closing.
2. Collect the data necessary for closing. Prepare checklist of expenses:
   a. Title company fee,
   b. Lender's fee,
   c. Attorney's fee,
   d. Taxes and water bills to be prorated,
   e. Tax escrow, discharge of liens.
3. Prepare and organize the documents for closing:
   a. Deed,
   b. Settlement statement,
   c. Note and deed of trust,
   d. Corporate resolutions,
   e. Performance bond,
   f. Waivers.
4. Check compliance with the disclosure requirements of the Real Estate Settlement Act.
5. Arrange for a rehearsal of the closing.
6. Attend and assist at the closing—for example, take minutes, notarize documents.

F. Foreclosure:
1. Order foreclosure certificate.
2. Prepare notice of election and demand for sale,
3. Compile a list of parties to be notified,
4. Monitor publication of the notice.
5. Assist with sale documents—for example, prepare bid letter.

G. Eminent Domain:
1. Photograph or videotape the property taken or to be taken by the state,
2. Prepare inventory of the property taken,
3. Help client prepare business records pertaining to the value of the property,
4. Arrange for appraisals of the property,
5. Order and review engineering reports regarding soil,

6. Review tax appeals records on values claimed by the property owner,

7. Mail out notice of condemnation.

H. Office management:

1. Maintain office tickler system,

2. Maintain individual attorney's calendar,

3. Be in charge of the entire client's file (opening it, keeping it up-to-date, knowing where parts of it are at all times),

4. Train other staff in the office system of handling real estate cases.

II. Tax-exempt Industrial Development Financing

A. Undertake a preliminary investigation to establish facts relevant to:

1. Project eligibility,

2. The local issuer,

3. Cost estimates of the financing.

B. Prepare a formal application to the issuer.

C. Prepare a timetable of approvals, meetings, and all other requirements necessary for closing.

D. Prepare a preliminary draft of portions of the proposal memorandum (relating to the legal structure of the financing) that is submitted to prospective bond purchasers.

E. Obtain confirmation from the Treasury Department that the company is in compliance with the financing covenants of current external debt instruments.

F. Obtain insurance certificates.

G. Write the first draft of the resolutions of the board of directors.

H. Write the preface and recital of documents for the legal opinion of the company.

I. Contact the bank to confirm the account numbers, amount of money to be transferred, and investment instructions.

J. Prepare a closing memorandum covering the following documents:

1. Secretary's certificate including resolutions of the board of directors, the certified charter and bylaws of the company, and the incumbency certificate,

2. UCC-1 financing statements,

3. Requisition forms,

4. Certificate of authorized company representative,

5. Deed,

6. Legal opinion of the company,

7. Transfer instruction letter,

8. Officer's certificate.

K. Confirm that the money has been transferred to the company's account on the day of closing.

L. Order an updated good-standing telegram.

M. Send a copy of the IRS election statement.

N. Assemble, monitor, and distribute documents to appropriate departments.

■ *Comment on Paralegal Work in this Area:*

"Although it may look boring to the untrained eye, and sound boring to the untrained ear, for those of us whose livelihoods depend upon it, real estate law is *interesting* and *exciting*. There is always something new to learn or a little flaw to resolve. What can be better than having clients come to you and thank you for your assistance in what would have been a complete disaster without your knowledge and expertise to get them through? I call that total job satisfaction. I am now capable of doing everything in a real estate settlement from opening the file to walking into the settlement room and disbursing the funds. It is not uncommon for me to receive calls from attorneys in the area asking me how certain problems can be solved. That boosts my ego more than any divorce case every could!" Jaeger, *Real Estate Law Is a Legal Profession Too!*, 14 On Point 9 (Nat'l Capital Area Paralegal Ass'n, June 1988).

At a paralegal conference, Virginia Henderson made a seminar presentation on her duties as a paralegal. Her "candor and energetic enthusiasm concerning her profession were encouraging and motivating. She was very explicit about her duties as a commercial real estate paralegal, explaining that attorney supervision is lessened once the paralegal assumes more responsibility and exhibits initiative as far as his/her duties are concerned. It was refreshing to listen to a veteran of the paralegal profession speak so optimistically about the profession's limitless potential. Here's to having more paralegals as seminar speakers!" Troiano, *Real Estate*, Newsletter 12 (Western New York Paralegal Ass'n, November/December 1987).

"As a foreclosure legal assistant, one of my worst fears is to have a client call and say, 'Remember the Jones property you foreclosed for us last year? Well, we're trying to close on this and it seems there's a problem with the title. . . .' Oh no, what *didn't* I do! Mortgage foreclosure litigation is fraught with all kinds of pitfalls for the inexperienced and the unwary. An improper or faulty foreclosure could not only be disastrous for the client, it can also be a malpractice nightmare for the law firm." Hubbell, *Mortgage Foreclosure Litigation: Avoiding the Pitfalls*, 16 Facts and Findings 10 (NALA, November 1989).

■ *Quotes from Want Ads:*

"Ideal candidate must possess exceptional organization, communication, writing and research skills and be willing to work overtime." "We need a team player with high energy." Position requires an ability to work independently on a wide variety of matters and to meet deadlines." "Experience in retail real estate or real estate financing a must." "Should be assertive and have excellent analytical skills." Position requires a "self-motivated person. We seek a TIGER who can accomplish much with a minimum of supervi-

sion." "Knowledge of state and federal securities law a plus." "Must be flexible and possess high integrity." Position requires a "self-starter able to deal effectively with executive management, outside counsel, escrow and title companies, brokers, leasing agents, and clients."

39. Social Security Law

(See also *administrative law, public sector,* and *welfare law*.)

I. Problem Identification

Identify whether:
A. Person is denied benefits.
B. Recipient is terminated from disability payments.
C. Recipient is charged with receiving overpayment.
D. Medicare waivers/appeals are involved.

II. Case Preparation

A. Investigate relevant facts.
B. Perform legal research.
C. Engage in informal advocacy with Social Security employees.

III. Representation

A. Represent clients at administrative hearings regarding SSI (Supplemental Security Income).
B. Represent clients at administrative hearings regarding SSD (Social Security Disability)

IV. Appeal

A. Help attorney prepare a court appeal of the agency's decision.

■ *Comment on Paralegal Work in this Area:*

"Paralegal representation of a claimant in a Social Security Disability hearing is the closest to a judicial setting that a paralegal may expect to become involved in. For the paralegal, this can be a very complex and challenging field. It can also be extremely rewarding, bringing with it the satisfaction of successfully representing a claimant in a quasi-judicial setting." Obermann, *The Paralegal and Federal Disability Practice in Maine,* MAP Newsletter (Maine Ass'n of Paralegals, January 1988).

40. Tax Law

(See also *corporate law, employee benefits law, estates law,* and *real estate law.*)

I. Compile all necessary data for the preparation of tax returns:

A.   Corporate income tax,

B.   Employer quarterly tax,

C.   Franchise tax,

D.   Partnership tax,

E.   Sales tax,

F.   Personal property tax,

G.   Individual income tax,

H.   Estate tax,

I.   Gift tax.

II. Communicate with client to obtain missing information.

III. Compile supporting documents for the returns.

IV. Draft extensions-of-time requests.

V. Make corrections in the returns based upon new or clarified data.

VI. Compute the tax liability or transfer client information to computer input sheets for submission to a computer service that will calculate the tax liability.

VII. Organize and maintain client binder.

VIII. Compute cash flow analysis for proposed real estate syndication.

IX. Compile documentation on the valuation of assets.

X. Maintain the tax law library.

XI. Read loose-leaf tax services and other periodic tax data to keep current on tax developments. Bring such developments to the attention of others in the office.

XII. Supervise and train other nonattorney staff within the tax department of the office.

■ *Comment on Paralegal Work in this Area:*

"A legal assistant with the firm for the past 13 years, Pat [Coleman] spends a lot of time in her office. She is surrounded by her work, and one gets the idea that Pat knows exactly what is in every file and could put her hand on any information that is needed. Notes are taped next to the light switch; the firm's monthly calendar highlighting important meetings is readily available, and helps her track her many deadlines. Pat is an Enrolled Agent (which permits her to practice before the Treasury Department) and has a lot of tax background, and is competent in that area as well as bookkeeping. One of her least favorite tax forms is the 990 required of not-for-profit organizations. The 990 tax form is second only to private foundation returns when it comes to being pesky and tricky." Howard, *Patricia Coleman of Chicago Creates Her Niche in Taxes, Trusts and ERISA,* 3 Legal Assistant Today 40 (Winter 1986).

41. Tort Law

A tort is a civil wrong that has injured someone. Paralegals who work on PI (personal injury) cases are mainly litigation assistants. The major torts are negligence, defamation, strict liability, and wrongful death. Paralegals in this area are also often involved in worker's compensation cases for injuries that occur on the job. (See *admiralty law, litigation,* and *worker's compensation.*)

■ *Comment on Paralegal Work in this Area:*

"Personal injury/products liability cases can be fascinating, challenging, and educational. They also can be stressful, aggravating and very sad. I have been involved in a great many cases in my career, on both sides of the plaintiff/defendant fence. Some of the cases seemed frivolous and somewhat 'ambulance chasing' in nature. Others were significant cases in which the plaintiff had wrongfully suffered injury. There are many talents a good personal injury/products liability paralegal must have. He or she must be creative, tenacious, observant and able to communicate well with people." Lee, *Personal Injury/Products Liability Cases,* 11 Newsletter 7 (Dallas Ass'n of Legal Assistants, November 1987).

"Recently, Mary Mann, a paralegal who works on product liability litigation, was asked by her attorney to track down a specific medical article [on a subject relevant to a current case]. The attorney only had a vague description of the article, a possible title, and the name of the organization that might have published it. In her search Mary spoke by phone to people in New York, Atlanta, Washington, and finally to a doctor in Geneva, Switzerland, who spoke very little English. In her effort to make herself understood by the doctor, Mary continued to speak louder and louder in very simplistic and basic English phrases, as people tend to do when confronted by a language barrier. She is sure her efforts to maintain a professional demeanor were humorous to those passing by her office. However, she did succeed in getting the article and in the process gained a friend in Switzerland!" Fisher, *Spotlight: Mary Mann,* 7 The Assistant 14 (Mississippi Ass'n of Legal Assistants, April/June 1988).

"Asbestos litigation . . . opened up in the late 1970's with the law suits initiated against the Johns-Mansville Corporation. In 1982 Mansville filed a Chapter 11 bankruptcy to protect its assets from the thousands of claims being filed against it." Huge numbers of paralegals were employed in this litigation. For those paralegals working *for* Johns-Mansville on the defense team, "the question of morality arose. I get asked about the morality of my job constantly. For me, personal moral judgment does not enter into it. Our legal system is based on the availability of equal representation for both sides. I think I play a small part in making that system work." Welsh, *The Paralegal in Asbestos Litigation,* 10 Ka Leo O' H.A.L.A. 6 (Hawaii Ass'n of Legal Assistants, February/March 1987) (reprint from newsletter of the East Bay Ass'n of Legal Assistants).

■ *Quotes from Want Ads:*

"Medical malpractice law firm seeks paralegal who is a self-starter, has good communication skills, is organized and detail-oriented." Position in PI [personal injury] firm requires "a take-charge person to handle case details from beginning to end." "Prefer person with experience in claims adjustment, medical records, or nursing." Position requires "dynamic, highly-motivated individual who will enjoy the challenge of working independently and handling a wide variety of responsibilities." "Excellent writing skills a must." "Should be able to perform under pressure." Manufacturer of consumer products "seeks paralegal with engineering background." Must be mature enough to handle "heavy client contact." Position requires "ability to read and summarize medical records."

42. Tribal Law

Tribal courts exist on Indian reservations that have jurisdiction over many civil and criminal cases in which both parties are Native Americans. Parties are often represented by tribal court advocates who are nonattorney Native Americans. In addition, the judges are often nonattorneys. (See *litigation.*).

43. Water Law[8]

(See also *administrative law* and *real estate law.*)

---

[8]See footnote 4.

I. Water Rights

Investigate and analyze specific water rights and water rights associated with property:

A. Do research at Department of Water Resources regarding decrees, tabulations, well permits, reservoirs, diversion records, maps, and statements.

B. Communicate in writing and orally with Department of Water Resources personnel regarding status of water rights and wells.

C. Communicate in writing and orally (including interviews) with District Water Commissioners regarding status of water rights and wells, historic use, and use on land.

D. Communicate in writing and orally (including interviews) with property owners and managers, ranch managers, ditch company personnel, etc. regarding status of water rights and wells, historic use, and use on land.

E. Do research at other agencies and offices (such as the Bureau of Land Management, state archives, historical societies, public libraries).

F. Prepare historic use affidavits.

G. Prepare reports regarding investigation and analysis of the status of water rights and wells, historic use, and use on land.

H. Prepare maps, charts, diagrams, etc. regarding status of water rights and wells, historic use, and use on land.

II. Real Estate Transactions

A. Draft documents for the purchase and sale, encumbrance, or lease of water rights and wells.

B. Perform standup title searches in county clerk and recorder's offices.

C. Perform due diligence investigations.

D. Prepare for and assist at closings.

III. Well Permit Applications

A. Prepare well permit documents for filing—applications, land ownership affidavits, statements of beneficial use, amendments to record, extensions of time.

B. Coordinate and monitor the well permitting and drilling process.

C. In writing and orally, communicate with Department of Water Resources personnel, well drillers, and client.

IV. Water Court Proceedings—

Certain district courts have special jurisdiction over water right proceedings. Proceedings are governed by the Rules of Civil Procedure for District Courts and by local water court and district court rules.

A. Prepare water court documents for filing applications, statements of opposition, draft rulings and orders, stipulations, withdrawals of opposition, and affidavits.

B. Maintain diligence filing tickler system. Work with client to record and maintain evidence of diligence.

C. Review, route, and maintain a file of water court resumes.

D. Review, route, and maintain a file of term day notices and orders. Prepare attorneys for term day and/or attend term day.

V. Monitor Publications

Read *Reporter*, water court resumes, and register for new water law cases and Department of Water Resources regulations.

44. Welfare Law

(See also *administrative law, pro bono work, public benefits,* and *social security law*.)

I. Problem Identification

A. Perform preliminary interview:

1. Identify nonlegal problems for referral to other agencies,

2. Open a case file or update it,

3. Using a basic fact sheet (or form), record the information collected during the interview,

4. Determine next appointment,

5. Instruct client on what to do next, such as obtain medical and birth records, etc.,

6. Arrange for client to see office attorney.

B. Categorize welfare problems:

1. Help client learn what benefits exist in programs such as:

   a. Welfare

   b. Social Security

   c. Medicare

2. Help client fill out application forms.

3. Deal with client who objects to home visits by caseworkers or attempt by welfare department to force him or her to take a job or enter a training program.

4. Help client when welfare department wants to reduce the amount of client's welfare check or terminate public assistance altogether.

II. Problem Resolution

A. Consult with attorney immediately:

1. Summarize facts for the attorney,

2. Submit the case record to the attorney,

3. Obtain further instructions from attorney.

B. Refer nonlegal problems to other agencies:

1. Give name and address of agency to client,

2. Search for an appropriate agency,

3. Contact agency for the client.

C. Investigate:

1. Verify information (call caseworker, visit welfare office, etc.)

2. Search for additional information.

3. Record relevant facts.

4. Consult with attorney on difficulties encountered.

D. Analyze laws:

1. Check office welfare law manual,

2. Consult with office attorneys,

3. Contact legal service attorneys outside office,

4. Do research in law library.

E. Be an informal advocate (to determine if the problem can be resolved without a hearing or court action).

1. Make sure everyone (welfare department, client, etc.) understands the issue,

2. Provide missing information,

3. Pressure the welfare department (with calls, letters, visits, etc.),

4. Maintain records such as current and closed files.

F. Be a formal advocate:

1. Prior hearing (administrative review)

   a. Determine if such hearing can be asked for and when request must be made,

   b. Draft letter requesting such hearing,

   c. Prepare for hearing (see "Fair Hearing" below),

   d. Conduct hearing (see "Fair Hearing" below),

   e. Follow-up (see "Fair Hearing" below).

2. Fair Hearing

   a. Determine if the hearing can be asked for and when request must be made,

   b. Draft letter requesting the hearing,

   c. Prepare for the hearing:

      i. In advance of hearing, request that the welfare department send the paralegal the documents it will rely on at the hearing.

      ii. In advance of hearing, make sure that everyone (department representatives, client, etc.) is going to the hearing on the same issues.

iii. Organize other relevant documents such as cancelled check stubs.

iv. Find witnesses (other than client).

v. Prepare all witnesses (for example, explain what hearing will be about; conduct a brief role-playing experience to acquaint them with the format and what the paralegal will be seeking from them as witnesses).

vi. Map out a preliminary strategy to use in conducting the hearing.

vii. Make a final attempt to resolve the issues without a hearing.

viii. Make sure client and other witnesses will appear (e.g., give address of the hearing, take them to the hearing on the date of the hearing).

d. Conduct the hearing:

i. Make sure the name, address, and title of everyone present is identified for the record.

ii. Make opening statement summarizing client's case.

iii. Ask for a postponement if the client has not appeared or if an emergency has arisen requiring more time to prepare.

iv. Clearly state what relief the client is seeking from the hearing.

v. If confusion exists on the issues, fight for a statement of the issues most favorable to the client.

vi. Take notes on the opening statement of the welfare department representative.

vii. Complain if welfare department failed to provide sufficient information in advance of the hearing.

viii. Present the client's case.

a. submit documents.

b. conduct direct examination of own witnesses.

c. conduct re-direct examination of own witnesses (if allowed).

d. cite the law.

ix. Rebut case of welfare department.

a. object to their documents.

b. object to their use of jargon.

c. object to their interpretation of the law.

d. cross-examine their witnesses.

e. re-cross-examine their witnesses (if allowed).

x. Make closing statement summarizing the case of the client and repeating the result the client is seeking.

e. Follow up:

i. Pressure the hearing officer to reach a result without undue delay.

ii. Request a copy of the transcript of the hearing.

iii. When a result is reached, pressure the welfare department to abide by it.

iv. Consult with attorney to determine whether the hearing result should be appealed in court.

3. Court
   a. Prepare preliminary draft of the legal argument to be made on appeal,
   b. Assist the attorney in gathering the documents for appeal; interview the witnesses for appeal, etc.,
   c. Be a general assistant for the attorney at court proceedings,
   d. File papers in court,
   e. Serve the papers on opponents.

G. Miscellaneous
   1. Train other paralegals.
   2. Write pamphlets on welfare law for distribution in the community.
   3. Organize the community around welfare issues.

45. Worker's Compensation Law

(See also *administrative law, labor and employment law,* and *litigation.*)

I. Interviewing

A. Collect and record details of the claim (date of injury, nature and dates of prior illness, etc.).
B. Collect or arrange for the collection of documents, such as medical records, employment contract, etc.
C. Schedule physical examination.

II. Drafting

A. Draft claim for compensation.
B. Draft request for hearing.
C. Draft medical authorization.
D. Draft demand for medical information in the possession of respondent or insurance carrier.
E. Draft proposed summary of issues involved.

III. Advocacy

A. Informal: Contact (call, visit, write a letter to) the employer and/or the insurance carrier to determine whether the matter can be resolved without a formal hearing or court action.

B. Formal: Represent claimant at the administrative hearing.

IV. Follow-up

A. Determine whether the payment is in compliance with the award.
B. If not, draft and file a statutory demand for proper payment.
C. If such a statutory demand is filed, prepare a tickler system to monitor the claim.

■ *Comment on Paralegal Work in this Area:*

"I have been working as a paralegal in this area for more than seven years. This is one of the areas of the law [in this state] in which a paralegal can perform almost all of the functions to properly process a Workers' Compensation claim. A Workers' Compensation practice must be a very high volume in order to be [profitable]. Thus paralegal assistance in handling a large case load is an absolute necessity. An extensive volume of paperwork is processed on a daily basis. Client contact is a major portion of a paralegal's responsibilities. With a large case load, it is physically impossible for an attorney to communicate with each and every client on a regular basis. It is not unusual for a paralegal in this field to work on several hundred files each week." Lindberg, *Virtually Limitless Responsibilities of a Workers' Compensation Paralegal,* Update 6 (Cleveland Ass'n of Paralegals, July 1989).

"The Company's two worker's compensation paralegals are responsible for reviewing each claimant's file, preparing a summary of medical reports, outlining the issues, and reviewing with the adjusters any questions or circumstances of the case before the claimant's disposition. In addition, they draft any necessary subpoenas, witness lists and settlement stipulations for their respective attorneys, and collect information and draft letters to the Special Disability Trust Fund outlining the Company's theory of reimbursement for second injury cases." Miquel, *Walt Disney World Company's Legal Assistants: Their Role in the Show,* 16 Facts and Findings 29, 30 (NALA, January 1990).

Note

A PARALEGAL IN THE WHITE HOUSE
MEG SHIELDS DUKE
NEW ROLES IN THE LAW CONFERENCE REPORT, 93 (1982)

[After working as a paralegal on the Reagan-Bush Campaign Committee], I'm a paralegal in the White House Counsel's office. I believe I'm the first paralegal in this office, in the White House. They've had law clerks in the past, but never have they hired a paralegal. There's one paralegal to nine attorneys at the moment. I think that's ridiculous and I hope we'll change that in the next several months to a year. But my responsibilities here are varied. Everybody is still trying to determine what their turf is. But for the first couple of months I've worked on a lot of transition matters, which might be expected. I was the coordinator for our transition audit, congressional transition audit, from the Hill, which just ended a few weeks ago. I have engaged in drafting correspondence concerning the use of the president's name, the use of his image, our policy on gifts acceptance by public employees; drafting standards of conduct for public employees in the White House; job freeze litigation; those few controversial things. The last few weeks of my time have been devoted to the Lefever nomination. It's all been fascinating. Anyway, there are a number of areas that we also get involved in, the ethics of government act, for example. It's the first time it has been applied across the board to a new administration. It has been very, very time consuming for all our staff. I've been assisting in that, reviewing each individual file for high level government employees. As I said, I'm in the counsel's office now and intend to stay for a couple of years. But I would like to start my own paralegal firm. I have a close friend who started her own paralegal firm in Florida and we've talked often in the past of expanding it to Washington and a few other cities West where we'd like to spend some time. We're investigating the possibilities of reopening another firm here in Washington at some point, maybe in the next year and a half. But I think there is a place for more paralegals in the public sector, at least in the White House area, and I understand the Department of Justice of course has many, but I'd like to see it expanded and I'd also like to see more people branching out and trying this independent approach because I think it's fun. It's risky, but it's worth it.

Key Terms

paralegal specialties	landmen	public benefits
conflicts specialist	private sector	PI cases
legalman	public sector	tort

CHAPTER

3

Finding a Job

■ Chapter Outline

■ Section A. General Strategies

The following strategies are primarily for individuals who have never worked with attorneys or held a paralegal job. Many of the strategies, however, are also relevant to people who have worked in law offices as secretaries or who are paralegals and wish to find other employment opportunities in the field.

Strategy 1: Begin Now

You should begin preparing for the job hunt on the first day of your first paralegal class. Do *not* wait until the program is almost over. Whether or not there is a placement office at your school, you should assume that obtaining a job will be your responsibility. For most students, the job you get will be the job *you* find.

"In my experience, most entry-level candidates are unprepared to effectively market themselves to law firms and corporations in this increasingly competitive marketplace. It is no longer enough simply to have a paralegal certificate. An individual must be able to sell him or herself effectively through the use of a well-written resume and cover letter, and be prepared to develop strong interviewing skills."

Tami M. Coyne, May 1990.

"Getting the job you want requires planning, determination, hard work, and follow-through. Don't give up!"

Lindi Massey, January 1991.

While in school, your primary focus should be on compiling an excellent academic record. *In addition,* start the job search now. It is not too early, for example, to begin compiling the lists called for in the Job Hunting Notebook that we will examine later. When school is over, be prepared to spend substantial additional time looking for employment. Since most students in the country will not have a job lined up before they graduate, time must be set aside for the search. How much time? There is no absolute answer to this question. It is clear, however, that a half-hearted, part-time effort will probably not be successful. Simply sending out a stack of resumes is rarely effective! Since this is a "buyer's market" where there are many more applicants than available jobs, a conscientious search could involve four to six hours a day for several months. This may surprise—and disappoint—many graduates of paralegal programs. Yet this time frame is a reality throughout the legal profession. It applies to the majority of attorneys and legal administrators looking for work as well as to paralegals. *Being* a paralegal requires determination, assertiveness, initiative, and creativity. *Finding* paralegal work will require these same skills. This is not a field for those who are easily discouraged.

It may be that there is still a lot of uncertainty in your mind about the kinds of employment options that exist. How can you begin looking for a job if you don't yet know what kind of job you would like to have? First of all, many of the suggested steps in this chapter will be helpful regardless of the kind of job you are pursuing. More important, however, the very process of going through these steps will help you clarify your employment objectives. As you begin seeking information and leads, the insights will come to you.

At this point, keep an open mind, be conscientious, and begin now.

Strategy 2: Begin Compiling a Job Hunting Notebook

Later in this chapter, you will find an outline for a Job Hunting Notebook that you should start preparing now. Following the outline, there are sample pages for the various sections in the Notebook. (See page 128.)

Strategy 3: Organize an Employment Workshop

In Figure 1.1 at the beginning of Chapter 1, you were given a list of the major categories (and subcategories) of paralegal employment. Begin organizing an employment conference or workshop consisting of a panel of paralegals from as many of the categories and subcategories of paralegals as you can locate in your area. Try to find at least one paralegal to represent each category and subcategory. The guest paralegals could be asked to come to an evening or Saturday session to discuss topics such as:

- How I obtained my job
- My recommendations for finding work
- Dos and don'ts in the employment interview
- What I do (what a typical day consists of)
- What were the most valuable parts of my legal education

While you might want to ask a teacher or the director of the program at your school to help organize the workshop, you should make it a student-run workshop. It will be good practice for you in taking the kind of initiative that is essential in finding employment. Consider asking the nearest paralegal association to co-sponsor the workshop with your class.

Have a meeting of your class in which a chairperson is selected to help coordinate the event. Then divide up the tasks of contacting participants, arranging for a room, preparing an agenda for the workshop, etc. You may want to invite former graduates of your school to attend as panel speakers or as members of the audience. The ideal time for such a workshop is a month or two after you begin your coursework. This means that you need to begin organizing immediately.

Strategy 4: Locate Working Paralegals

Perhaps the most significant step in finding employment is to begin talking with paralegals who are already employed. They are the obvious experts on how to find a job! They are probably also very knowledgeable about employment opportunities in their office and in similar offices in the area. (See Job Hunting Notebook, p. 137.)

Attend paralegal association meetings. See Appendix D for a list of paralegal associations. Contact the one nearest you and ask about joining. There may be a special dues or fee structure for students.

Ask if the association has a *job bank* service. Here is what a paralegal who recently used this service had to say:

> I gained access to an opening to a wonderful job at a law firm exclusively listed in the Minnesota Association of Legal Assistants (MALA) Job Bank. . . . I would never have heard about the position if I hadn't been a member of MALA. *Merrill Advantage* (Spring 1990).

Not all associations, however, have job bank services, and those that do have them may not make them available to students.

Try to obtain copies of current and past issues of the monthly or bimonthly newsletters of all the local paralegal associations in your area. Some of these newsletters give listings of job openings that mention specific employers. If so, try to contact the employers to determine if the position is still open. If it is no longer open, ask if you could send your resume to be kept on file in the event a position becomes available in the future. Also, try to speak to the paralegal who filled the position in order to ask for leads to openings elsewhere.

Ask the local paralegal association if it has a job-finding manual for paralegals in your area. Find out about attending various association meetings. Try to participate in committees. The more active you are as a student member, the more contacts you will make. If there is no paralegal association near you, organize one—beginning with your own student body and past graduates of your school.

Paralegal newsletters often announce continuing education conferences and seminars for paralegals. Similar announcements are found in the newsletters of the two major national paralegal associations: the National Federation of Paralegal Associations *(National Paralegal Reporter),* and the National Association of Legal Assistants *(Facts and Findings).* Employed paralegals attend these events in large numbers. Hence they are excellent ways in which to meet experienced paralegals.

Paralegals sometimes attend continuing education conferences conducted by the local bar association, particularly those bar associations where paralegals are allowed to become associate members. You should also find out if there is an association of legal secretaries and of legal administrators in your area. If so, they might conduct workshops or meetings that you can attend. At such meetings and elsewhere, try to talk with individual legal secretaries and legal administrators about employment opportunities for paralegals where they work.

Strategy 5: Go on Informational Interviews

An *informational interview* is an opportunity for you to sit down with someone, preferably where he or she works, to learn about a particular kind of employment. Unlike a job interview, where you are the one interviewed, *you* do the interviewing in an informational interview. You ask questions that will help you learn what life is like working at that kind of office. Your goal is to find out if a particular kind of paralegal practice interests you.

> If, for example, you are a real "people" person who finds antitrust theory fascinating, you should listen to antitrust paralegals discussing their day-to-day work. You may hear that most of them spend years in document warehouses with one lawyer, two other paralegals and a pizza delivery man as their most significant personal contacts. That information may influence your decision about antitrust as a career path.[1]

Do *not* try to turn an informational interview into a job interview. While on an informational interview, it is inappropriate to ask a person for a job. Toward the end of the interview, you can delicately ask for leads to employment

---

[1]Gainen, *Information Interviews: A Strategy,* Paradigm (Baltimore Ass'n of Legal Assistants, November/December 1989).

and you can ask how the person obtained his or her job, but these inquiries should be secondary to your primary purpose of obtaining information about the realities of work at that kind of office. Do not use an informational interview as a subterfuge for a job interview that you are having difficulty obtaining.

The best people to interview are employed paralegals whom you have met through the steps outlined in Strategy 4. While attorneys and legal administrators may also be willing to grant you informational interviews, the best people to talk to are those who were once in your shoes. Simply say to a paralegal you have met, "Would it be possible for me to come down to the office where you work for a brief informational interview?" If he or she is not familiar with this kind of interview, explain its limited objective. Some may be too busy to grant such interviews, but you have nothing to lose by asking, even if you are turned down. As an added inducement, consider offering to take the paralegal to lunch. In addition to meeting this paralegal, you also want to try to have at least a brief tour of the office where he or she works. Observing how different kinds of employees interact with each other and with available technology in the office will be invaluable.

Here are some of the questions you should ask on an informational interview.

- What is a typical day for you in this office?
- What kinds of assignments do you receive?
- How much overtime is usually expected? Do you take work home with you?
- How do the attorneys interact with paralegals in this kind of practice? Who does what? How many different attorneys does a paralegal work with? How are assignment priorities set?
- How do the paralegals interact with secretaries and other support staff in the office?
- What is the hierarchy of the office?
- What kind of education best prepares a paralegal to work in this kind of office? What courses are most effective?
- What is the most challenging aspect of the job? The most frustrating?
- How are paralegals perceived in this office?
- Are you glad you became this kind of paralegal in this kind of office? Would you do it over again?
- What advice would you give to someone who wants to become a paralegal like yourself?

Several of these questions are also appropriate in a job interview, as we will see later.

One final word of caution. Any information you learn at the office about clients or legal matters must be kept confidential, even if the person you are interviewing is casual about revealing such information to you. This person may not be aware that he or she is disclosing confidential information. Carelessness in this regard is not uncommon.

Strategy 6: Locate Potential Employers

There are a number of ways to locate attorneys:

a. Placement office

b. Personal contacts

c. Ads

d. Through other paralegals

e. Employment agencies

f. Directories and other lists

g. Courts and bar association meetings

(See Job Hunting Notebook, p. 137).

For every attorney that you contact, you want to know the following:

■ Has the attorney hired paralegals in the past?

■ If so, is the attorney interested in hiring more paralegals?

■ If the attorney has never hired paralegals before, might he or she consider hiring one?

■ Does the attorney know of other attorneys who might be interested in hiring paralegals?

The last point is particularly important. Attorneys from different firms often talk with each other about their practice, including their experiences with paralegals or their plans for hiring paralegals. Hence always ask about other firms. If you obtain a lead, begin your contact with the other firm by mentioning the name of the attorney who gave you the lead. You might say, "Mary Smith told me that you have hired paralegals in the past and might be interested in hiring another paralegal," or "John Jones suggested that I contact you concerning possible employment at your firm as a paralegal."

a. Placement Office.   Start with the placement office of your paralegal school. Talk with staff members and/or check the bulletin board regularly. If your school is part of a university that has a law school, you might want to check the placement office of the law school as well. While paralegal jobs are usually not listed there, you may find descriptions of law firms with the number of attorneys and paralegals employed. (See Figure 1.2.) It would be useful for you to identify the major resources for obtaining attorney jobs, such as special directories, lists or ads in bar publications, legal newspapers, etc. In particular, try to find the following resource used by unemployed attorneys and law students: *Directory of Legal Employers,* which is published by the National Association of Law Placement. (The Directory can also be used on WESTLAW, see Figure 3.1, if you have access to this computer legal research system.) Such resources might provide leads on contacting offices about paralegal employment.

b. Personal Contacts.   Make a list of attorneys who fall into the following categories:

- Personal friends
- Friends of friends
- Attorneys you have hired
- Attorneys your relatives have hired
- Attorneys your former employers have hired
- Attorneys your friends have hired
- Teachers
- Politicians
- Neighbors
- Etc.

You should consider contacting these attorneys about their own paralegal hiring plans as well as for references to other attorneys. Don't be reluctant to take advantage of any direct or indirect association that you might have with an attorney. Such contacts are the essence of networking. (See Job Hunting Notebook, page 137).

c. Ads.   You should regularly check the classified pages of your daily newspaper as well as the legal newspaper for your area. If you are seeking employment in another city, the main branch of your public library and the main library of large universities in your area may have out-of-town newspapers. If you have friends in these other cities, they might be willing to send you clippings from the classified ads of their newspapers. There are several *national* legal newspapers that sometimes have paralegal employment ads. These include the *National Law Journal* and the *American Lawyer*. Law libraries often subscribe to such newspapers.

Look for ads under the headings "Paralegal" or "Legal Assistant." For example

> **PARALEGAL**
> **TRUST ACCOUNTANTS**
> For details see our ad in this section headed
> **ACCOUNTANT**

> **PARALEGALS** Fee Pd. Salary Open. Corporate & Real Estate positions. Superior writing ability is a necessity. Must be able to work under pressure. Superior opportunities. Contact . . .

> **PARALEGAL**
> **(CORPORATE)**
> Large downtown Boston law firm seeks expd Corporate Paralegal. Oppty for responsibility and growth. Must have strong academic background. Computer literacy a plus. Salary commensurate with exp. Send resume in confidence to: X2935 TIMES

> **LEGAL ASSISTANT**
> Large West Palm Beach, Florida, firm wishes to employ legal assistant with immigration/naturalization experience, in addition to civil litigation, research & pleading abilities. Knowledge of Germanic languages helpful. Full fringe benefits/profit sharing. Salary negotiable. Contact . . .

For detailed quotes from want ads for a variety of different kinds of paralegal jobs, see pages 54–93.

Some ads are placed by private employment agencies that specialize in legal placements. The ad may not give the name and address of the employer seeking the paralegal. Instead, it will direct interested parties to an intermediary, such as a newspaper, which forwards all responses to the employer. Such ads are called "blind ads."

You will find that most want ads seek paralegals with experience in a particular area of practice. Hence if you are a recent graduate of a paralegal school who is looking for a beginning or entry-level position, you may not meet the qualifications sought in the ads.[2] Should you apply for such positions nevertheless? Suppose, for example, that an add seeks "a corporate paralegal with two years of experience." You might consider answering such an ad as follows:

> I am responding to your ad for a corporate paralegal. I do not have the experience indicated in the ad, but I did take an intensive course on corporate law at my paralegal school, and I'm wondering whether I could send you my resume so that you could consider what I have to offer.

If the answer is no, you can certainly ask for leads to anyone else who might be hiring individuals like yourself.

When reading want ads, do not limit yourself to the entries for "Paralegal" and "Legal Assistant." Also look for headings for positions that may be law related, such as "Research Assistant," "Legislative Aide," "Law Library Assistant." For example:

RESEARCH ASSISTANT	PROOFREADER	LEGISLATIVE ASSIS-
IMMEDIATE POSITION Social Science Research Institute in downtown looking for coder/editor of survey instruments. Post Box L3040.	Leading newspaper for lawyers has an immediate opening for a proofreader of manuscripts and galleys. Attention to detail, some night work. Past experience preferred. Low teens. Call Nance, 964-9700, Ext. 603.	TANT/SECRETARY Good skills essential, dwntwn location, send resume/sal. requirements to Post Box M 8341.

Of course, such jobs may not be what you are looking for. They may not be directly related to your legal training and experience. Nevertheless, you should read such ads carefully. Some might be worth pursuing.

On most classified pages, you will find many ads for legal secretaries or word processors. You might want to respond to such ads as follows:

> I saw your ad for a legal secretary. I am a trained paralegal and am wondering whether you have any openings for paralegals. If not, I would greatly appreciate your referring me to any attorneys you know who may be looking for paralegals.

---

[2]At the end of this chapter, we will examine the catch-22 problem of "no job/no experience" and "no experience/no job" when we discuss "your second job."

What about applying for a clerical position in a law office? Many paralegals take the view that this would be a mistake. In a tight employment market, however, some paralegals believe that a secretarial or typing job would be a way to "get a foot in the door," and hope that they will eventually be able to graduate into a position in the office that is commensurate with their paralegal training. Such a course of action is obviously a very personal decision that you must make on your own. It is not uncommon for clerical staff to be promoted to paralegal positions in a firm. It is also not uncommon, however, to get stuck in a clerical position.

Should you ever respond to want ads *for attorneys?* Such ads are common in legal newspapers and magazines. Of course, a paralegal cannot claim to be an attorney. But any office that is looking for attorneys obviously has a need for legal help. Hence, consider these possible reasons for responding to such ads, particularly when they give the name and address of the office seeking the attorney:

■ Perhaps the office is *also* looking for paralegal help but is simply not advertising for it (or you have not seen the want ad for paralegals).

■ Perhaps the office is having difficulty finding the attorney it is seeking and would consider hiring a paralegal for a temporary period of time to perform paralegal tasks *while* continuing the search for the attorney.

■ Perhaps the office has never considered hiring a paralegal *instead of* an attorney, but would be interested in exploring the idea.

Many of these employers may be totally uninterested in a response by a paralegal to an ad for an attorney. Yet none of the possibilities just described is irrational. The effort might be productive. Even if you are given a flat rejection, you can always use the opportunity to ask the person you contact if he or she knows of any other offices that are hiring paralegals.

Finally, a word about want ads placed *by a paralegal* seeking employment. Should you ever place an ad in a publication read by attorneys, such as the journal of the bar association, or the legal newspaper for your area? Such ads can be expensive and are seldom productive. Nevertheless, if you have a particular skill—for example, if you are a former nurse trained as a paralegal and are seeking a position in a medical malpractice firm, an ad might strike a responsive chord.

d. Through Other Paralegals. In Strategy 4 above, we discussed methods to contact working paralegals. Once you talk with a paralegal, you can, of course, obtain information about contacting the employing attorney of that paralegal.

e. Employment Agencies. There have always been employment agencies for the placement of attorneys. Many of these agencies also handle paralegal placement. Recently, a number of agencies have been opened to deal primarily with paralegal placement. Here is an example of an ad from such an agency:

Help Wanted

Paralegal Agency   **Fee Paid**

Paralegal Placement Experts Recognized by
Over 200 Law Firms and Corporations

PENSIONS

Outstanding law firm seeks 1+yrs pension paralegal exper. Major responsibilities, quality clients & liberal benefits. Salary commensurate w/exper.

LITIGATION

SEVERAL positions open at LAW FIRMS for litigation paralegals. Major benefits incl bonus.

MANAGING CLERK

Midtown law firm seeks 1+ yrs exper as a managing clerk. Work directly w/top management. Liberal benefits.

These are just a few of the many paralegal positions we have available. Call us for professional career guidance.

Look for such ads in the classified pages of general circulation and legal newspapers. Check your yellow pages under "Employment Agencies." If you are not sure which of the listed agencies cover legal placements, call several at random and ask which agencies in the city handle paralegal placement or legal placement in general. Caution is needed, however, in using such agencies. Some of them know very little about paralegals, in spite of their ads claiming to place paralegals. You may find that the agency views a paralegal as a secretary with a little extra training.

All employment agencies charge a placement fee. You must check whether the fee is paid by the employer or by the employee hired through the agency. Read the agency's service contract carefully before signing. Question the agency about the jobs they have available—for instance, whether evening work is expected or what typing requirements there are, if any.

Finally, you should find out if a paralegal *staffing agency* exists in your area. This is an employment agency that provides part-time employment at law offices. Most of the people placed are paralegals with experience in a particular area of practice. The paralegals are often paid by the agency, which in turn is paid by the offices. Law firms and corporate law departments may prefer part-time paralegals because of the low overhead costs involved, the availability of experienced people on short notice for indefinite periods, and the ability to end the relationship without having to go through the sometimes wrenching experience of terminating permanent employees.

f. Directories and Other Lists of Attorneys.   Find out whether there is a directory or list of attorneys in your area. Ask a librarian at any law library in your area. Your yellow pages will also list attorneys generally or by specialty.

Also check with a librarian about national directories of attorneys. One of the major directories is the *Martindale-Hubbell Law Directory* which gives descriptions of law firms by state and city or county (see Figure 3.1). For each firm, you are given brief biographies of the attorneys (listing bar memberships, colleges attended, etc.) as well as the areas of practice for the firm. (In 1992, Martindale-Hubbell started to include information on paralegals and other legal support personnel in law firms.) Also inquire about the availability of specialty lists of attorneys. Examples include criminal law attorneys, corporate counsel, bankruptcy attorneys, black attorneys, women attorneys, etc. Read whatever biographical data is provided on the attorneys. If there is something you have in common with a particular attorney (for example, you were both born in the same small town or you both went to the same school), you might want to mention this fact in a cover letter or phone conversation.

If you have access to either of the two major computer research systems—WESTLAW or LEXIS—you can locate attorneys online. LEXIS gives you the entire *Martindale-Hubbell Law Directory*. WESTLAW has created its own directory: *West's Legal Directory*. See Figure 3.2.

Finally, you may want to examine the *Directory of Legal Employers*, published by the National Association of Law Placement. As mentioned earlier, it lists the names and addresses of law firms and corporations that hire attorneys. But it will also indicate the number of paralegals employed by the offices listed in the directory. There are two places where you can find this directory: in the placement offices of most law schools and on WESTLAW.

g. Courts and Bar Association Meetings.   You can also meet attorneys at the courts of your area—for example, during a recess or at the end of the day. Bar association committee meetings are sometimes open to nonattorneys. When the other strategies for contacting attorneys do not seem productive, consider going to places where attorneys congregate. Simply introduce yourself and ask if they know of paralegal employment opportunities at their firms or at other firms. If

FIGURE 3.1   Excerpt from a Page in Martindale-Hubbell Law Directory

POYATT, ROYCROFT & MACDONALD
Established In 1968

731 SHADY LANE
DALLAS, TEXAS 75202
Telephone: 214-555-6720
Fax: 214-555-6730
Fort Worth, Texas Office: 34 Main Street, Suite 10, 77001
Telephone: 817-555-9224.   Fax: 817-555-9220

Poyatt, Roycroft & MacDonald was founded in 1968 by Kathleen Poyatt, Greg Roycroft and Julie MacDonald, former classmates and graduates of the University of Texas Law School. Starting with a local general practice, the firm now serves the entire state and maintains two fully-staffed offices offering a wide range of legal services. The firm encourages continuing professional development, and all partners and associates participate in continuing legal education seminars, professional association activities and civic affairs.

MEMBERS OF FIRM

KATHLEEN POYATT, born Plano, Texas, May 13, 1940; admitted to bar, 1967, Texas and U.S. Court of Appeals, Fifth Circuit. *Education:* Tulane University (B.A., with honors, 1962); University of Texas (J.D., cum laude, 1967). Phi Beta Kappa; Phi Delta Phi; Order of the Coif. Associate Editor, Texas Law Review, 1966–1967. Certified Public Accountant, Texas, 1971. Member, Advisory Board, Dallas Family Planning Council, 1982–1984. Legal Counsel, Dallas Board of Realtors, 1986–1987. *Member:* Dallas and American Bar Associations; State Bar of Texas (Chair, Committee on Trust Administration, Estate Planning and Probate Section, 1989–); American Judicature Society. (Board Certified, Estate Planning and Probate Law, Texas Board of Legal Specialization). LANGUAGES: Spanish and French. SPECIAL AGENCIES: Texas Council on Charitable Trusts. REPORTED CASES: Mastalia v. Fairty, 145 S.E. 2d 1405. TRANSACTIONS: Bankruptcy of Braniff Airlines, 1982; The Keepwell Foundation, 1990. AREAS OF CONCENTRATION: Trust Administration, Banking and Creditors' Rights, Trial, Litigation and Real Estate.

JULIE MACDONALD, born Nashville, Tennessee, August 29, 1940; admitted to bar, 1967, Texas and U.S. District Court, Northern District of Texas. *Education:* University of Tennessee at Memphis (B.A., with honors, 1962); University of Texas (J.D., with honors, 1967). Alpha Lambda Delta; Phi Kappa Phi; Phi Beta Kappa. Member, Tennessee State Board of Professional Responsibility, 1983–1984; The Association of Trial Lawyers of America. *Member:* Dallas (*Member:* Real Estate and Commercial Real Estate Morning Section; Continuing Education Committee) and American (*Member:* Real Property Section; Continuing Education Committee). Bar Associations; State Bar of Texas; Dallas Association of Young Lawyers; The Association of Trial Lawyers of America, LANGUAGES: Spanish and Italian. SPECIAL AGENCIES: Texas Council on Taxation Trusts. REPORTED CASES: Cuneo v. Banks, 466 S.E. 2d 6609; Kyle v. Smily, 432 S.E. 2d 4599. TRANSACTIONS: The Hines foundation, 1989. AREAS OF CONCENTRATION: Trials and Appeals, Estate Planning, Real Estates, Banking and Taxation.

LEGAL SUPPORT PERSONNEL
PARALEGAL

LINDA DAVIS, born Maurice, Louisiana, August 16, 1962. *Education:* Interstate Paralegal Institute. Certified Legal Assistant, Texas, 1985. President, Dallas Paralegal Association, 1987. Secretary, Texas State Paralegal Association, 1988. *Member:* National, State and Local Paralegal Association. Legal Research, Drafting Legal Pleadings, Client Correspondence, Deposition Summaries and File Investigations.

you meet an attorney who practices in a particular specialty, it would be helpful if you could describe your course work or general interest in that kind of law. If you are doing some research in that area of the law, you might begin by asking for some research leads before you ask about employment.

FIGURE 3.2

Sample Screen from West's Legal Directory

Name:	Jones, James E
City:	Boston
State:	Massachusetts
Position:	Partner
Firm:	Smith, Jones & White
Address:	1000 State Street, Exchange Plaza, Boston, MA 90001
Phone:	(617)722-7777
Electronic Mail:	Fax Area Code (617) Phone 722-7776
Born:	May 20, 1947, Dallas, TX. U.S.A.
Education:	Baylor University, Waco, Texas (J.D., 1973), Cum Laude
	University of Texas, Austin, Texas (B.A., 1969)
Admitted:	Massachusetts 1975
	Texas 1973
	Federal Court 1979
Fraternities:	Phi Alpha Delta
Directorships:	Massachusetts Commerce Association, 1980–Present
Affiliations:	American Bar Association
	State Bar of Massachusetts
Representative Clients:	Semi-Conductor, Inc.
	BCA National Bank
Representative Cases:	Thayer v. Smith, 560 S.W.2d 137 (1989)
Practice:	50% Patent, Trademark, Copyright
	25% Corporations Law
	25% Litigation
Foreign Languages:	Russian
Certified Specialty:	Patent, Trademark, Copyright--U.S. Patent & Trademark Office
Published Works:	*Corporations and Business Law,* 1981, CAB Publishing Company

h. Miscellaneous. Go to a recent reporter volume (or to its advance sheet) containing court opinions of your state. At the beginning of each opinion, there is a list of the attorneys who represented the parties in that case. You can obtain their addresses from standard directories such as those mentioned above. If the opinion is on an area of law that interests you, call the attorneys after you have read the opinion. Ask questions about the case and that area of the law. Then ask about job opportunities for paralegals in that area.

Look for ads in legal newspapers in which an attorney is seeking information about a particular product involved in a suit that is contemplated or underway. Or read feature stories in this newspaper on major litigation that is about to begin. If the area of the law interests you, contact the law firms involved to ask about employment opportunities for paralegals. Many firms hire additional paralegals, particularly for large cases.

Find the bar journal of your local or state bar associations in the law library. The articles in the journal are often written by attorneys from the state.

If the subject of an article interests you, read it and call the author. Ask a question or two about the topic of the article and the area of the law involved. Then ask about employment opportunities for paralegals in that area.

Strategy 7: Prepare Your Resume, Cover Letter, and Writing Sample

The cardinal principle of resume writing is that the resume must fit the job you are seeking. Hence, you must have more than one resume or you must rewrite your resume for each kind of paralegal job you are seeking. A resume is an *advocacy* document. You are trying to convince someone (a) to give you an interview and ultimately (b) to offer you a job. You are not simply communicating information about yourself. A resume is *not* a summary of your life or a one-page autobiography. It is a very brief *commercial* in which you are trying to sell yourself as a person who can make a contribution to a particular prospective employer. Hence the resume must stress what would appeal to this employer. You are advocating (or selling) yourself effectively when the form and content of the resume has this appeal. Advocacy is required for several reasons. First, there are probably many more applicants than jobs available. Second, most prospective employers ignore resumes that are not geared to their particular needs.

Before examining sample resumes, we need to explore some general guidelines that apply to *any* resume.

Guidelines on Drafting an Effective Resume

1. Be concise and to the point. Generally, the resume should fit on one page. A longer resume is justified only if you have a unique education or experience that is directly related to law or to the particular law firm or company in which you are interested.

2. Be accurate. Studies show that about 30% of all resumes contain inaccuracies. Recently, a legal administrator felt the need to make the following comment (to other legal administrators) about job applicants: "I'm sure we have all had experiences where an applicant has lied on an application about experience, previous salary scales, length of time with previous employers, training, skills, and anything else they can think of that will make them appear more attractive." [3] While you want to present yourself in the best possible light, it is critical that you not jeopardize your integrity. All of the data in the resume should be verifiable. Prospective employers who check the accuracy of resumes usually do so themselves, although some use outside organizations such as the National Credential Verification Service.

3. Include personal data—that is, name, address, zip code, and phone (with area code) where you can be reached. (If someone is not always available to take messages while you are away, invest in an answering machine.) Do not include a personal photograph or data on your health, height, religion, or political party. You do not have to include information that might give a prospective

---

[3] Jacobi, *Back to Basics in Hiring Techniques,* The Mandate, 1 (Ass'n of Legal Administrators, San Diego Chapter, October 1987).

employer a basis to discriminate against you illegally, such as your marital status or the names and ages of your children. Later we will discuss how to handle such matters in a job interview.

4. Provide a concise statement of your career objective at the top of the resume. (It should be pointed out, however, that some people recommend that this statement be included in the cover letter rather than in the resume.) The career objective should be a quick way for the reader to know whether your goal fits the needs of the prospective employer. Hence, *the career objective should be targeted to a particular employer.* An overly general career objective gives the unfortunate effect of a "mass-mailing resume." Suppose, for example, you are applying for a position as a litigation paralegal at a forty-attorney law firm that is looking for someone to help with scheduling and document handling on several cases going on simultaneously.

Don't say: **Career Objective**—A position as a paralegal at an office where there is an opportunity for growth.

Do say: **Career Objective**—A position as a litigation paralegal at a medium-sized law firm where I will be able to use and build on the organization skills I developed in my prior employment and the case management skills that I have learned to date.

The first statement is too flat and uninformative. Its generalities could fit just about *any* paralegal job. Even worse, its focus is on the needs of the applicant. The second statement is much more direct. While also referring to the needs of the applicant, the second statement goes to the heart of what the employer is looking for—someone to help create order out of the complexity of events and papers involved in litigation.

5. Next, state your prior education and training.[4] (See Job Hunting Notebook, page 132, page 133.) List each school or training institution and the dates attended. Use a reverse chronological order—that is, start the list with the most current and work backwards. Do not include your high school unless you attended a prestigious high school, you have not attended college, or you are a very recent high school graduate. When you give your legal education:

a. List the major courses.

b. State specific skills and tasks covered in your courses that are relevant to the job you are applying for. Also state major topic areas covered in the courses that demonstrate a knowledge of (or at least exposure to) material that is relevant to the job. For example, if you are applying for a corporate paralegal job, relevant courses could be stated as follows:

Corporate Law: This course examined the formation of a corporation, director and shareholder meetings, corporate mergers, and the dissolution of corporations; we also studied sample shareholder minutes and prepared proxy statements. Grade received: B+.

Legal Bibliography: This course covered the basic law books relevant to researching corporate law, including the state code. We also covered the

---

[4]If you already have experience as a paralegal and are seeking to change jobs, the next section of the resume should be work experience, followed by education and training.

skills of using practice books, finding cases on corporate law through the digests, etc. Grade received: A — .

c. List any special programs in the school, such as unique class assignments, term papers, extensive research, moot court, internship, or semester projects. Give a brief description if any of these programs are relevant to the job you are applying for.

d. State any unusually high grades: give overall grade point average (GPA) if it is distinctive.

List any degrees, certificates, or other recognition that you earned at each school or training institution. Include high aptitude or standard test scores. If the school or institution has any special distinction or recognition, mention this as well.

6. State your work experience. (See Job Hunting Notebook, pages 130–132.) List the jobs you held, your job title, the dates of employment, and the major duties that you performed. (Do not state the reason you left each job, although you should be prepared to discuss this if you are granted an interview.) Again, work backwards. Start with the most current (or your present) employment. The statement of duties is particularly important. If you have legal experience, emphasize specific duties and tasks that are directly relevant to the position you are seeking—for example, include that you drafted corporate minutes or prepared incorporation papers. Give prominence to such skills and tasks on the resume. Nonlegal experience, however, can also be relevant. Every prior job says something about you as an individual. Phrase your duties in such jobs in a manner that will highlight important personality traits. (See p. 132.) In general, most employers are looking for people with the following characteristics:

- Emotional maturity
- Intelligence
- Willingness to learn
- Ability to get along with others
- Ability to work independently (someone with initiative and self-reliance who is not afraid of assuming responsibility)
- Problem-solving skills
- Ability to handle time pressures and frustration
- Loyalty
- Stability, reliability
- Energy

As you list duties in prior and current employment settings, do *not* use any of the language just listed. But try to state duties that tend to show that these characteristics apply to you. For example, if you had a job as a camp counselor, state that you supervised 18 children, designed schedules according to predetermined objectives, prepared budgets, took over in the absence of the director of the camp, etc. A listing of such duties will say a lot about you as a person. You are someone who can be trusted, you know how to work with people, you are flexible, etc. These are the kind of conclusions that you want the reader of your resume to reach. Finally, try to present the facts to show a growth in your accomplishments, development, and maturity. Note that *action verbs* were used in examples just given: supervised, designed, prepared, took over. Concentrate on such verbs. Avoid weak verbs such as "involved in" or "was related to."

7. State other experience and skills that do not fall within the categories of education and employment mentioned above. (See Job Hunting Notebook, p. 131.) Perhaps you have been a homemaker for 20 years, you raised five children, you worked your way through college, you were the church treasurer, a cub scout volunteer,. etc In a separate category on the resume called "Other Experience," list such activities and state your duties in the same manner mentioned above to demonstrate relevant personality traits. Hobbies can be included (without using the word "hobby") when they are distinctive and illustrate special talents or achievement.

8. State any special abilities (for example, that you can design a database or speak a foreign language), awards, credentials, scholarships, membership associations, leadership positions, community service, publications, etc., that have not been mentioned elsewhere on the resume.

9. No one has a perfect resume. There are facts about all of us that we would prefer to downplay or avoid, e.g., sudden change in jobs, school transfer because of personal or family difficulties, low aptitude test scores. There is no need to point out these facts, but in a job interview you must be prepared to discuss any obvious gaps or problems that might be evident from your resume. Thus far we have been outlining the format of a *chronological resume* in which your education, training, and experience are presented in a chronological sequence from the present backwards. (See Figure 3.4.) Later we will examine how a *functional resume* might be more effective than a chronological resume in handling difficulties such as sudden changes or gaps in employment. (See Figure 3.5.)

10. At the end of the resume, say, "References available on request." On a separate sheet of paper, type the names and addresses of people who know your abilities and who could be contacted by a prospective employer. If the latter is seriously considering you for a position, you will probably be asked for the list. This will most likely occur during a job interview. Generally, you should seek the permission of people you intend to use as references. Call them up and ask if you can list them as references in your job search.

11. Do not include salary requirements or your salary history on the resume. Leave this topic for the interview.

12. The resume should be neatly typed, grammatically correct, and readable. Be sure that there are no spelling errors or smudge spots from erasures or fingerprints. In this regard, if you can't make your resume *perfect*, don't bother submitting it. Avoid abbreviations except for items such as street, state, degrees earned, etc. Do not make any handwritten corrections. Proofread carefully. Ask someone else to proofread the resume for you to see if you missed anything.

You do not have to use complete sentences in the resume. Sentence fragments are adequate as long as you rigorously follow the grammatical rule on parallelism. For example, say, "researched securities issues, drafted complaints, serv*ed* papers on opposing parties." Do not say, "researched securities, drafting complaints, and I served papers on opposing parties." When you present a series or a list, be consistent in using words ending in "ed" or ending in "ing," etc. Do not suddenly change from an "ed" word to an "ing" word or add personal pronouns on only some of the items in the series or list.

Leave generous margins. Cluster similar information together and use consistent indentation patterns so that readers can easily scan the resume and quickly find those categories of information in which they are most interested.

The resume should have a professional appearance. Consider having your resume typeset on quality paper (with matching envelopes) by a commercial printing company or word processing service. Obtain multiple copies of your resume. Avoid submitting a resume that was obviously reproduced on a poor-quality Xerox machine at a corner drugstore. The resume is often the first contact that a prospective employer will have with you. You want to convey the impression that you know how to write and organize data. Furthermore, it is a sign of respect to the reader when you show that you took the time and energy to make your resume professionally presentable. Law offices are *conservative* environments. Attorneys like to project an image of propriety, stability, accuracy, and order. Be sure that your resume also projects this image.

13. Again, the resume concentrates on those facts about you that show you are particularly qualified *for the specific job you are seeking*. The single most important theme you want to convey in the resume is that you are a person who can make a contribution to *this* organization. As much as possible, the reader of the resume should have the impression that you prepared the resume for the particular position that is open. In style and content, the resume should emphasize what will be pleasing to the reader and demonstrate what you can contribute to a particular office. (See Figure 3.3.)

The last guideline is very important. You cannot comply with it unless you have done some *background research* on the law office where you are applying and, if possible, on the person who will be receiving the resume. How do you do this background research? First and foremost, you want to try to contact employees, particularly paralegals, who work there now or who once worked there. That's why Strategy 4, outlined above, on ways to locate working paralegals is so important.

In addition, consult one of the directories of attorneys, such as the *Martindale-Hubble Law Directory* or *West's Legal Directory,* discussed earlier. Ask a librarian for a current directory of attorneys used in your state. Many large firms have brochures on their firms which are part of marketing strategies to find new clients. They may also have newsletters that they send to their current clients. Such brochures and newsletters may not be available to the general public unless someone within the firm gives you access to them.

FIGURE 3.3   The Resume as an Advocacy Document

What you are seeking		Background research		What the prospective employer wants to read about applicants		What your resume should contain
	+		+		>	

If you are applying for a position in the law department of a large corporation, call the public relations office of the corporation and ask for promotional literature and a copy of its annual report. Many law libraries have directories of corporate counsel which you should check. In addition, most general libraries have directories, such as *Standard & Poor's Register of Corporations, Directors and Executives* and *Moody's Bank and Finance Manual*, that provide information on such companies. Ask the librarian what other sources provide profiles of businesses.

Here is a partial checklist of information you want to obtain through background research on a prospective employer or job (see also page 124):

- Why has the office decided to hire a paralegal now? What needs or problems prompted this decision?
- What kind of law is practiced at the office? What are its specialties?
- How is the office structured and governed? By management committee?
- How old is the office? Has it expanded recently? If so, in what areas?
- What kinds of clients does the office have? A variety of small clients? Several large clients that provide most of the fees?
- If the office is the law department of a corporation, what are the company's main products or services?
- How many attorneys are in the office?
- How many paralegals? What kind of work do they do? Does the office understand the role of paralegals? What kinds of complaints have the paralegals had about the office? What are the advantages and disadvantages of working in the office?
- Has the office had personnel problems? High turnover?
- Does the office operate through systems? If not, how does it feel about developing such systems?

If you do your homework on a prospective employer, you will have begun collecting answers to such questions so that you can tailor your resume to these answers. You will select those aspects of your prior employment or education, for example, that suggest or demonstrate you are able to handle the demands of the job.

Of course, for many jobs, you will *not* be able to obtain answers to these questions, no matter how much background research you do. You will simply have to do the best you can to predict what the "correct" answers are and structure your resume, cover letter, and writing samples accordingly.

The main point, however, is that a lot of preparation is needed before you approach a prospective employer. Much time and energy must be expended. A conscientious and organized job search will be good preparation for the career ahead of you. *The same kind of motivation, creativity, and aggressiveness that is needed to find a good job is also needed to perform effectively as a paralegal and to advance in this field.* The cornerstone of achievement and success is a heavy dosage of old-fashioned hard work.

Figure 3.4 is an example of a *chronological resume,* the most common and traditional format used by many applicants today. As indicated earlier, this resume presents your education, training, and work history in reverse chronological sequence, beginning with the most recent events and working backwards.

A *functional resume,* on the other hand, clusters certain skills or talents together regardless of the period in which they were developed. See Figure 3.5. This style of resume can be particularly useful when you want to downplay large gaps in education, when you are making a radical change of careers, or when your skills were not gained in paralegal education, training, or employ-

FIGURE 3.4   Sample Chronological Resume

JOHN J. SMITH
43 BENNING ROAD SE
SALEM, MARYLAND 21455
(301) 456-0427

Career Objective	Position as a paralegal at a small law firm in the area of probate, trusts, and estates in a firm where my accounting and legal skills will be used and where there are opportunities for growth.
Education	Jan. 1989–Jan. 1990 Maynard Paralegal Institute.

Courses:

Trusts and Estates: The course presented an overview of probate procedure in Maryland. We covered how to conduct a client conference to collect the basic facts and how to prepare the 105 short form.

Tax I: An introduction to the taxation of estates and general income tax; fundamentals of accounting; valuation of personal and real assets.

Introduction to Law	Civil Procedure	Litigation
Family Law	Legal Research	

Internship: Part of the curriculum at Maynard involved a six-week internship placement at a law firm; I was placed at Donaldson and Tannance, a general practice firm in Salem. Tasks undertaken at the internship: drafted answers to interrogatories in a divorce case on the ground of mental cruelty; maintained the office's tickler system; completed cite checking and shepardizing for an appellate brief.

Sept. 1987–June 1988 Jefferson Junior College Courses:

Business Law	Sociology	French
English I, II	Chemistry	Creative Writing
Introduction to Psychology		

Employment	1985–1988 Teller, Salem National Bank

Responsibilities: received deposit and withdrawal requests; trained new tellers, supervised note department in the absence of the assistant manager.

1980–1984 Driver, ABC Biscuit Company

Honors	1985 Junior Achievement Award for Outstanding Marketing
Associations	Financial Secretary, Salem Paralegal Association Regional Representative, National Federation of Paralegal Associations Member, National Association of Legal Assistants
References	Available on request.

FIGURE 3.5   Sample Functional Resume[5]

> Jane Doe
> 18 East 7th Avenue
> Denver, Colorado 80200
> 303-555-1198
>
> **JOB OBJECTIVE**
>
> A position in a legal office requiring skills in communications, research, and organization, leading toward training for and work as a paralegal.
>
> **BRIEF SUMMARY OF BACKGROUND**
>
> Bachelor of Arts and Bachelor of Science (Education) with major in English and minor in Library Science. Taught creative writing and communications to high school juniors and seniors; worked several years as research and index assistant in records and research department of large, international organization; worked part-time on a volunteer basis in schools and libraries as librarian and reading tutor.
>
> **PROFESSIONAL SKILLS RELATED TO CAREER OBJECTIVE**
>
> **Communications Skills**
>
> Taught communications to high school seniors; read extensively in international publications during nonworking years; conducted workshops on library skills and storytelling to children and young adults; participated in workshops with educators on reading skills; served as Circulation Representative for *The Christian Science Monitor,* which included promoting and selling subscriptions by telephone and in person. Gained writing experience while working toward college degree in English.
>
> **Clerical Skills**
>
> Facility with [a] vocabulary and spelling; [b] rules of diction and usage; [c] typing (80 wpm); [d] filing (helped revise and maintain many files including administrative, subjective, alpha-chrono combinations); [e] systems (maintained and circulated library collections and maintained catalog card files).
>
> **Research Skills**
>
> As librarian: helped students and teachers research information and materials on various subjects; ordered, received, processed, and shelved library materials.
>
> As research assistant: indexed correspondence; researched files for information using subject index; collated information on various subjects.
>
> **Analytical and Organizational Skills**
>
> Handled all phases of management of school library; planned for materials needed; ordered to meet those needs; supervised assistants; set up revised filing systems; helped engineer departmental move to new quarters.
>
> **EMPLOYMENT HISTORY**
>
> 9/84–Present   Lincoln Elementary School
>   100 Oak Street, Denver, Colorado 80000
>   *Title:* Teacher's Aide (Part-time)
>
> 6/76–6/84   International Church Center
>   Executive Department, Records and Research Section
>   465 E. 8th St., Boston, Massachusetts 02127
>   *Title:* Research and Index Assistant (1 year full-time; 7 years part-time)
>
> 4/84–6/84   Latin Preparatory School
>   16 Adams Court, Dorchester, Massachusetts 02139
>   *Title:* School Librarian (substitute)

Continued

FIGURE 3.5   Sample Functional Resume[5]—*Continued*

2/83–6/84	James P. O'Reilly Elementary School 74 Statler Road, Boston, Massachusetts 02140 *Title:* School Librarian (volunteer)
9/74–6/75	Roosevelt High School 16 Main St., Minneapolis, Minnesota 55162 *Title:* English Teacher

EDUCATION

1983–1984	University of Massachusetts, Boston Campus Special courses included: Library and Urban Children; Design Management
1979–1980	Harvard Extension, Problems in Urban Education
1969–1973	University of Minnesota, Minneapolis, B.S. and B.A., *Major:* English *Minor:* Library Science

SCHOOL ACTIVITIES

National Honor Society; Dramatic Club; Creative Writing Club; YWCA; Member, Minnesota Dance Company, 1969–1973.

REFERENCES

Available on request.

ment. The functional resume should not, however, ignore the chronological sequence of the major training and work events of your life, since a prospective employer will want to know what this sequence is. Note that the functional resume in Figure 3.5 has a skill cluster early in the resume, after which there is the historical overview in reverse chronological order. Because of this format, the emphasis of the resume is on the skills or abilities highlighted at the beginning.

Cover Letter

The *cover letter* should state how you learned of the office. It should also highlight and amplify those portions of the resume that are relevant to the position you are seeking. Without being unduly repetitive of the resume, explain how you are qualified for the job. Like the resume itself, the cover letter should give the impression that you are a professional. It is also important that you communicate a sense of enthusiasm about the position.

Note that the cover letter in Figure 3.6 is addressed to a specific person. It would be inappropriate to send a "To Whom It May Concern" letter. Find out the exact name of the person to whom the resume should be sent. If you are not sure, call the office and ask.

One final, critically important point about the cover letter: it must be grammatically correct and contain no spelling errors. Your standard must be perfec-

---

[5]Rocky Mountain Legal Assistants Association, *Employment Handbook for Legal Assistants,* 26–8 (1979).

FIGURE 3.6   Cover Letter

43 Benning Road SE
Salem, Maryland 21455
301/456-0427
March 13, 1990

Linda Stenner, Esq.
Stenner, Skidmore & Smith
438 Bankers Trust Bldg.
Suite 1200
Salem, Maryland 21458

Dear Ms. Stenner:

Michael Diamond, Esq. told me that your firm may have an opening for a trusts and estates paralegal. I am enclosing my resume for your consideration. I am very interested in working in the field of probate, trusts, and estates. The course work that I did at Maynard Institute and my prior work at the Salem National Bank provided me with an appreciation of the complexity of this area of the law. I find the field fascinating.

I am fully aware of the kind of attention to detail that a paralegal in this field must have. If you decide to check any of my references, I am confident that you will be told of the high level of discipline and responsibility that I bring to the tasks I undertake.

I have two writing samples that may be of interest to you: a draft of a will that I prepared in my course on trusts and estates, and a memorandum of law on the valuation of stocks. These writing samples are available on request.

I would appreciate the opportunity to be interviewed for the paralegal position at your firm. I feel confident that my training and experience have prepared me for the kind of challenge that this position would provide.

Sincerely,

John J. Smith

tion. While this is also true of the resume, it is particularly true of the cover letter. When the envelope is opened, the first thing that is read is the cover letter. Most of us are *unaware of how poor our grammar is*. We have been lulled into a sense of security because readers of what we write—including teachers—seldom complain unless we make an egregious error. People read primarily for content; they do not focus on grammar and spelling. Hence you must provide this focus on your own. In the section on studying at the beginning of this book, there are suggestions for improving your writing skills. In the meantime, proofread, proofread, proofread; and then find others to proofread everything that you intend to submit in writing to a prospective employer.

Writing Samples

You should be constantly thinking about writing samples based upon the course work you do and any legal employment or internship experiences you have had. If your writing sample comes from a prior job or internship, be sure that the confidentiality of actual parties is protected by "whiting out" or changing their names.[6] In addition, consider preparing other writing samples *on your own*. For example:

- a brief memorandum of law on the application of a statute to a set of facts that you make up
- a pleading such as a complaint
- a set of interrogatories
- articles of incorporation and bylaws for a fictitious corporation
- an analysis of a recent court opinion
- an in-take memorandum of law based on an interview that you role-play with another student
- an annotated bibliography on a particular topic
- a brief article that you write for a paralegal newsletter on an aspect of your legal education or work experience as a paralegal

Prepare a file of all your writing samples. (See Job Hunting Notebook, page 136.) If possible, try to have a teacher, practicing attorney, or paralegal review each sample. Rewrite it based on their comments. You must take the initiative in preparing writing samples and in soliciting feedback from knowledgeable contacts that you make. You need to have a large pool of diverse writing samples from which to choose once you begin the actual job hunt. Start preparing these samples now.

Strategy 8: The Job Interview

Once you have overcome the hurdles of finding a prospective employer who will read your cover letter and resume, the next problem is to arrange for a job interview. In your cover letter, you may want to add the following sentence at the end: "Within the next two weeks, I will give you a call to determine whether an interview would be possible." This strategy does not leave the matter entirely up to the prospective employer as to whether there will be further contact with you. You must be careful, however, not to appear too forward. Some may resent this approach. On the other hand, you have little to lose by trying it several times to see what response you obtain.

Always try to have a paralegal, attorney, administrator, or secretary in the office arrange the interview for you with the person who will be doing the hiring and/or interviewing. Hopefully, your background research into the office will enable you to identify such an in-house person who will put in a word for you.

---

[6] "It is always inappropriate to hand a prospective employer anything that has current, active case information anywhere in it: case names and numbers, court and internal file numbers, names, addresses, telephone numbers of deponents, names of plaintiffs, defendants, and third parties in the body of the document." Fitzgerald, *Ethics and the Job Hunting Paralegal,* 18 Reporter (Los Angeles Paralegal Ass'n, November 1989).

Job Interview Guidelines

(See Job Hunting Notebook, page 138.)

"Attired in your best interviewing suit, you nervously navigate your way to the reception area of what you hope will be your future employer's office. You are a comfortable ten minutes early. Upon arrival you are directed to the office of the interviewer, whom you greet with a smile and pleasant handshake. She offers you a cup of coffee, which you wisely refuse, since you may spill it. She then looks you in the eye and poses her first question. 'Why are you interested in working for this company?' [Suddenly you go blank!] All thoughts leave your mind as you pray for the ability to speak." Cunningham, *A Planned Approach to Interviewing,* 5 The LAMA Manager 1 (Legal Assistant Management Association, Fall 1989).

1. Be sure you have the exact address, room number, and time of the interview. Give yourself sufficient time to find the office. If the area is new to you, be sure that you have precise directions. It would be unfortunate to start your contact with the office by having to provide excuses for being late. Arrive at least ten minutes early. You will probably be nervous and will need to compose yourself before the interview. It is important that you are as relaxed as possible.

2. Try to find out in advance who will be interviewing you. Don't be surprised, however, if the person who greets you is a substitute for the person originally scheduled to conduct the interview. There are a number of different kinds of people who might conduct the interview: the law office manager, the managing attorney, the supervising attorney for the position, the paralegal supervisor, a staff paralegal, or a combination of the above if you are interviewed by different people on the same day or on different days. The style of the interview may be quite different depending on who conducts it. Someone with management responsibility might stress the interpersonal dimensions of the position, whereas a trial attorney might give you the feeling that you are being cross-examined. Try to determine whether you are being interviewed by the person who has the final authority to hire you. In many offices, you will be interviewed by someone whose sole task is to screen out unacceptable applicants. If you make it through this person, the next step will usually be an interview with the ultimate decision-maker. Whenever you know or suspect that you will be interviewed by an attorney, try to obtain his or her professional biography through *Martindale-Hubbell* or other directories. You might be lucky enough to get to talk with someone who has been interviewed by this person before (such as a paralegal now working at the office, a fellow job seeker, or someone at the local paralegal association) so that you can obtain a sense of what to expect.

3. Although relatively uncommon, you may have to face a *group interview.* There could be several interviewers questioning you at once. Alternatively, one or more interviewers could interview you along with, and at the same time as, other candidates for the job.

4. Make sure that you are prepared for the interview. Review the guidelines discussed above on writing your resume. In the resume and in the interview, you are trying to sell yourself. Many of the principles of resume writing apply to the interview. Know the kinds of questions you will probably be asked.

Rehearse your responses. Write down a series of questions (tough ones) and ask a friend to role-play an interview with you. Have your friend ask you the questions and critique your responses. Also take the role of the interviewer of your friend so that you can gauge both perspectives. Be prepared to handle a large variety of questions. See Figure 3.7. Keep in mind, however, that no matter how much preparation you do, you may still be surprised by the course the interview takes. Be flexible enough to expect the unexpected. If you are relaxed, confident, *and prepared,* you will do fine.

5. You are not required to answer potentially illegal questions—for instance, "Are you married?" Some employers use the answers to such irrelevant questions to practice illegal sex discrimination. You need to decide in advance how you will handle them if they are asked. You may want to ask why the question is relevant. Or you may simply decide to steer the interview back to the qualifications that you have and the commitment that you have made to a professional career. A good response might be, "If you're concerned that my marital status may affect my job performance, I can assure you that it will not." Follow this up with comments about dedication and job commitment. It may be the perfect time to offer references.[7] Whatever approach you take, be sure to remain courteous.

6. Avoid being critical of anyone. Do not, for example, "dump on" your prior employer or school. Criticizing or blaming other organizations, even if justified, is likely to give the interviewer the impression that you will probably end up blaming *this* organization if you get the job and difficulties arise.

7. What about being critical of yourself? You will be invited to criticize yourself when you are asked the seemingly inevitable question, "What are your weaknesses?" You may want to pick a *positive* trait and express it as a negative. For example: "I tend to get frustrated when I'm not given enough to do. My goal is not just to collect a paycheck. I want to make a contribution." Or: "I think I sometimes have expectations that are too high. There is so much to learn, and I want it all now. I have to pace myself, and realize that the important goal is to complete the immediate task, even if I can't learn every conceivable aspect of that task at the present time." Or: "I get irritated by carelessness. When I see someone turn in sloppy work, or work that is not up to the highest standards, it bothers me."

If you use any of these approaches, be sure that you are able to back them up when you are asked to explain what you mean. You will probably be asked to give concrete examples of such "weaknesses."

8. If you have done the kind of background research on the office mentioned earlier, you will have a fairly good idea what the structure and mission of the office is. Interviewers are usually impressed by applicants who demonstrate this kind of knowledge during the interview. It will be clear to them which applicants have done their homework. A major goal of the interview is to relate your education and experience to the needs of the office. To the extent possible, you want to know what these needs are before the interview so that you can

---

[7]Reitz, *Be Steps Ahead of Other Candidates: Understand the Interview Game,* 5 Legal Assistant Today 24, 84 (March/April 1988).

FIGURE 3.7   The Six Categories of Job Interview Questions

- **Open-Ended Questions** (which are calculated to get you to talk, giving the listener an idea of how you organize your thoughts)

  (1) Tell me about yourself.

  (2) What kind of position are you seeking?

  (3) What interests you about this job?

- **Closed-Ended Questions** (which can be answered by one or two words)

  (4) When did you receive your paralegal certificate?

  (5) Did you take a course in corporate law?

- **Soft-Ball Questions** (which should be fairly easy to answer if you are prepared)

  (6) What are your interests outside of school and work?

  (7) What courses did you enjoy the most? Why? Which were least rewarding? Why?

  (8) Do your grades reflect your full potential? Why or why not?

  (9) Why did you leave your last job?

  (10) How have you grown or developed in your prior jobs? Explain.

  (11) How were you evaluated in your prior jobs?

  (12) What are your strengths as a worker?

  (13) Describe an ideal work environment. What would your "dream job" be?

  (14) What factors make a job frustrating? How would you handle these factors?

  (15) What do you hope to be doing in ten years? What are your long-term goals?

  (16) If you are hired, how long are you prepared to stay?

  (17) Are you interested in a job or a career? What's the difference?

  (18) Why did you become a paralegal?

  (19) What problems do you think a paralegal might face in a busy law office? How would you handle these problems?

  (20) Can you work under pressure? When have you done so in the past?

  (21) How flexible are you in adapting to changing circumstances? Give examples of your flexibility in the last year.

  (22) How do you feel about doing routine work?

  (23) Do you prefer a large or a small law office? Why?

  (24) What accomplishment in your life are you most proud of? Why?

  (25) What salary expectations do you have? What was your salary at your last position?

  (26) What other questions should I ask to learn more about you?

  (27) What questions would you like to ask me about this office?

- **Tension Questions** (which are calculated to put you on the spot in order to see how you handle yourself)

  (28) No one is perfect. What are your weaknesses as a worker?

  (29) Have you ever been fired from a position? Explain the circumstances.

  (30) Why have you held so many jobs?

  (31) Name some things that would be unethical for an attorney to do. What would you do if you found out that the attorney supervising you was doing these things?

Continued

FIGURE 3.7   The Six Categories of Job Interview Questions—*Continued*

(32) Are you a competitive person? If not, why not? If you are, give some examples over the last six months that demonstrate this characteristic.

(33) Is there something in this job that you hope to accomplish that you were not able to accomplish in your last job?

(34) Do you type? If not, are you willing to learn?

(35) Do you smoke? If so, how would you handle a work environment that is totally smoke-free, including the washrooms?

(36) Where else have you interviewed for a job? Have you been turned down?

(37) Why wouldn't you want to become an attorney now?

(38) Everyone makes mistakes. What is the biggest mistake that you made in any of your prior jobs and how did you handle it?*

(39) No job is perfect. What is the least appealing aspect of the job you are seeking?

(40) There are over 50 applicants for this one position. Why do you think you are the most qualified?

(41) If you are offered this position, what are the major concerns that you would have about taking it?

(42) What would make you want to quit a job?

(43) Give some examples of when you have shown initiative over the last six months in school or at your last job.

■ **Hypothetical Questions** (in which you are asked how you would handle a stated fact situation)

(44) If you were told, "This isn't any good, do it again, and get it right this time," what would you do?

(45) If you find out on Friday afternoon that you're expected to come in on Saturday, what would you do?**

(46) Assume that you are given the position here and that you work very closely on a day-to-day basis with an attorney. After a six-month period, what positive and negative comments do you think this attorney would make about you as a worker?

(47) Suppose that your first assignment was to read through and summarize 4,000 documents over an eight-month period. Could you do it? Would you want to do it?

(48) Assume that two airplanes crash into each other and that your firm represents one of the passengers who was killed. What kind of discovery would you recommend?

■ **Potentially Illegal Questions** (because the questions are not relevant to the candidate's fitness and ability to do most jobs)

(49) Are you married? Do you plan to marry?

(50) Do you have any children? If so, how old are they? Who takes care of your children?

(51) If you do not have any children now, do you plan to have any in the future?

(52) How old are you?

(53) What is your religion?

(54) What is your political affiliation?

---

*Moralez, *Sample Interview Questions*, 11 Paragram (Oregon Legal Assistant Ass'n, May 1988).
**Wendel, *You the Recruiter*, 5 Legal Assistant Today 31 (September/October 1987).

quickly and forcefully demonstrate that you are the person the office is looking for. Most offices decide to hire someone because they have a problem—for example, they need someone with a particular skill, they need someone to help them expand, or they need someone who can get along with a particularly demanding supervising attorney. If you are not sure, ask the interviewer directly why the office has decided to add a paralegal. The success of the interview is directly related to your ability to identify the problem of the office and to demonstrate how you can solve it for them.

9. If the paralegal job is in a certain specialty, such as probate or corporate law, you must be prepared to discuss that area of the law. You may be asked questions designed to assess your familiarity with the area. Prior to the interview, spend some time reviewing your class notes. Skim through a standard practice book for that area of the law in the state. Be sure that you can back up anything you said in your resume about prior involvement with the area in your school or work experience. Such discussions are always an excellent opportunity for you to present writing samples in that field of the law. (Be sure to bring extra copies of such writing samples and of your resume).

10. Dress conservatively. "It is recommended that a man be clean shaven, wear a dark suit (gray or navy blue), a white shirt, and a muted-tone tie. Shoes should be polished. A woman should wear a skirt-suit or a blazer and skirt, plain blouse, neutral-colored stockings, and a simple hairdo. A minimal amount of jewelry and no perfume are the rule. . . . To complete these 'uniforms,' a briefcase is a necessity. It symbolizes that you are a professional. Women may want to keep their purses in their briefcases." [8]

11. Be sure that you project yourself positively. Take the initiative in greeting the interviewer. A firm handshake is recommended. Maintain good posture and eye contact. Remember that everything you do will be evaluated. The interviewer will be making mental notes on your body language. Avoid appearing ill at ease or fidgety. Many feel that the practice of law is a battlefield. The interviewer will be forming an opinion of whether you "fit in."

12. Try to avoid the topic of salary until the end of the interview when you have completed the discussion of the job itself. Preferably, let the interviewer raise the issue. Think through how you will handle the topic, but try to avoid discussing it until the appropriate time arises. If asked what salary you are seeking, give a salary range rather than a single rigid figure. Always relate salary to the specific skills and strengths that you would be able to bring to the office, rather than to the "going rate." You need to know what the going rate is— check recent salary surveys of local and national paralegal associations—so that the salary range you seek is realistic. But avoid using the going rate as the first and sole reason for your position on salary.

13. Be an active participant in the interview even though you let the interviewer conduct the interview. Help keep the discussion going.

14. Be enthusiastic, but not overly so. You want to let the office know that you really want the job, not because you are desperate but because you see it as a challenge offering professional development. You are qualified for the job and

---

[8]Berkey, *Successful Interviewing*, 5 Legal Assistant Today 66 (September/October 1987).

you feel that the office is the kind of place that recognizes valuable contributions from its workers.

15. Be yourself. Do not try to overwhelm the interviewer with your cleverness and charm.

16. Be prepared to leave the following documents with the interviewer: extra copies of your resume, a list of references, and writing samples.

17. Ask the interviewer if you can be given the opportunity to talk with one or more paralegals currently working at the office. It will be another sign of your seriousness.

18. Ask your own questions of the interviewer. In effect, you are interviewing the office as much as the other way around. Come with a written list and don't be afraid to let the interviewer see that you have a checklist of questions that you want to ask. It is a sign of an organized person. There is a great deal of information about the job that you could inquire about. From your background research about the job, you should already have some of this information, but you can now verify what you know. You want to ask pertinent and intelligent questions that will communicate to the interviewer that you are serious about the paralegal field, that you are prepared, and that you grasp what the interviewer has been telling you about the job and the office.

Below are some of the topics that you could cover in your own questions. See also Figure 3.8 and Figure 3.9 for ideas on questions.

- What type of person is the office seeking to hire?
- What prompted the office to seek this type of person?
- What are some examples of paralegal responsibilities? Will the paralegal specialize in certain tasks or areas of the law? (Ask for a description of a typical workday of a paralegal at the firm.)
- What skills will the paralegal need for the job? Digesting? Investigation? Research? Drafting? Interviewing?
- How many attorneys are in the firm? Is the number growing, declining, remaining constant?
- How is the firm managed or governed? Managing partner? Management committees? Legal administrator? Is there a policy manual for the firm?
- How many paralegals are in the firm? Is the number growing, declining, remaining constant? Are all the paralegals at the firm full-time? Does the firm use part-time or freelance paralegals? Has the firm considered hiring a paralegal coordinator?
- Is there a career ladder for paralegals in the firm?
- How long has the firm used paralegals? What is the average length of time a paralegal stays with the firm? What are the feelings of firm members on the value of paralegals to the firm? Why is this so? How would firm members describe an ideal paralegal employee? Do all members of the firm feel the same about paralegals? What reservations, if any, do some members of the firm have about paralegals?

■ What other personnel does the firm have (secretaries, computer staff, library staff, clerks, messengers, part-time law students, etc.)? How many of each are there? What relationship does the paralegal have with each?

■ What kind of supervision does a paralegal receive? Close supervision? From one attorney? Several?

■ Will the paralegal work for one attorney? Several? Will the paralegal have his or her own case load? Is there a paralegal pool available to many attorneys?

■ What kind of client contact will the paralegal have? Phone? Meetings? Interviews? Document inspection at client's office?

■ What kind of correspondence will the paralegal be preparing? Letters that the paralegal will sign? Letters for attorney to sign? Memos?

■ What opportunities does a paralegal have for further learning? Office training programs? (Do paralegals attend new-attorney training sessions?) Does the firm encourage outside training for paralegals, e.g., from paralegal associations, bar associations, area schools?

■ Will the paralegals be attending staff meetings? Strategy sessions with attorneys?

■ How are paralegals evaluated in the office? Written evaluations? Oral? How often?

■ Are paralegals required to produce a set number of billable hours? Per day? Per week? Per month? Annually? What is the hourly rate at which a paralegal's time is billed to a client? Do different paralegals in the office bill at different rates? If so, what determines the difference?

■ How often are paralegals required to record their time? Daily, hourly, in tenminute segments, etc.?

■ What secretarial assistance is available to the paralegal? None? A personal secretary? Secretary shared with an attorney? Use of a secretarial pool? Will the paralegal do any typing? Light typing? His or her own typing? Typing for others?

■ Does the job require travel?

■ What equipment will the paralegal be using? Word processor, typewriter, copier, dictaphone, research computer?

■ Office space for the paralegal? Private office? Shared office? Partitioned office?

■ Compensation and benefits—See Figure 3.8, Checklist of Possible Paralegal Fringe Benefits.

19. After you have thoroughly explored the position during the interview, if you still want the job, ask for it. Be sure that you make a specific request. Some interviewers go out of their way to stress the difficult aspects of the job in order to gauge your reaction. Don't leave the interviewer with the impression that you may be having second thoughts if in fact you still want the job after you have had all your questions answered.

FIGURE 3.8   Checklist of Possible Paralegal Fringe Benefits

Compensation:
_____ Salary Increases (amount? criteria to determine? frequency of review? who reviews?)
_____ Overtime (frequency? method of compensation?)
_____ Bonus (method for determining? frequency?)
_____ Cost-of-Living Adjustment (frequency? method for determining?)
_____ Other Incentive Programs, like Profit Sharing Plan
_____ Pension/Retirement Plan (defined benefit? defined contribution? other?)
_____ Tax Deferred Savings Plan

Insurance:
_____ Basic Medical (full coverage? partial?)
_____ Major Medical (full coverage? partial?)
_____ Dependent Medical Insurance (fully paid? partially paid?)
_____ Supplemental Medical (fully paid? partially paid?)
_____ Dental (full coverage? partial?)
_____ Maternity Leave (full coverage? partial?)
_____ Eye Care/Glasses (full coverage? partial?)
_____ Life Insurance (full coverage? partial?)
_____ Physical Disability (short term? long term? full coverage? partial?)
_____ Sick Days (number? carry-over of unused sick leave allowed?)

Professional Activities:
_____ Time Off for Association Events
_____ Association Dues Paid
_____ Association Dinner Events Paid
_____ Tuition Reimbursement for Paralegal Classes
_____ Tuition Reimbursement for Law School

Other:
_____ Vacation (number of days? carry over of unused vacation allowed?)
_____ Personal Leave Days (number allowed?)
_____ Child Care Assistance
_____ Paid Holidays (number?)
_____ Parking (fully paid? partially paid?)
_____ Leased Car
_____ Mileage Allowance
_____ Club Membership
_____ Fitness Center
_____ Refreshments on the Job
_____ Sports Tickets
_____ Entertainment Allowance
_____ Free Legal Advice and Representation by the Firm on Personal Matters

Comparability:
_____ Paralegal Fringe Benefits Similar to Those of New Attorneys?
_____ Paralegal Fringe Benefits Similar to Those of Secretaries?

FIGURE 3.9   Checklist of Factors that Help Determine the Quality of the Work Environment of a Paralegal

_____ Policy Manual on Paralegal Use in Office (available?)

_____ Evaluation (method? frequency?)

_____ Career Ladder for Paralegals in Office (criteria for advancement?)

_____ Supervision of Paralegal (by attorney? by paralegal manager? by legal administrator?)

_____ Supervision by Paralegal (secretary? assistant to paralegal?)

_____ Work Assignments (who delegates? one attorney? several? paralegal manager?)

_____ Availability of Secretarial Assistance

_____ Paralegal Turnover in Office (low? high?)

_____ Client Contact (frequent? rare?)

_____ Attendance at Trials (frequent? rare?)

_____ Sit at Counsel's Table (frequent? rare?)

_____ Billable Hours: hourly rate?

_____ Billable Hours: quota? (monthly quota? annual quota?)

_____ Time Spent on Non-Billable Matters (frequent? rare? type?)

_____ Office Space (private? shared?)

_____ Use of Computers (frequent? rare?)

_____ Availability of Word Processing Department to Paralegal (frequent? rare?)

_____ Typing (own work? attorney's work?)

_____ How Management Perceives Paralegals (professionals? administrative? support staff? combination?)

_____ Flexible Work Schedule

_____ Travel Required (frequent? rare? type?)

_____ Attendance at Attorney Strategy Meetings (frequent? rare?)

_____ Attendance at Management Meetings (frequent? rare?)

_____ Office Training for Paralegals (kind? frequency?)

_____ In-House Attorney Training Available to Paralegals (frequent? rare?)

_____ CLE _(Continuing Legal Education)_ for Attorneys Available to Paralegals (frequent? rare?)

_____ Business Cards Provided

_____ Name on Door

_____ Name on Letterhead Stationery of Law Office

_____ Has Own Letterhead Stationery

_____ Office Correspondence (does paralegal ever sign under own name?)

_____ Attendance at Attorney Retreats (frequent? rare?)

_____ Attendance at Attorney Social Functions (frequent? rare?)

Follow-Up Letter

After the interview, always send a letter to the person who interviewed you. In a surprising number of cases, the follow-up letter is a significant factor in obtaining the job. In the letter:

■ Thank the person for the interview.

■ Tell the person that you enjoyed the interview and the opportunity to learn about the office.

■ State that you are still very interested in the position.

■ Briefly restate why you are qualified for the position.

■ Clarify any matters that arose during the interview.

■ Submit references or writing samples that may have been asked for during the interview.

Keep a copy of all such letters. In a notebook, maintain accurate records on the dates you sent out resumes, the kinds of resumes you sent, the dates of interviews, the names of people you met, your impressions, the dates when you made follow-up calls, etc. (See page 140.)

If you are turned down for a job, find out why. Call the office to try to obtain more information than is provided in standard rejection statements. Politely ask what could have improved your chances. Finally, use the occasion to ask for any leads to other prospective employers.

■ ASSIGNMENT

Role-play an interview in class. The instructor will decide what kind of job the interview will be for, and will select students to play the role of interviewer and interviewee. The interviewer should ask a variety of questions such as those presented above in the guidelines for handling a job interview. The rest of the class will evaluate the performance of the interviewee. What mistakes did he or she make? How should he or she have dealt with certain questions? Was he or she confident? Overconfident? Did he or she ask the right questions of the interviewer? Were these questions properly timed? What impressions did the interviewee convey of himself or herself? Make a list of dos and don'ts for such interviews.

■ Section B. Job Hunting Notebook

Purchase a large three-ring, loose-leaf notebook for your Job Hunting Notebook. Include in it the outline of sections listed below. Following the outline, create at least one page for each section.

There are a number of purposes for the Notebook:

■ To help you identify your strengths based on past legal or nonlegal employment, training, and other life experience.

■ To help you organize this data for your resumes.

■ To provide you with checklists of contacts that you should start making immediately.

■ To help you prepare for job interviews.

■ To provide a place to store copies of resumes, cover letters, writing samples, follow-up letters, notes on job leads and strategies, personal impressions, etc.

■ To keep a calendar on all aspects of the job search.

The Notebook is your own personal document. No one else will see it unless you choose to share its contents with others.

Outline of Job Hunting Notebook

Part I. Resume & Writing Sample Preparation

1. Prior and Current Nonlegal Employment—Analysis Sheet
2. Prior and Current Legal Employment—Analysis Sheet
3. Prior and Current Volunteer Activity—Analysis Sheet
4. Other Life Experiences—Analysis Sheet
5. Nonlegal Education & Training—Analysis Sheet
6. Legal Education & Training—Analysis Sheet
7. Notes on Resume Writing
8. Draft of General Resume
9. Drafts of Specialized Resumes
10. Writing Samples

Part II. Contacts for Employment

11. Contacts—Attorneys You Already Know or with Whom You Have Indirect Association
12. Contacts—Employed Paralegals
13. Contacts and Tasks—General

Part III. Legwork in the Field

14. Job Interview Checklist
15. Job Interview—Analysis Sheet
16. Record Keeping

. . . .

1. Prior and Current Nonlegal Employment—Analysis Sheet

2. Prior and Current Legal Employment—Analysis Sheet

3. Prior and Current Volunteer Activity—Analysis Sheet

We begin by analyzing your experience in nonlegal jobs (e.g., cashier, truck driver); then in legal jobs (e.g., legal secretary, investigator); and finally in volunteer activity (e.g., church sale coordinator, political campaign assistant). Make a list of these jobs and volunteer activities. Start a separate sheet of paper for each entry on your list, and then do the following:

■ State the name, address, and phone number of the place of employment or location of the volunteer work.

■ State the exact dates you were there.

■ State the names of your supervisors there. (Circle the name of supervisors who had a favorable impression of you. Place a double circle around the name of each supervisor who would probably write a favorable recommendation for you, if asked.)

■ Make a list of every major task you performed there. Number each task, starting with number 1. (As you write this list, leave a three-inch *left-hand margin* on the paper. In front of the number for each task, place as many of the following letters that apply to that task. When an explanation or description is called for, provide it on attached sheets of paper.)

B   The task required you to conform to a *budget*. (Briefly describe the budget, including its size and who prepared it.)

C   There was some *competition* in the office about who is the person most qualified to perform it. (Briefly describe why you were the most qualified.)

E   You were *evaluated* on how well you performed the task. (Briefly describe the evaluation of you.)

EI   To perform the task, you occasionally or always had to *exercise initiative;* you did not just wait for detailed instructions. (Briefly describe the initiative you took.)

ET   You occasionally or frequently had to devote *extra time* to perform the task. (Briefly describe the circumstances.)

J/C   It was not a mechanical task; you had to exercise some *judgment* and/or *creativity* to perform it. (Briefly describe the kind of judgment or creativity you exhibited.)

M   *Math* skills were involved in performing the task. (Briefly describe what kind of math you had to do).

OD   *Others depended* on your performing the task well. (Briefly describe who had to rely on your performance and why.)

OT   You always or regularly performed the task *on time.*

OW   To perform the task, you had to coordinate your work with *other workers;* you did not work alone. (Briefly describe the nature of your interaction with others.)

P   You had some role in *planning* how the task would be performed; you were not simply following someone else's plan. (Briefly describe your planning role.)

PI   You did not start out performing the task; you were formally or informally *promoted into* it. (Briefly describe what you did before being asked to perform this task and the circumstances of the promotion.)

PP   You are *personally proud* of the way you performed the task. (Briefly describe why.)

R   You made *recommendations* on how the task could be more efficiently performed or better integrated into the office. (Briefly describe the recommendations you made and what effect they had.)

RR   You *received recognition* because of how well you performed the task. (Briefly describe what recognition you received and from whom.)

SE   To perform the task, you had to operate *some equipment* such as computers or motor vehicles. (Briefly describe the equipment and the skills needed to operate it.)

SO   To perform the task, you had to *supervise others* or help supervise others. (Briefly describe whom you supervised and what the supervision entailed.)

T   You *trained* others to perform the task. (Briefly describe this training.)

TP   You had to work under *time pressures* when you performed the task; you didn't have forever to perform it. (Briefly describe these pressures.)

W   There was some *writing* involved in performing the task. (Briefly describe what kind of writing you did.)

Include other characteristics of the task that are not covered in this list.

4. Other Life Experiences—Analysis Sheet

Circle *each* of the following experiences that you have had. Do not include experiences that required schooling, since these experiences will be covered elsewhere in the Notebook. Do not include experiences that involved volunteer work unless you have not already included them elsewhere in the Notebook. Attach additional sheets as indicated and where more space is needed.

- Raised a family alone
- Helped raise a family
- Traveled extensively
- Read extensively in a particular field on your own
- Learned to operate a computer on your own
- Learned a language on your own
- Learned a craft on your own, such as weaving or fixing cars
- Learned an art on your own, such as painting or sculpture
- Developed a distinctive hobby requiring considerable skill
- Other life experiences (list each)

Attach a separate sheet of paper for *each* of the life experiences or activities that you listed above. Write the activity at the top of the sheet. Answer the following questions for each activity:

a. How long did you engage in this activity?

b. Have you ever tried to teach this activity to someone else? If so, describe your efforts.

c. Do you think you could teach this activity to others? Explain your answer.

d. Which of the following characteristics do you think are necessary or helpful in being able to perform the activity competently? Do not focus at this point on whether you possess these characteristics. Simply compile a list of what would be helpful or necessary.

Intelligence	Compassion	Patience
Creativity	Responsibility	Dependability
Perseverance	Punctuality	Determination
Drive	Self-confidence	Stamina
Independence	Poise	Self-control
Talent	Efficiency	Grace
Understanding	Skill	Dexterity
Cleverness	Competitiveness	Sophistication
Spirit	Congeniality	Stick-to-itiveness
Conviction	Judgment	Will power
Fortitude	Strength	Zeal
Ambition	Know-how	Experience
Ability to work with others	Imagination	Others? (list)

e. Ask *someone else* (whom you trust and who is familiar with you) to look at the list. Ask this person if he or she would add anything to the list. Then ask him or her to identify which of these characteristics apply to *you* for this activity.

f. Now it's your turn. Which of these characteristics do *you* think apply to you for this activity?

g. If there are any major differences in the answers to (e) and (f) above, how do you explain the discrepancy? Are you too hard on yourself? Do you tend to put yourself down and minimize your strengths?

5. *Nonlegal Education and Training—Analysis Sheet*

On a separate sheet of paper, list every school or training program *not* involving law that you have attended or are now attending (whether or not you completed it), starting with the most recent. Include four-year colleges, two-year colleges, vocational training schools, weekend seminars, work-related training programs, internships, church training programs, hobby training programs, self-improvement training, etc. Include everything since high school.

Devote a separate sheet of paper to each school or training program, writing its name at the top of the sheet and answering the following questions for it. If more than one course was taught, answer these questions for two or three of the most demanding courses.

a. What were the exact or approximate dates of attendance?

b. Did you complete it? What evidence do you have that you completed it? A grade? A certificate? A degree?

c. Were you required to attend? If so, by whom? If not, why did you attend?

d. How did you finance your attendance?

e. What requirements did you meet in order to attend? Was there competition to attend? If so, describe in detail.

f. Describe the subjects taught. What was the curriculum?

g. How were you evaluated?

h. What evidence of these evaluations do you have? Could you obtain copies of them?

i. Describe in detail any writing that you had to do, such as exams or reports. Do you have copies of any of these written items? If not, could you obtain copies? Could any of these items be rewritten now for use as a writing sample?

j. What skills other than writing did you cover, such as organization, research, speaking, reading, manual dexterity, machine operation, interpersonal relations?

k. What evidence do you have or could you obtain that shows you covered these skills and how well you did in them?

l. Did you receive any special award or distinction? If so, describe it and state what evidence you have or could obtain that you received it.

m. Make a list of every favorable comment you can remember that was made about your work. What evidence of these comments do you have or could you obtain?

n. Was the experience meaningful in your life? If so, explain why. How has it affected you today?

o. What, if anything, did you do that called for extra effort or work on your part beyond what everyone else had to do?

p. Have you ever tried to teach someone else what you learned? If so, describe your efforts. If not, could you? Describe what you could teach.

q. List each teacher who knew you individually. Circle the name of each teacher who would probably write you a letter of recommendation if asked.

r. Would any other teacher or administrator be able to write you a letter of recommendation based on the records of the school or program? If so, who?

s. Does the school or program have a reputation for excellence? If so, describe its reputation.

6. Legal Education and Training—Analysis Sheet

On a separate sheet of paper, list every *legal* course or training program that you have ever taken—formal or informal. Include individual classes, seminars, internships, etc., at formal schools, on the job, or through associations. Devote a separate sheet of paper to each course or program, writing its name at the top of the sheet and answering the following questions for it.

a. What were the exact dates of attendance?

b. Did you complete it? What evidence do you have that you completed it? A grade? A certificate?

c. What requirements did you meet in order to attend? Was there competition to attend? If so, describe in detail.

d. What text(s) did you use? Photocopy the table of contents in the text(s) and circle those items that you covered.

e. Attach a copy of the syllabus and circle those items in the syllabus that you covered.

f. Make two lists: a list of the major themes or subject areas that you were required to *know* or understand (content) and a list of the things that you were asked to *do* (skills).

g. Make a detailed list of everything that you were asked to write for the course or program, such as exams, memos, research papers, other reports. For every written work product other than exams, give the specific topic of what you wrote. Describe this topic in at least one sentence.

h. Which of these written work products could you now *rewrite* as a writing sample? Whom could you ask to evaluate what you rewrite to insure that it meets high standards?

i. Describe in detail everything else you were asked to do other than mere reading assignments. Examples: role-play a hearing, visit a court, verbally analyze a problem, interview a client, evaluate a title abstract, search a title, operate a computer, find something in the library, investigate a fact.

j. How were you evaluated? What evidence do you have or could you obtain of these evaluations?

k. Did you receive any special award or distinction? If so, describe it and state what evidence you have or could obtain that you received it.

l. Make a list of favorable comments that were made about your work. What evidence of these comments do you have or could you obtain?

m. What, if anything, did you do that called for extra work or effort on your part beyond what everyone else had to do?

n. Describe the most valuable aspect of what you learned.

o. Have you ever tried to teach anyone else what you learned? If so, describe your efforts. If not, could you? Describe what you could teach.

p. Describe every individual who evaluated you. Could you obtain a letter of recommendation from these individuals?

7. Notes on Resume Writing

It is important that you have an open mind about resumes. There is no correct format. Different people have different views. In the best of all worlds, you will be able to do some background research on the law office where you are applying for work and you will learn what kind of resume (in form and content) that office prefers. When this type of research is not possible, you must do the best you can to predict what kind of a resume will be effective .

On this page in the Notebook, you should collect ideas about resumes from a wide variety of people such as:

Teachers	Program administrators
Working paralegals	Unemployed paralegals
Paralegal supervisors	Legal administrators
Fellow students	Attorneys whom you know
Personnel officers	Authors of books and articles on finding employment
Placement officers	
Legal secretaries	Others

You want to collect divergent viewpoints on questions such as the following:

- What is an ideal resume?
- What are the major mistakes that a resume writer can make?
- What is the best way to phrase a career objective?
- How long should the resume be?
- In what order should the data in the resume be presented?
- How detailed should the resume be?
- What kind of personal data should be included and omitted?
- How do you phrase educational experiences to make them relevant to the job you are seeking?
- How do you phrase employment experiences to make them relevant to the job you are seeking?
- How do you show that nonlegal experiences (school or work) can be relevant to a legal job?
- How do you handle potentially embarrassing facts, e.g., frequent job changes, low course grades?
- What should the cover letter for the resume say?

8. Draft of General Resume

Prepare a general resume and include it here. We are calling it general because it is not directed at any specific job. It should be comprehensive with no page limitation. Use the guidelines, questions, and checklists in this Notebook to help you identify your strengths. The resumes you write for actual job searches will be shorter, specialized, and tailored to the job you are seeking. Before you write specialized resumes, however, you should write a general one that will be your main point of reference in preparing these other resumes. The general resume will probably never be submitted anywhere. Take at least one full day to compile and carefully think about the data needed for the general resume.

9. Drafts of Specialized Resumes

Every time you write a resume that is tailored to a specific job, include a copy here. Also include several practice copies of specialized resumes. While taking a course in corporate law, for example, write a resume in which you pursue an opening at a law office for a corporate paralegal. For each resume that you write (practice or real), solicit the comments of teachers, administrators, fellow students, working paralegals, attorneys, etc. Include these comments in this section of the Notebook.

10. Writing Samples

The importance of collecting a large pool of writing samples cannot be overemphasized. Even if you eventually use only a few of them, the value of preparing them is enormous. The following characteristics should apply to *each* writing sample:

- It is your own work.
- It is clearly and specifically identified. The heading at the top tells the reader what the writing is.
- It is typed (handwritten work should be typed).
- There are no spelling or grammatical errors in it.
- Its appearance is professional.
- Someone whom you respect has evaluated it before you put it in final form.
- You feel that it is a high-quality product.
- It does not violate anyone's right to privacy or confidentiality. (If the sample pertains to real people or events, you have disguised all names or other identifying features.)

There are two main kinds of writing samples: those that are assigned in school or at work and those you generate on your own.

Examples of Required Work That You Could Turn into a Writing Sample

- A memorandum of law
- A legal research memo
- An answer to a problem in a textbook
- An exam answer
- An intake memorandum of law
- A complaint
- An answer to a complaint
- A motion
- A set of interrogatories
- Answers to a set of interrogatories
- An index to discovery documents
- A digest of one or more discovery documents
- Other memos or reports
- Articles of incorporation and bylaws

Any of the above writing samples could be generated on your own if they are not required in your coursework. Ask your teachers or supervisors to help you identify written pieces that you could create. Also consider writing an article for a paralegal newsletter (see Appendix D). The article could cover an aspect of your education or work experience. Or write a review of a recent paralegal book. Even if what you write is not published in a newsletter, it might still become a writing sample if it meets the criteria listed above.

11. Contacts—Attorneys You Already Know or with Whom You Have Indirect Association

Make a list of attorneys as described in Strategy 6 in this chapter, page 100. Not only do you want to know whether any of these attorneys are interested in hiring paralegals, but equally important, you want to know if they can give you any leads to other employers who might be interested in hiring.

12. Contacts—Employed Paralegals

You want to talk with as many employed paralegals as you can in order to obtain leads to possible positions, as well as general guidelines for the job search. Make a list of all the paralegals that you contact and what they tell you. If they have nothing useful to say at the present time, ask them if you could check back with them in several months and if you could leave your name and number with them in the event that they come across anything in the future. See page 97 for ideas on how to locate employed paralegals.

13. Contacts and Tasks—General

Below you will find a general checklist of contacts and tasks that you should consider in your job search. Take notes on the results of these contacts and tasks and include these notes here if they are not included elsewhere in the Notebook. Your notes should include what you did, when, whom you contacted, what was said, what follow-up is still needed, etc.

- Attorneys with whom you already have a direct or indirect association
- Employed paralegals
- Other paralegals searching for work; they may be willing to share leads that were unproductive for them, especially if you do likewise
- Contacts provided by your placement office
- Want ads in general circulation newspapers
- Want ads in legal newspapers
- Want ads and job bank openings listed in paralegal newsletters
- General directories of attorneys, such as *Martindale-Hubbell*
- Special directories of attorneys, such as the *Directory of Corporate Counsel*
- Information from placement offices of local law schools
- Employment agencies specializing primarily in attorney placement
- Employment agencies specializing in paralegal placement

- Staffing agencies specializing in support staff and paralegal placement
- Bar association meetings open to the public
- Legal secretaries who may have leads
- Legal administrators who may have leads
- Local attorneys of record printed in reporter volumes
- Local attorneys who have written articles in bar journals
- Stories in legal newspapers on recent large cases that are in litigation or are about to go into litigation (page 107)
- Local and national politicians who represent your area
- Service companies and consulting firms (page 52)

14. *Job Interview Checklist*

1. _____ Exact location of interview
2. _____ Time of arrival
3. _____ Professional appearance in dress
4. _____ Extra copies of resume
5. _____ Extra copies of writing samples
6. _____ Name of person(s) who will conduct interview
7. _____ Background research on the firm or company so that you know the kind of law it practices, why it is considering hiring paralegals, etc.
8. _____ Role-playing of job interview in advance with a friend
9. _____ Preparation for difficult questions that might be asked, such as why you left your last job so soon after starting it
10. _____ Preparation of questions that you will ask regarding:
    _____ Responsibilities of position
    _____ Skills needed for the position
    _____ Methods of supervision
    _____ Office's prior experience with paralegals
    _____ Career ladder for paralegals
    _____ Relationship between paralegals, secretaries, and other clerical staff
    _____ Client contact
    _____ Opportunities for growth
    _____ Methods of evaluating paralegals
    _____ Continuing education
    _____ Billable hours expected of paralegals
    _____ Availability of systems
    _____ Working conditions (typing, photocopying, office, etc.)
    _____ Travel

_____ Overtime

_____ Equipment use

_____ Compensation and fringe benefits (see Figure 3.8)

11. _____ Follow-up letter

15. Job Interview—Analysis Sheet

Write out the following information *after* each job interview that you have.

1. Date of interview
2. Name, address, and phone number of firm or company where you interviewed
3. Name(s) and phone number(s) of interviewer(s)
4. Kind of position that was open
5. Date you sent the follow-up letter
6. What you need to do next (send list of references, send writing samples, provide missing information that you did not have with you during the interview, etc.)
7. Your impressions of the interview (how you think you did, what surprised you, what you would do differently the next time you have an interview)
8. Notes on why you did not get the job

16. Record Keeping

You need a system to keep track of the steps taken to date. See Figure 3.10, Record Keeping & the Job Search. In addition, keep a calendar in which you record important future dates, such as when you must make follow-up calls, when the local paralegal association meets, etc.

■ Section C. Your Second Job

If you examine want ads for paralegals (p. 101), you will find that most prospective employers want paralegals with experience. The market for such individuals is excellent. But if you are *new* to the field, you are caught in the dilemma of not being able to find a job without experience and not being able to get experience without a job. How do you handle this classic Catch-22 predicament?

■ You work even harder to compile an impressive resume. You make sure that you have collected a substantial writing-sample file. Such writing samples are often the closest equivalent to prior job experience available to you.

■ When you talk to other paralegals, you seek specific advice on how to present yourself as an applicant for the first job.

■ You consider doing some volunteer work as a way to acquire experience for your resume. Legal service offices (page 30) and public interest law firms

FIGURE 3.10 Record Keeping & the Job Search

CALLS MADE TO:	DATE	RESUME SENT TO:	DATE	FOLLOW-UP	DATE	WRITING SAMPLES PROVIDED TO:	DATE	INTERVIEW	DATE	FOLLOW-UP	DATE

FIGURE 3.11   Positions for Experienced Paralegals

- Paralegal supervisor
- Law office administrator (Legal administrator)
- Law firm marketing administrator
- Paralegal consultant
- Freelance/independent paralegal
- Law librarian/assistant
- Paralegal teacher
- Paralegal school administrator
- Placement officer
- Bar association attorney referral coordinator
- Court administrator
- Court clerk
- Sales representative for legal publisher/vendor
- Investigator
- Customs inspector
- Compliance and enforcement inspector
- Occupational safety and health inspector
- Lobbyist
- Legislative assistant
- Real estate management consultant
- Real estate specialist
- Real estate portfolio manager
- Land acquisitions supervisor
- Title examiner
- Independent title abstractor
- Abstractor
- Systems analyst
- Computer analyst
- Computer sales representative
- Bank research associate
- Trust officer (Trust administrator)
- Trust associate
- Assistant loan administrator
- Fiduciary accountant
- Financial analyst/planner
- Investment analyst
- Assistant estate administrator
- Enrolled agent
- Equal employment opportunity specialist
- Employee benefit specialist/consultant
- Pension specialist

Continued

FIGURE 3.11   Positions for Experienced Paralegals—*Continued*

- Pension administrator
- Compensation planner
- Corporate trademark specialist
- Corporate manager
- Securities analyst
- Securities compliance officer
- Insurance adjustor
- Actuarial associate
- Claims examiner
- Claims coordinator
- Director of risk management
- Environmental specialist
- Editor for a legal or business publisher
- Recruiter, legal employment agency
- Personnel director
- Administrative law judge
- Arbitrator
- Mediator
- Internal security inspector
- Evidence technician
- Demonstrative evidence specialist
- Fingerprint technician
- Polygraph examiner
- Probation officer
- Parole officer
- Corrections officer
- Politician
- Etc.

(page 50) often encourage volunteer work. A recent law school graduate struggling to start a practice may be another option.

▦ You may have to reassess what you will accept for your first job. Perhaps you can eventually turn the first job into a more acceptable position. You may simply use it to gain the experience necessary for landing a better second job.

▦ Pray for luck.

Once you have had several years of experience and have demonstrated your competence, you will find many more employment options available to you. You will find it substantially easier to negotiate salary and articulate your skills in a job interview. You can also consider other kinds of employment where your legal training, skills, expertise, and experience are valuable. It is not uncommon for a paralegal to be recruited by former or active clients of a first employer.

Numerous business contacts are made in the course of a job; these contacts could turn into new careers. In Figure 3.11 you will find a list of some of the types of positions that paralegals have taken after they demonstrated their ability and acquired legal experience.

In short, you face a different market once you have acquired a record of experience and accomplishment. You are in greater demand in law firms and businesses. Furthermore, your legal skills are readily transferable to numerous law-related positions.

Key Terms

job bank
National Paralegal
    Reporter
Facts & Findings
informational interview
networking

blind ad
staffing agency
Martindale-Hubbell
chronological resume
functional resume
cover letter

group interview
open-ended question
closed-ended question
hypothetical question
CLE

APPENDIX

How to Start a Freelance Paralegal Business

by Linda Harrington

The best way to get into business is to do it, not talk forever about it. In fact, you may be doing it before you know that you are actually running a business.

The conservative approach to getting into freelance business it to take work on the side while you maintain a salaried position. When your side business interferes with your job, then you must decide whether or not the business is enticing enough to promote. If it is not, give up the business, keep the salaried job, and be thankful to have learned a lesson in an undramatic way about running a business.

If the business is satisfying and if you enjoy it, the time has come to devote more time and energy to it. Therefore, you will be resigning your salaried job to tackle a business.

Perhaps you have impressed your current employer enough so that he, she, or it will be your client after you resign.

Preliminary Considerations in Getting Started

What is your area of expertise? Is it likely to generate some cash for you if you go freelance? One of the areas to avoid is claimants' personal injury work where it's contingent, that is, the attorney will get a fee contingent upon success in court. It's been my experience that attorneys will pay you when they get paid on a case. So if you're working for an attorney who will pay you when that attorney gets paid and that attorney loses the case, then it's likely you won't get paid.

I work in probate. Everyone knows that death and taxes are inevitable. That being the case, I find it a very lucrative and interesting area.

An extremely important aspect of being a freelance paralegal is having a network. A network can be one of two kinds: first, a network of prior employers who respect your skills a lot and will use you when you go freelance; second, the network of your peers that's developed through paralegal associations and contacts. Both are equally important; one does not substitute for the other. I found that my activities in the local association have been extremely rewarding.

They have given me leadership opportunities, the ability to learn current law from the people who work in large law firms, and a chance to meet friends who have the same kind of responsibilities I do. For the most part, my job leads have come from people I worked for before I became a freelancer.

The other part of the network to explore is the school system. The local paralegal programs can assist you a great deal in establishing a freelance business. For one thing you can teach there, and that provides some of the income you need when you're first starting a business. (The income does come slowly in a new business.) Second, if you're teaching, you're meeting people who will one day be your peers—and that's expanding your professional network. Third, many paralegal programs have work-study experiences available for the students. The students are placed in offices where they get on-the-job training. I have lots of them come to my office. That keeps my overhead down. I give the student on-the-job training in all aspects of probate and death taxes, and in return, I have people to staff my office. It benefits the school, my office, and the students as well. So there are resources, lots of resources, available from the local schools.

A high level of expertise is something that I would like to stress. I have seen a lot of people come out of paralegal training programs and not get their dream job. They then decide that they're going to open freelance business operations, knowing not too much about the practical reality of dealing with attorneys, not to mention the practical reality of working as a paralegal. *I would think that you'd need about four or five years' experience in your field before attempting to go freelance.* The first reason, of course, is that you want to have strength in your practice area and be able to handle some of the problems that you will later encounter as a freelance paralegal.

The second reason is that you have to know about attorneys. You have to know about their personalities, you have to be able to manage the problems that they often present. I tell all my students that attorneys now have to pass "arrogance" before they are allowed to take the Bar exam, and you have to learn how to deal with this attitude in as cheerful a manner as you possibly can. Dealing with attorneys is just as important an area of expertise to develop as any other aspect of expertise in a practice field. If you're going to go freelance, you have to handle the situation of hundreds of attorneys calling you up, each one considering himself or herself the most important person in the world. You have to deal with that reality.

The most important things I had to learn were to keep a sense of humor and to remember to be compulsive. Some people say that I'm a workaholic; I prefer to state that I work hard. I work very, very hard. The things that most people think are available in freelance work are independence and free time. The reality is that they don't always exist. If your office does not get the work done, the buck stops with you. You can't blame your staff. The final responsibility rests on your shoulders. If everybody else leaves and the computer breaks down, you must still perform. If you don't get it done, you face the possibility of jeopardizing your entire business operation.

Other Practical Suggestions

Step 1. Have business cards printed. The cards should state your name, area of specialty, and telephone number.

Have an answering service. A business answering service provides a real, live voice to a caller, not a recording. It is reassuring to a potential customer to hear "a live one" on the line. Limit the service to the hours 9–5 to keep the cost of the service down.

Have "call waiting" installed by the phone company. This feature enables one line to handle several calls at once by a mere flick of a button.

Have "call forwarding" installed by the phone company. This feature enables you to have incoming calls automatically forwarded to the telephone number of your choice. If you are waiting for an important call but have a visit to make, you can have your call forwarded to your destination automatically.

Step 2. Systematize your operation immediately. The systems you will need are:

1. Calendar system
2. Timekeeping system
3. Billing system
4. Filing system for both open and closed matters
5. Procedural manual for your area of specialty

A *calendar system* should include: a master calendar that is easily spotted among clutter; a pocket calendar, which you must carry at all times; and some sort of statute-of-limitations reminder system. Many companies offer calendar systems at relatively low cost. Two are: Safeguard Business Systems and Lawfax System.

A *timekeeping system* should include: a master time record repository (separate from the case file), time slips, and decision-making on your part concerning standard charges for services and costs. It is easiest to assign a set charge for a particular service, subject to increases for complications or quirks. For example, typical time charges will be incurred for telephone calls. Assign a minimum charge for each call. Each duty should have a minimum charge assigned to it. In this way, your billing will reflect all applicable charges for the particular service involved in the transaction as well as your research, investigation, and other "write up" expenses. Costs such as photocopies should also reflect the time involved to perform the service. Therefore, standard mark-up for costs is advisable. Naturally, these are matters that are internal to the business. Therefore, establish your standards and then keep your mouth shut.

A *billing system* should include a retainer, which is received when the case work comes in, and a statement for services submitted at an advantageous time and in a personal manner which makes it clear that a bill is an important document to the sender. Set up a system for billing that is realistic. If your clients are most likely to pay on the 30th of the month, send your bills on the 25th. If your clients will not pay the bill until the receipts from the case are received, bill at the end of the work. Billing is as much psychology as anything else. Figure out when the client will want to pay and bill at that time.

A *filing system* for open cases will include: a repository for case documents, an identification system for file labels, a spot for the files to be stored; and a case matter sheet that generally describes the client, the case, and the work to be done, as well as the billing arrangements between you and the client. Casework can be stored in file folders, in binders, in boxes, and a number of other places. Make sure that all cases are stored in the same fashion and that the case files are easily located.

Closed cases should be stored and retained. A closed file system should be a numerical system. For this type of system, you need: file folders, a card file to store the case name and closed file number (retained in alphabetical order by case), and a central register to show the numbers used for previously closed files, so that the number chosen for a closed file will not have been used previously.

A *procedural manual* will contain: standard correspondence sent for the particular areas of law you specialize in, standard (completed) court forms used in your field, instructions to others concerning processing the documents. A procedural manual can also contain information concerning special and standard requirements of area courts, if your work involves preparing and filing court papers. The latter will help you avoid procedural errors and will save time, if it is updated regularly.

Step 3.   Fix your goals, make a budget, and prepare to stick to them.

Fixing a goal involves knowing why you want to run a business. There are many reasons to want to be in business for yourself. Some are: ego gratification—now you are going to get recognition for how great you've always known you are; free time—now you can set your own hours and go to the beach whenever you want; money—now you are going to get a piece of the action and get rich.

Caution: be prepared for reality. None of your original goals will be unchanged if you are still in business one year later. Most of the people you work for will never be impressed by your brilliance—you said you could do the work, you did do the work, so what's the big deal? If you are successful, the last thing you will have is free time. Even in the beginning, your clients will want to see you or talk to you when *they* want to do so, not when you want them to. Most attorneys feel that if you only knew that they wanted to talk to you, you would jump to attention at four in the morning and be grateful for the phone call. All the money you earn will be hard earned. When it comes, some of it goes to your staff, some to your landlord, some to the IRS, and some to you.

To keep your wits about you, you must budget and you must set limits. How much of what you want do you have to receive in order to stick with it? If you want ego gratification, how many clients have to tell you you are great to make the business worthwhile? If you want free time, how much free time do you have to have to make the business worthwhile? If you want money, how much profit must you make to make the business worthwhile? The "how much" is your minimum. Obviously, the sky is the limit.

If you do not get your minimum, are you willing to quit? If not, do not go into business.

You can generally figure out how you are doing by using the following calculation: Monthly gross × 12 = Year's gross. Do not count on new business to get you by. Count on the status quo as far as income is concerned to figure out how much money you will make by December 31 and budget accordingly. If you need income from the business to pay your personal bills, how much do you need monthly? Does this leave any money to run the business? Of the money that is left, how much will be required for telephone, answering service, supplies, and other fixed expenses? Now how much is left? Use the rest for expansion of your business (equipment purchases, rent, personnel, etc.).

Step 4. Develop realistic employee relationships.

If you have done everything you can do to avoid hiring your first employee and that is not enough to keep pace with your work or to allow you the time off you desire, then it is time to hire help.

Accept what you are. You are the owner of a very small business and cannot offer big-firm benefits to your employee. Also, you are a person who wishes to protect your business position, so you do not want to hand your business over to a potential competitor. Last, you are a person who has certain expectations on job performance, productivity, and attendance. You have developed your own ideas about what constitutes a good job in your field.

Do not hire a friend. Being someone's boss does not improve a friendship when you also own the business.

Hire someone trainable. A trainable person is likely to be a recent graduate from a paralegal school. The fact that an applicant has sought education in the field and completed some or all of it is a strong indication that the person has an interest in the field and a desire for practical experience.

Do not hire someone just like you. You are the person who decided to start up the business, who worked (slaved?) to get it going, who knows everything, and who does not want to work so hard now. If you hire someone just like you, you will have two people not wanting to work so hard (you and your employee) *or* one who wants to start a business and has access to all your clients.

Establish a trial employment first. Whether you're hiring a work-study student at minimum wage from a local paralegal program or hiring an experienced person from some other source, set a review period or termination period for the relationship. Tell your employee what that period is and stick to it.

Be realistic about your employee. Because you are a small business, you cannot compete with larger firms that will offer your employee a better deal after the employee has experience and training. Therefore, accept the fact that the employee will probably move on. Tell the employee that you accept this fact and will help the person find a better position after the training has been completed (one to two years, usually). This will motivate the employee to learn as much as possible and to do a good job. This will also avoid you taking the job move personally, which any sensible employee will consider after becoming competent on the job.

Be sure you understand the tax and insurance requirements for your employee. You must have an employer I.D. number, you must withhold taxes and social security and state disability insurance, you must file quarterly reports with the taxing authorities and provide your employee with a W-2 at year end, you must have Worker's Compensation Insurance, and you must contribute as the employer into the unemployment fund and to Social Security. Each employee's salary is hardly your total cost in keeping that employee.

Have your employee work on your premises. This is mandatory during the training period, at bare minimum, so that you can become familiar with the employee's work habits and control work production.

Review the employee's time slips. The time slip review will educate you concerning how long a particular job takes the employee to perform, how many hours during the day the employee devotes to office matters, and how the cases are progressing.

Fire the hopeless. When you know that an employee is not going to work out, do not wait for the realization to come to the employee. It never will. Call the person into your office, look the person in the eyes, and tell the person how wonderful he or she is and how many fantastic qualities he or she has and how unfortunate it is that the job is so miserable for such a terrific individual and that the job just isn't good enough for such a talented person. *Or* call the person in and tell him or her that the employment is not working out and that you wish to ask for his or her resignation, to avoid the stigma to the employee of being fired. *Or* call the person in and tell him or her that you can no longer tolerate his or her presence and that he or she is fired. In whatever way you can do it, be sure that it gets done as soon as you have given up hope for improvement. That's your money that your employee is taking home every two weeks. Nothing rankles so much as feeling that you are paying for a mistake again and again.

Reward the hearty. Go out to lunch for a chat and pay the bill. Send the employee home early or give him or her a surprise day off after a hard week. Leave town yourself and let him or her have the office to himself or herself. Give bonuses when a difficult case is completed. Give a raise of one-day off a week. Compliment the employee for work well done.

Accept criticism. Your employee will probably be compelled to express criticism of the systems in your office or, perhaps, your own style. So what? This is how good ideas get born. Think about the recommendations and, if they are good ones, change your office systems.

Conclusion

The worst way to get into business is to assume that there is no way you can fail (90% of all new businesses do fail, the Small Business Administration says), to buy the most expensive equipment, rent the most costly office space, get the most sophisticated telephone system, and generally count on the birds in the bushes before they land in your hand. Hope that you are able to start building your business slowly so that you will have time to learn about building and problem solving. Give it a good try. If it works out and if you like it, keep going. If it works out and you do not like it, or if it does not work out, then give it up and congratulate yourself on having given it a good try-out.

Federal Job Information

Office of Personnel Management Federal Job Information Centers

Contact the Federal Job Information Center, which is nearest the location where you would like to work, for information on the job opportunities in that area and the forms needed to apply.

ALABAMA
Huntsville:
Building 600, Suite 341
3322 Memorial Pkwy., South
35801-5311
(205) 544-5802

ALASKA
Anchorage:
222 W. 7th Ave., #22,
99513-7572
(907) 271-5821

ARIZONA
Phoenix:
Century Plaza Bldg., Rm. 1415
3225 N. Central Ave., 85012
(602) 640-5800

ARKANSAS
(See Oklahoma Listing)

CALIFORNIA
Los Angeles:
9650 Flair Drive
Ste. 100A
El Monte, 91731
(818) 575 6510

Sacramento:
4695 Watt Ave., North Entrance
95660-5592
(916) 551-1464

San Diego:
Federal Bldg., Room 4-S-9
880 Front St., 92188
(619) 557-6165

San Francisco:
P.O. Box 7405, 94120
(Located at 211 Main St.,
2nd Floor, Room 235)
(415) 974-5627

COLORADO
Denver:
P.O. Box 25167, 80225
(303) 969-7050
(Located at 12345 W. Alameda Pkwy.,
Lakewood)

For Job Information (24 hours a day) in the following States, dial:
Montana: (303) 969-7052
Utah: (303) 969-7053
Wyoming: (303) 969-7054
For forms and local supplements, dial:
(303) 969-7055

CONNECTICUT
Hartford:
Federal Bldg., Room 613
450 Main St., 06103
(203) 240-3096 or 3263

DELAWARE
(See Philadelphia Listing)

DISTRICT OF COLUMBIA
Metro Area:
1900 E St., N.W., Room 1416, 20415
(202) 606-2700

FLORIDA
Orlando:
Commodore Bldg., Suite 150
3444 McCrory Pl., 32803-3701
(407) 648-6148

GEORGIA
Atlanta:
Richard B. Russell Federal Bldg., Room
940A, 75 Spring St., S.W., 30303
(404) 331-4315

HAWAII
Honolulu (and other Hawaiian Islands
and Overseas):
Federal Bldg., Room 5316
300 Ala Moana Blvd., 96850
(808) 541-2791
Overseas Jobs—(808) 541-2784

IDAHO
(See Washington Listing)

ILLINOIS
Chicago:
175 W. Jackson Blvd., Room 530 60604
(312) 353-6192
(For Madison & St. Clair Counties, see
St. Louis, MO listing)

INDIANA
Indianapolis:
Minton-Capehart Federal Bldg.,
575 N. Pennsylvania St., 46204
(317) 226-7161
(For Clark, Dearborn, & Floyd Counties,
see Ohio listing)

IOWA
(816) 426-7757
(For Scott County see Illinois listing; for
Pottawattamie County, See Kansas
listing)

KANSAS
Wichita:
One-Twenty Bldg., Room 101

120 S. Market St., 67202
(316) 269-6794
(For Johnson, Leavenworth, and
Wyandotte Counties, dial
(816) 426-5702)

KENTUCKY
(See Ohio listing: for Henderson County,
see Indiana listing)

LOUISIANA
New Orleans:
1515 Poydras St., Suite 680, 70112
(504) 589-2764

MAINE
(See New Hampshire Listing)

MARYLAND
Baltimore:
Garmatz Federal Building
101 W. Lombard Street, 21201
(301) 962-3822

MASSACHUSETTS
Boston:
Thos. P. O'Neill, Jr. Federal Bldg.
10 Causeway St., 02222-1031
(617) 565-5900

MICHIGAN
Detroit:
477 Michigan Ave., Rm. 565, 48225
(313) 226-6950

MINNESOTA
Twin Cities:
Federal Building, Room 501
Ft. Snelling, Twin Cities, 55111
(612) 725-3430

MISSISSIPPI
(See Alabama Listing)

MISSOURI
Kansas City:
Federal Building, Rm. 134
601 E. 12th Street, 64106
(816) 426-5702
(For Counties west of and including
Mercer, Grundy, Livingston, Carroll,
Saline, Pettis, Benton, Hickory, Dallas,
Webster, Douglas, and Ozark)

St. Louis:
400 Old Post Office Bldg.

815 Olive St., 63101
(314) 539-2285
(For all other Missouri counties not listed under Kansas City above)

MONTANA
(See Colorado Listing)

NEBRASKA
(See Kansas Listing)

NEVADA
(See Sacramento, CA Listing)

NEW HAMPSHIRE
Portsmouth:
Thomas J. McIntyre Federal Bldg.
Room 104
80 Daniel Street, 03801-3879
(603) 431-7115

NEW JERSEY
Newark:
Peter W. Rodino, Jr., Federal Bldg.
970 Broad Street, 07102
(201) 645-3673
In Camden, dial (215) 597-7440

NEW MEXICO
Albuquerque:
Federal Building
421 Gold Avenue, S.W., 87102
(505) 766-5583

NEW YORK
New York City:
Jacob K. Javits Federal Bldg.
26 Federal Plaza, 10278
(212) 264-0440, 0441, or 0442

Syracuse:
James M. Hanley Federal Building
100 S. Clinton Street, 13260
(315) 423-5660

NORTH CAROLINA
Raleigh:
P.O. Box 25069
4505 Falls of the Neuse Rd.
Suite 450, 27611-5069
(919) 856-4361

NORTH DAKOTA
(See Minnesota Listing)

OHIO
Dayton:

Federal Building, Rm. 506
200 W. 2nd Street, 45402
(513) 225-2720
(For Van Wort, Auglaize, Hardin, Marion, Crawford, Richland, Ashland, Wayne, Stark, Carroll, Columbiana counties and all counties north of these see Michigan listing)

OKLAHOMA
Oklahoma City:
(Mail or phone only)
200 N.W. Fifth St., 2nd Floor, 73102
(405) 231-4948
TDD-(405) 231-4614
For Forms, dial (405) 231-5208

OREGON
Portland:
Federal Bldg., Room 376
1220 S.W. Third Ave., 97204
(503) 326-3141

PENNSYLVANIA
Harrisburg:
Federal Bldg., Room 168
P.O. Box 761, 17108
(717) 782-4494

Philadelphia:
Wm. J. Green, Jr., Federal Bldg.
600 Arch Street, 19106
(215) 597-7440

Pittsburgh:
Federal Building
1000 Liberty Ave., Rm. 119, 15222
(412) 644-2755

PUERTO RICO
San Juan:
Federico Degetau Federal Building
Carlos E. Chardon Street
Hato Rey, P. R. 00918
(809) 766-5242

RHODE ISLAND
Providence:
Pastore Federal Bldg.
Room 310, Kennedy Plaza, 02903
(401) 528-5251

SOUTH CAROLINA
(See Raleigh, NC Listing)

SOUTH DAKOTA
(See Minnesota Listing)

TENNESSEE
Memphis:
200 Jefferson Avenue
Suite 1312, 38103-2335
(901) 521-3958

TEXAS
Dallas:
(Mail or phone only)
1100 Commerce St., Rm. 6B12, 75242
(214) 767-8035

San Antonio:
8610 Broadway, Rm. 305, 78217
(512) 229-6611 or 6600

UTAH
(See Colorado Listing)

VERMONT
(See New Hampshire Listing)

VIRGINIA
Norfolk:
Federal Building, Room 500
200 Granby St., 23510-1886
(804) 441-3355

WASHINGTON
Seattle:
Federal Building
915 Second Ave., 98174
(206) 442-4365

WEST VIRGINIA
Phone only:
(513) 225-2866

WISCONSIN
For Dane, Grant, Green, Iowa, Lafayette,
Rock, Jefferson, Walworth, Milwaukee,
Waukesha, Racine, and Kenosha counties
call
(312) 353-6189

(For all other Wisconsin counties not
listed above see Minnesota listing)

WYOMING
(See Colorado Listing)

Proposed Legislation to Increase Paralegal Employment in the Government

Below you will find two bills that are designed to increase paralegal employment and use in the government. The first was introduced in the House of Representatives of Congress, and the second in the Assembly of the California legislature.

Neither bill was enacted into law. They are of interest, however, as an indication of the growing recognition of the value of paralegals.

99th CONGRESS
2d Session

H. R. 5107

To increase Government economy and efficiency and to reduce the deficit by implementing certain recommendations of the President's Private Sector Survey on Cost Control regarding the increased use of paralegals by the Department of Justice, and for other purposes.

IN THE HOUSE OF REPRESENTATIVES

June 26, 1986

Mr. Carr (for himself, Mr. Brown of Colorado, Mr. Gunderson, Mr. Crane, Mr. Stenholm, Mr. Miller of Washington, Mr. Armey, Mr. Roth, Mr. Dornan of California, Mr. Pease, Mr. Packard, Mr. Roemer, Mr. Fawell, Mr. Gekas, Mr. Coleman of Texas, Mr. Boulter, Mr. Bartlett, Mr. Barnard, Mr. DioGuardi, Mr. Strang, and Mr. Neal) introduced the following bill; which was referred to the Committee on the Judiciary.

A BILL

To increase Government economy and efficiency and to reduce the deficit by implementing certain recommendations of the President's Private Sector Survey on Cost Control regarding the increased use of paralegals by the Department of Justice, and for other purposes.

1   *Be it enacted by the Senate and House of Representatives of the*
2   *United States of America in Congress assembled, That this Act may be*
3   *cited as the "Paralegal Coordination and Activities Act of 1986."*
4   PURPOSE
5   Sec. 2. In order to increase the productivity and cost-efficiency in the
6   Department of Justice, this Act—
7   (1) establishes an Office of Paralegal Coordination and Activi-
8   ties to coordinate Justice's utilization of paralegals in the areas of
9   legal research, litigation, legal support, and other legal activities;
10   (2) directs such office to study the potential for greater use of
11   paralegals in Justice; and
12   (3) requires the Attorney General to report to Congress and the
13   President the findings of the study to include recommendations to
14   increase the efficient utilization of paralegals within the Department
15   of Justice.
16   USE OF PARALEGALS
17   Sec. 3. (a) Chapter 31 of title 28, United States Code, is amended by
18   adding at the end thereof the following new section:
19   **"§ 530A. Use of paralegals**
20   "(a) According to such rules and regulations as may be prescribed by
21   the Attorney General of the United States, there shall be established within
22   the Department of Justice an Office of Paralegal Coordination and Activi-
23   ities. The principal purposes of such Office shall be—
24   "(1) to coordinate efforts to increase utilization of paralegals in
25   the areas of legal research, litigation support, and other legal activi-
26   ties within the Department not requiring the skill of an attorney, and
27   "(2) to coordinate paralegal training programs within the
28   Department.
29   "(b) The Office established in subsection (a) shall study the possibility
30   of increasing the use of paralegals within each legal division or office in
31   the Department. Within one year after the date of the enactment of this
32   section, the Attorney General of the United States shall report to the Con-
33   gress and to the President of the United States on the findings of such
34   study. The report shall include the following information for each legal
35   division or legal office within the Department—
36   "(1) a summary of the division's or office's current utilization of
37   paralegal services and the current job description for paralegal
38   positions;
39   "(2) a description of the nonlitigative functions and responsibil-
40   ities currently performed within each division or office by attorneys
41   which could be performed successfully by trained paralegals, the ex-
42   tent of additional training and attorney supervision that may be re-
43   quired if paralegals are to assume such new duties, and correspond-
44   ing job descriptions;

45 "(3) as dictated by the individual needs of each division or of-
46 fice, an estimate of the optimal ratio of paralegals to attorneys in
47 terms of productivity and economy, including the potential cost sav-
48 ings which could be achieved from adoption of these ratios;
49 "(4) an estimate of the extent to which the optimal ratios deter-
50 mined in paragraph (3) could be achieved through administrative
51 action by the Department without compromising the quality and
52 quantity of legal service provided by the Department's legal staff,
53 and if such administrative action would be insufficient to achieve
54 these ratios, the extent to which the Department must raise its
55 personnel-ceilings by making application to the Office of Manage-
56 ment and Budget;
57 "(5) an evaluation of the benefits and problems associated with
58 the current methods used to fill paralegal positions within the De-
59 partment and any recommendations the Attorney General believes
60 would facilitate the hiring of qualified personnel in a timely manner;
61 and
62 "(6) any additional recommendations which the Attorney Gen-
63 eral believes would be useful in increasing efficient utilization of
64 paralegals within the Department.".
65 (b) The table of sections for such chapter is amended by adding at the
66 end thereof the following new item:
67 "530A. Use of paralegals.".
68   EFFECTIVE DATE
69 Sec. 4. This Act and the amendments made by this Act shall become
70 effective on the date of enactment.

• • • • • • • • • • • • • •

ASSEMBLY BILL (CALIFORNIA)   No. 2729

Introduced by Assembly Member Areias

January 21, 1986

An act to add Section 18715 to the Government Code, relating to public employment.

LEGISLATIVE COUNSEL'S DIGEST

AB 2729, as introduced, Areias. Public employees.

Existing law does not contain provisions governing the ratio of attorneys to paralegals to be employed by the state.

This bill would require each state agency and department that employs attorneys to begin to utilize a combination of hiring practices and attrition which will result in a ratio of one paralegal, or legal analyst, as defined, to every 5 attorneys employed by the state by January 1, 1990.

This bill would require the Office of the Legislative Analyst to report by July 1, 1990, on whether agencies and departments are complying with the requirements of the bill.

Vote: majority. Appropriation: no. Fiscal committee: yes. State-mandated local program: no.

The people of the State of California do enact as follows:

1   SECTION 1. The Legislature finds and declares that attorneys are
2   currently being used to perform a wide variety of tasks.
3   While recognizing that the complexity of modern life often calls for
4   legal interpretation and the assistance of competent legal specialists, the
5   Legislature declares that the use of attorneys should be restricted to those
6   situations in which their services are essential.
7   It is the intent of the Legislature that the state employ only that num-
8   ber of attorneys necessary to adequately serve the needs of the state.
9   It is also the intent of the Legislature that the state employ paralegals
10   to perform all tasks for which their legal expertise is sufficient in order to
11   free attorneys to do the work for which they have been trained.
12   It is the intent of the Legislature to improve the efficiency of state
13   government and produce cost savings by the state's employment of legal
14   professionals whose training and salaries are commensurate with the
15   tasks they perform.
16   SEC. 2. Section 18715 is added to the Government Code, to read:
17   18715. (a) All state agencies and departments which employ attor-
18   neys shall immediately begin to utilize a combination of hiring practices
19   and attrition that will result in a ratio of one paralegal, or legal analyst, as
20   defined in Personnel Board Class Specifications Schematic Code LE 18
21   and Class Code 5237 to every five attorneys employed by the state by
22   January 1, 1990.
23   (b) On or before July 1, 1990, the Office of the Legislative Analyst
24   shall review all state agencies and departments which employ attorneys to
25   determine whether they have complied with this section and shall report
26   the findings to the Legislature.
27
28

APPENDIX

Paralegal Associations

PARALEGAL ASSOCIATIONS (NATIONAL)

(Membership statistics, where known, are presented in brackets.)

National Association of Legal Assistants
[15,000]
1601 S. Main St., Suite 300
Tulsa, OK 74119
918-587-6828

National Federation of Paralegal
Associations [17,500]
P.O. Box 33108
Kansas City, MO 64114
816-941-4000

(NALA and NFPA have numerous affili-
ated local paralegal associations. NALA

affiliates are indicated by one asterisk (*)
below; NFPA affiliates are indicated by
two asterisks below (**). The addresses of
these local associations change frequently.
If the address given below turns out to be
incorrect, contact the national office of
NALA or NFPA for a more current address. Local associations without an asterisk are unaffiliated at the time of
publication.)

PARALEGAL ASSOCIATIONS (STATE)

ALABAMA

Alabama Association of Legal Assistants
(*) [215]
P.O. Box 55921
Birmingham, AL 35255

Huntsville Association of Paralegals
P.O. Box 244
Huntsville, AL 35804-0244

Mobile Association of Legal Assistants
[75]
P.O. Box 1988
Mobile, AL 36633

ALASKA

Alaska Association of Legal Assistants
(**) [130]
P.O. Box 101956
Anchorage, AK 99510-1956

Fairbanks Association of Legal Assistants
(*)
P.O. Box 73503
Fairbanks, AK 99707

Juneau Legal Assistants Association (**)
[20]
P.O. Box 22336
Juneau, AK 99802

ARIZONA

Arizona Association of Professional
  Paralegals (**) [50]
P.O. Box 25111
Phoenix, AZ 85002

Arizona Paralegal Association (*)
P.O. Box 392
Phoenix, AZ 85001
602-258-0121

Legal Assistants of Metropolitan Phoenix
  (*)
P.O. Box 13005
Phoenix, AZ 85002

Southeast Valley Association of Legal
  Assistants (*)
% Sandy Slater
1707 N. Temple
Mesa, AZ 85203

Tucson Association of Legal Assistants
  (*)
P.O. Box 257
Tucson, AZ 85702-0257

ARKANSAS

Arkansas Association of Legal Assistants
  (*)
P.O. Box 2162
Little Rock, AR 72203-2162

CALIFORNIA

California Alliance of Paralegal
  Associations [4000]
P.O. Box 2234
San Francisco, CA 94126
415-576-3000

California Association of Freelance
  Paralegals [94]
P.O. Box 3267
Berkeley, CA 94703-0267
213-251-3826

Central Coast Legal Assistant Association
  (**) [70]
P.O. Box 93
San Luis Obispo, CA 93406

Central Valley Paralegal Association
P.O. Box 4086
Modesto, CA 95352

East Bay Association of Paralegals [200]
P.O. Box 29082
Oakland, CA 94604

Inland Counties Paralegal Association
P.O. Box 292
Riverside, CA 92502-0292

Kern County Paralegal Association [63]
P.O. Box 2673
Bakersfield, CA 93303

Legal Assistants Association of Santa
  Barbara (*)
P.O. Box 2695
Santa Barbara, CA 93120
805-965-7319

Los Angeles Paralegal Association (**)
  [1150]
P.O. Box 241928
Los Angeles, CA 90024
213-251-3755

Marin Association of Legal Assistants
P.O. Box 13051
San Rafael, CA 94913-3051
415-456-6020

Orange County Paralegal Association
  (**) [490]
P.O. Box 8512
Newport Beach, CA 92658-8512
714-744-7747

Paralegal Association of Santa Clara
  County (*)
P.O. Box 26736
San Jose, CA 95159

Redwood Empire Association of Legal
  Assistants
1275 4th St. Box 226
Santa Rosa, CA 95404

Sacramento Association of Legal
  Assistants (**) [271]
P.O. Box 453
Sacramento, CA 95812-0453

San Diego Association of Legal Assistants
  (**) [450]
P.O. Box 87449
San Diego, CA 92138-7449
619-491-1994

San Francisco Association of Legal
  Assistants (**) [975]

P.O. Box 26668
San Francisco, CA 94126-6668
415-777-2390

San Joaquin Association of Legal
   Assistants
P.O. Box 1306
Fresno, CA 93715

Sequoia Paralegal Association
P.O. Box 3884
Visalia, CA 93278-3884

Ventura County Association of Legal
   Assistants (*)
P.O. Box 24229
Ventura, CA 93002

COLORADO

Association of Legal Assistants of
   Colorado (*) [106]
% Alma Rodrigues
4150 Novia Dr.
Colorado Springs, CO 80911

Rocky Mountain Legal Assistants
   Association (**) [440]
P.O. Box 304
Denver, CO 80201
303-369-1606

CONNECTICUT

Central Connecticut Association of Legal
   Assistants (**) [290]
P.O. Box 230594
Hartford, CT 06123-0594

Connecticut Association of Paralegals,
   Fairfield County (**) [135]
P.O. Box 134
Bridgeport, CT 06601

Connecticut Association of Paralegals,
   New Haven (**) [100]
P.O. Box 862
New Haven, CT 06504-0862

Legal Assistants of Southeastern
   Connecticut (**) [55]
P.O. Box 409
New London, CT 06320

DELAWARE

Delaware Paralegal Association (**)
   [295]
P.O. Box 1362
Wilmington, DE 19899

DISTRICT OF COLUMBIA

National Capital Area Paralegal
   Association (**) [620]
1155 Connecticut Ave. N.W.
Wash. D.C. 20036-4306
202-659-0243

FLORIDA

Broward County Paralegal Association
% Leigh Williams
Ruden, Barnett, McClosky
P.O. Box 1900
Ft. Lauderdale, FL 33302

Dade Association of Legal Assistants (*)
% Maxine Stone
14027 S.W. 84th St.
Miami, FL 33183

Florida Legal Assistants (*)
% Nancy Martin
P.O. Box 503
Bradenton, FL 34206

Jacksonville Legal Assistants (*)
P.O. Box 52264
Jacksonville, FL 32201

Orlando Legal Assistants (*)
% Roxane MacGillivray
Akerman, Senterfitt & Eidson
P.O. Box 231
Orlando, FL 32802

Pensacola Legal Assistants (*)
% Deborah Johnson
Levin, Middlebrooks & Mabie
226 S. Palafox St.
Pensacola, FL 32581

Volusia Association of Legal Assistants
   (*)
P.O. Box 15075
Daytona Beach, FL 32115-5075

GEORGIA

Georgia Association of Legal Assistants
 (**) [820]
P.O. Box 1802
Atlanta, GA 30301

Southeastern Association of Legal
 Assistants of Georgia (*)
% Debra Sutlive
2215 Bacon Park Drive
Savannah, GA 31406

South Georgia Association of Legal
 Assistants (*)
% Martha Tanner
L. Andrew Smith, P.C.
P.O. Box 1026
Valdosta, GA 31603-1026

HAWAII

Hawaii Association of Legal Assistants
 (**) [150]
P.O. Box 674
Honolulu, HI 96809

IDAHO

Idaho Association of Legal Assistants (*)
 [54]
P.O. Box 1254
Boise, ID 83701

ILLINOIS

Central Illinois Paralegal Association (*)
% Debra Monke
GTE North Inc.
1312 E. Empire St.
Bloomington, IL 61701

Illinois Paralegal Association (**) [1059]
P.O. Box 857
Chicago, IL 60690
312-939-2553

Independent Contractors Association of
 Illinois
6400 Woodward Ave.
Downers Grove, IL 60516

Peoria Paralegal Association
% Sharon Moke
1308 Autumn Lane
Peoria, IL 60604

INDIANA

Indiana Legal Assistants (*)
% Dorothy French
14669 Old State Rd.
Evansville, IN 47711

Indiana Paralegal Association (**) [300]
P.O. Box 44518, Federal Station
Indianapolis, IN 46204

Michiana Paralegal Association (**) [40]
P.O. Box 11458
South Bend, IN 46634

IOWA

Iowa Association of Legal Assistants
 [400]
P.O. Box 335
Des Moines, IA 50302-0337

Paralegals of Iowa, Ltd.
P.O. Box 1943
Cedar Rapids, IA 52406

KANSAS

Kansas Association of Legal Assistants (*)
 [138]
% Jimmie Sue Marsh
Foulston & Siefkin
700 Fourth Financial Center
Wichita, KS 67202

Kansas City Association of Legal
 Assistants (**)
P.O. Box 13223
Kansas City, MO 64199
913-381-4458

Kansas Legal Assistants Society (**)
 [190]
P.O. Box 1657
Topeka, KS 66601

KENTUCKY

Kentucky Paralegal Association [232]
P.O. Box 2675
Louisville, KY 40201-2657

Lexington Paralegal Association (**) [80]
P.O. Box 574
Lexington, KY 40586

Louisville Association of Paralegals (**)
[182]
P.O. Box 962
Louisville, KY 40201

LOUISIANA

Baton Rouge Paralegal Association
P.O. Box 306
Baton Rouge, LA 70821

Lafayette Paralegal Association
P.O. Box 2775
Lafayette, LA 70502

Louisiana State Paralegal Association
[200]
P.O. Box 56
Baton Rouge, LA 70821-0056

New Orleans Paralegal Association (**)
[190]
P.O. Box 30604
New Orleans, LA 70190

Northwest Louisiana Paralegal
Association (*)
P.O. Box 1913
Shreveport, LA 71166-1913

Southwest Louisiana Association of
Paralegals
P.O. Box 1143
Lake Charles, LA 70602-1143

MAINE

Maine Association of Paralegals (*)
P.O. Box 7554
Portland, ME 04112

MARYLAND

Baltimore Association of Legal
Assistants (**) [140]
P.O. Box 13244
Baltimore, MD 21203
301-576-BALA

MASSACHUSETTS

Berkshire Association for Paralegals and
Legal Secretaries
℅ Nancy Schaffer
Stein, Donahue & Zuckerman

54 Wendell Ave.
Pittsfield, MA 01201

Central Massachusetts Paralegal
Association (**) [80]
P.O. Box 444
Worcester, MA 01614

Massachusetts Paralegal Association (**)
[440]
P.O. Box 423
Boston, MA 02102
617-642-8338

Western Massachusetts Paralegal
Association (**) [50]
P.O. Box 30005
Springfield, MA 01102-0005

MICHIGAN

Legal Assistants Association of Michigan
(*)
℅ Cora Webb
Woll, Crowley, Berman
315 S. Woodward
Royal Oak, MI 48067

Legal Assistant Section [400]
State Bar of Michigan
440 E. Congress, 4th Fl.
Detroit, MI 48226

Legal Assistants Section
State Bar of Michigan
306 Townsend St.
Lansing, MI 48933-2083
517-372-9030

MINNESOTA

Minnesota Association of Legal
Assistants (**) [972]
P.O. Box 15165
Minneapolis, MN 55415

Minnesota Paralegal Association (*)
℅ Tracy Blanshan
Kennedy Law Office
724 SW First Ave.
Rochester, MN 55902

MISSISSIPPI

Gulf Coast Paralegal Association
942 Beach Drive
Gulfport, MS 39507

Mississippi Association of Legal
Assistants (*)
P.O. Box 996
600 Heritage Bldg.
Jackson, MS 39205

Paralegal Association of Mississippi
P.O. Box 22887
Jackson, MS 39205

MISSOURI

Gateway Paralegal Association
P.O. Box 50233
St. Louis, MO 63105

Kansas City Association of Legal
Assistants (**) [470]
P.O. Box 13223
Kansas City, MO 64199
913-381-4458

Southwest Missouri Paralegal Association
[80]
2148 South Oak Grove
Springfield, MO 65804-2708

St. Louis Association of Legal Assistants
(*) [434]
P.O. Box 9690
St. Louis, MO 63122

MONTANA

Big Sky Paralegal Association
P.O. Box 2753
Great Falls, MT 59403

Montana Paralegal Association
P.O. Box 693
Billings, MT 59101

NEBRASKA

Nebraska Association of Legal Assistants
(*)
P.O. Box 24943
Omaha, NE 68124

NEVADA

Clark County Organization of Legal
Assistants (*)
% Angel A. Price
3800 S. Nellis #235
Las Vegas, NV 89121

Sierra Nevada Association of Paralegals
(*)
P.O. Box 40638
Reno, NV 89504

NEW HAMPSHIRE

Paralegal Association of New Hampshire
(*)
% Frances Dupre
Wiggin & Nourie
P.O. Box 808
Manchester, NH 03105

NEW JERSEY

Central Jersey Paralegal Association
P.O. Box 1115
Freehold, NJ 07728

Legal Assistants Association of New
Jersey (*) [260]
P.O. Box 142
Caldwell, NJ 07006

South Jersey Paralegal Association (**)
[160]
P.O. Box 355
Haddonfield, NJ 08033

NEW MEXICO

Legal Assistants of New Mexico (**)
[200]
P.O. Box 1113
Albuquerque, NM 87103-1113
505-260-7104

NEW YORK

Adirondack Paralegal Association
% Maureen Provost
Bartlett, Pontiff, Stewart
One Washington Street
Box 2168
Glen Falls, NY 12801

Legal Professionals of Dutchess County
51 Maloney Rd.
Wappingers Falls, NY 12590

Long Island Paralegal Association (**)
[130]
P.O. Box 31
Deer Park, NY 11729

Manhattan Paralegal Association [515]
200 Park Ave., Suite 303 East
New York, NY 10166
212-986-2304

Paralegal Association of Rochester (**)
   [170]
P.O. Box 40567
Rochester, NY 14604

Southern Tier Association of Paralegals
   (**) [45]
P.O. Box 2555
Binghamton, NY 13902

Western New York Paralegal Association
   (**) [275]
P.O. Box 207
Buffalo, NY 14202
716-862-6132

West/Roc Paralegal Association (**)
   [130]
Box 101
95 Mamaroneck Ave.
White Plains, NY 10601

NORTH CAROLINA

Cumberland County Paralegal
   Association
P.O. Box 1358
Fayetteville, NC 28302

Metrolina Paralegal Association
P.O. Box 36260
Charlotte, NC 28236

North Carolina Paralegal Association (*)
% T. William Tewes
Fuller & Corbett
P.O. Box 1121
Goldsboro, NC 27533-1121

Professional Legal Assistants
P.O. Box 31951
Raleigh, NC 27622
919-821-7762

Raleigh Wake Paralegal Association
P.O. Box 1427
Raleigh, NC 27602

Triad Paralegal Association
Drawer U
Greensboro, NC 27402

NORTH DAKOTA

Red River Valley Legal Assistants (*)
P.O. Box 1954
Fargo, ND 58106

Western Dakota Association of Legal
   Assistants (*)
P.O. Box 7304
Bismarck, ND 58502

OHIO

Cincinnati Paralegal Association (**)
   [380]
P.O. Box 1515
Cincinnati, OH 45201
513-244-1266

Cleveland Association of Paralegals (**)
   [480]
P.O. Box 14247
Cleveland, OH 44114

Greater Dayton Paralegal Association
   (**) [160]
P.O. Box 515, Mid City Station
Dayton, OH 45402

Legal Assistants of Central Ohio (**)
   [270]
P.O. Box 15182
Columbus, OH 43215-0812
614-224-9700

Northeastern Ohio Paralegal Association
P.O. Box 9236
Akron, OH 44305

Toledo Association of Legal Assistants (*)
   [176]
P.O. Box 1322
Toledo, OH 43603

OKLAHOMA

Oklahoma Paralegal Association (*)
P.O. Box 18476
Oklahoma City, OK 73154

Tulsa Association of Legal Assistants (*)
P.O. Box 1484
Tulsa, OK 74101

OREGON

Oregon Legal Assistants Association (**)
   [340]

P.O. Box 8523
Portland, OR 97207

Pacific Northwest Legal Assistants (*)
P.O. Box 1835
Eugene, OR 97440

PENNSYLVANIA

Berks County Paralegal Association
544 Court St.
Reading, PA 19601
215-375-4591

Central Pennsylvania Paralegal
Association (**) [70]
P.O. Box 11814
Harrisburg, PA 17108

Keystone Legal Assistant Association (*)
% Catrine Nuss
3021 Guineveer Drive, Apt. B4
Harrisburg, PA 17110

Lancaster Area Paralegal Association
% Rosemary Merwin
Gibble, Kraybill & Hess
41 East Orange St.
Lancaster, PA 17602

Paralegal Association of Northwestern
Pennsylvania (**) [40]
P.O. Box 1504
Erie, PA 16507

Philadelphia Association of Paralegals
(**) [775]
1411 Walnut St., Suite 200
Philadelphia, PA 19102
215-564-0525

Pittsburgh Paralegal Association (**)
[400]
P.O. Box 2845
Pittsburgh, PA 15230

Wilkes-Barre Area Group
% Tom Albrechta
6 East Green St.
West Hazelton, PA 18201

RHODE ISLAND

Rhode Island Paralegal Association (**)
[200]
P.O. Box 1003
Providence, RI 02901

SOUTH CAROLINA

Charleston Association of Legal
Assistants
P.O. Box 1511
Charleston, SC 29402

Columbia Association of Legal Assistants
(**)
P.O. Box 11634
Columbia, SC 29211-1634

Greenville Association of Legal Assistants
(*)
P.O. Box 10491 F.S.
Greenville, SC 29603

Paralegal Association of the Pee Dee [31]
P.O. Box 5592
Florence, SC 29502-5592

SOUTH DAKOTA

South Dakota Legal Assistants
Association (*) [61]
% Louise Peterson
May, Johnson, Doyle
P.O. Box 1443
Sioux Falls, SD 57101-1443

TENNESSEE

Memphis Paralegal Association (**)
[105]
P.O. Box 3646
Memphis, TN 38173-0646

Middle Tennessee Paralegal Association
(**) [145]
P.O. Box 198006
Nashville, TN 37219

Southeast Tennessee Paralegal
Association
% Calecta Veagles
P.O. Box 1252
Chattanooga, TN 37401

Tennessee Paralegal Association (*)
P.O. Box 11172
Chattanooga, TN 37401

TEXAS

Alamo Area Professional Legal Assistants
[245]

P.O. Box 524
San Antonio, TX 78292

Capital Area Paralegal Association (*)
[252]
% Chris Hemingson
Pope, Hopper, Roberts & Warren
111 Congress, Suite 1700
Austin, TX 78701

Dallas Association of Legal Assistants
(**) [799]
P.O. Box 117885
Carrollton, TX 75011-7885

El Paso Association of Legal Assistants
(*) [106]
P.O. Box 121
El Paso, TX 79941-0121

Fort Worth Paralegal Association [226]
P.O. Box 17021
Fort Worth, TX 76102

Houston Legal Assistants Association
P.O. Box 52266
Houston, TX 77052

Legal Assistant Division [2046]
State Bar of Texas
P.O. Box 12487
Austin, TX 78711
512-463-1383

Legal Assistants Association/Permian
Basin (*)
P.O. Box 10683
Midland, TX 79702

Legal Assistants Professional Association
(Brazos Valley)
P.O. Box 925
Madisonville, TX 79702

Northeast Texas Association of Legal
Assistants (*) [29]
P.O. Box 2284
Longview, TX 75606

Nueces County Association of Legal
Assistants (*)
% Joyce Hoffman
Edwards & Terry
P.O. Box 480
Corpus Christi, TX 78403

Southeast Texas Association of Legal
Assistants (*) [130]
% Janie Boswell

8335 Homer
Beaumont, TX 77708

Texarkana Association of Legal
Assistants (*) [40]
P.O. Box 6671
Texarkana, TX 75505

Texas Panhandle Association of Legal
Assistants (*) [63]
% Lisa Clemens
Morgan, Culton
P.O. Box 189
Amarillo, TX 79105

Tyler Area Association of Legal
Assistants [94]
P.O. Box 1178
Tyler, TX 75711-1178

West Texas Association of Legal
Assistants (*) [44]
P.O. Box 1499
Lubbock, TX 79408

UTAH

Legal Assistants Association of Utah (*)
P.O. Box 112001
Salt Lake City, UT 84147-2001
801-531-0331

VERMONT

Vermont Paralegal Association [80]
% Trudy Seeley
Langrock, Sperry & Wool
P.O. Drawer 351
Middlebury, VT 05753

VIRGINIA

American Academy of Legal Assistants
1022 Paul Avenue N.E.
Norton, VA 24273

Peninsula Legal Assistants (*)
% Diane Morrison
Jones, Blechman, Woltz & Kelly
P.O. Box 12888
Newport News, VA 23612

Richmond Association of Legal Assistants
(*) [318]
% Vicki Roberts

McGuire, Woods, Battle & Boothe
One James Center
Richmond, VA 23219

Roanoke Valley Paralegal Association
(**) [70]
P.O. Box 1505
Roanoke, VA 24001
703-224-8000

Tidewater Association of Legal Assistants
(*)
% Claire Isley
Wilcox & Savage
1800 Sovran Center
Norfolk, VA 23510

VIRGIN ISLANDS

Virgin Islands Paralegals (*)
% Eloise Mack
P.O. Box 6276
St. Thomas, VI 00804

WASHINGTON

Washington Legal Assistants Association
(**) [453]
2033 6th Ave., Suite 804
Seattle, WA 98121
206-441-6020

WEST VIRGINIA

Legal Assistants of West Virginia (*)
% Mary Hanson
Hunt & Wilson
P.O. Box 2506
Charleston, WV 25329-2506

WISCONSIN

Paralegal Association of Wisconsin (**)
[380]
P.O. Box 92882
Milwaukee, WI 53202
414-272-7168

WYOMING

Legal Assistants of Wyoming (*)
% Nancy Hole
Brown & Drew
123 West First St.
Casper, WY 82601

Glossary

AAfPE American Association for Paralegal Education.

ABA American Bar Association.

Adjudication The process by which a court resolves a legal dispute through litigation. The verb is *adjudicate*.

Administrative Agency A unit of government whose primary mission is to carry out or administer the statutes of the legislature and the executive orders of the chief of the executive branch.

Administrative Code A collection of administrative regulations organized by subject matter.

Administrative Hearing A proceeding at an administrative agency presided over by a hearing officer (e.g., an Administrative Law Judge) to resolve a controversy.

Administrative Law Judge A hearing officer who presides over a hearing at an administrative agency.

Administrative Procedure Act The statute that governs aspects of procedure before administrative agencies.

Administrative Regulation A law of an administrative agency designed to explain or carry out the statutes and executive orders that govern the agency. Also called a *rule*.

Admiralty Law An area of the law that covers accidents and injuries on navigable waters. Also called *maritime law*.

ADR Alternative dispute resolution.

Advance Sheet A pamphlet that comes out before (in advance of) a later volume.

Adversarial System Justice and truth have a greater chance of emerging when parties to a controversy appear before a neutral judge and jury to argue their conflicting positions.

Advocacy An attempt to influence actions of others.

Affiant *See* Affidavit.

Affidavit A written statement of fact in which a person (called the affiant) swears that the statement is true.

Affiliate Member *See* Associate Member.

Affirmation of Professional Responsibility A statement of the ethical guidelines of the National Federation of Paralegal Associations.

Agency Practitioner An individual authorized to practice before an administrative agency. This individual often does not have to be an attorney.

ALA Association of Legal Administrators.

Allegation A claimed fact.

Answer The pleading that responds to or answers the allegations of the complaint.

Antitrust Law The law governing unlawful restraints of trade, price fixing, and monopolies.

APA *See* Administrative Procedure Act.

Appearance Going to court to act on behalf of a party to the litigation. The first time this is done, the attorney files a *notice of appearance*.

Appellant The party bringing an appeal because of dissatisfaction with something the lower tribunal did.

Appellate Brief A document submitted to an appellate court containing arguments on whether a lower court made errors of law.

Appellate Jurisdiction The power of a court to hear an appeal of a case from a lower tribunal to determine whether it made any errors of law.

Appellee The party against whom an appeal is brought. Also called the *respondent*.

Apprentice A person in training for an occupation under the supervision of a full member of that occupation.

Arbitration In lieu of litigation, both sides agree to allow a neutral third party to resolve their dispute.

Arraignment A court proceeding in which the defendant is formally charged with a crime and enters a plea.

Arrest To take someone into custody in order to bring him or her before the proper authorities.

Assertive Confident, prepared, and tactfully demonstrative about one's accomplishments and needs.

Assigned Counsel An attorney appointed by the court and paid with government funds to represent an individual who cannot afford to hire an attorney.

Associate An attorney employee of a law firm who hopes eventually to become a partner.

Associated Pertaining to an attorney who is an associate in a law firm.

Attorney–Client Privilege A client and an attorney can refuse to disclose communications between them whose purpose was to facilitate the provision of legal services for the client.

Attorney General The chief attorney for the government. *See also* Opinion of the Attorney General.

Attorney of Record The attorney who has filed a notice of appearance. *See also* Appearance.

Attorney Work Product *See* Work-Product Rule.

Background Research Checking secondary sources to give you a general understanding of an area of law that is new to you.

Bail Property or a sum of money deposited with the court to ensure that the de-

fendant will reappear in court at designated times.

Bailiff A court employee who keeps order in the courtroom and renders general administrative assistance to the judge.

Bar Prevent or stop.

Barrister A lawyer in England who represents clients in the higher courts.

Bill A proposed statute.

Billable Tasks Those tasks requiring time that can be charged to a client.

Blind Ad A want ad that does not print the name and address of the prospective employer. The contact is made through a third party, e.g., the newspaper.

Career Ladder A formal promotion structure within a company or office.

Case (1) A legal matter in dispute or potential dispute. (2) The written decision of a court. *See also* Opinion.

Case Clerk An assistant to a paralegal; an entry-level paralegal.

Case Manager An experienced legal assistant who can coordinate or direct legal assistant activities on a major case or transaction.

Cause of Action A legally acceptable reason for suing.

Certificated Having met the qualifications for certification from a school or training program.

Certification The process by which a nongovernmental organization grants recognition to an individual who has met qualifications specified by that organization. *See also* Specialty Certification.

Certified Having complied with or met the qualifications for certification.

Certified Legal Assistant (CLA) The title bestowed by the National Association of Legal Assistants on a paralegal who has passed the CLA exam and has met other criteria of NALA. *See also* Specialty Certification.

Certified PLS A Certified Professional Legal Secretary. This status is achieved after passing an examination and meeting other requirements of NALS, the National Association of Legal Secretaries.

CFLA Certified Florida Legal Assistant. To earn this title, a paralegal must first pass the CLA (Certified Legal Assistant) exam of NALA, and then pass a special exam on Florida law.

Citation A reference to any written material. It is the "address" where the material can be found in the library. Also called a *cite*.

Cite (1) A citation. (2) To give the volume and page number, name of the book, etc. where written material can be found in a library.

Cite Checking Reading every cite in a document to determine whether the format of the cite conforms to the citation rules being used (e.g., the Bluebook rules), whether the quotations in the cite are accurate, etc.

Civil Dispute One private party suing another, or a private party suing the government, or the government suing a private party for a matter other than the commission of a crime.

CLA *See* Certified Legal Assistant.

CLAS Certified Legal Assistant Specialist (an advanced certification status of NALA).

CLE Continuing Legal Education. Undertaken after an individual has received his or her primary education or training in a law-related occupation.

Closed-Ended Question A relatively narrow question (e.g., how old are you?) that discourages the interviewee from rambling. Also called a *directed question*.

Closing The event during which steps are taken to finalize the transfer of an interest in property.

Code A set of rules, organized by subject matter.

Complaint The pleading filed by the plaintiff that tries to state a claim or cause of action against the defendant.

Confidential That which should not be revealed; pertaining to information that others do not have a right to receive.

Conflict of Interest Divided loyalty that actually or potentially places one of the participants to whom undivided loyalty is owed at a disadvantage. *See also* Divided Loyalty.

Conflicts Check A check of the client files of a law firm to help determine whether a conflict of interest might exist between a prospective client and current or past clients. The person performing this check is often called a *conflicts specialist*.

Conflicts of Law An area of the law that determines what law applies when a choice must be made between the laws of different, coequal legal systems, e.g., two states.

Contingent Fee A fee that is dependent on the outcome of the case.

Contract Attorney *See* Project Attorney.

Contract Paralegal A self-employed paralegal who often works for several different attorneys on a freelance basis. *See also* Freelance Paralegal.

Corporate Counsel The chief attorney of a corporation. Also called the *general counsel*.

Corporate Legal Department The law office within a corporation containing salaried attorneys (in-house attorneys) who advise and represent the corporation.

Counterclaim A claim or cause of action against the plaintiff stated in the defendant's answer.

Criminal Dispute A suit brought by the government for the alleged commission of a crime.

Cross-examination Questioning the witness called by the other side after direct examination.

Damages   An award of money paid by the wrongdoer to compensate the person who has been harmed.

Deep Pocket   Slang for the person or organization with enough money or other assets to be able to pay a judgment.

Default Judgment   A judgment for the plaintiff because the defendant failed to appear or to file an answer before the deadline.

Defense   An allegation of fact or the presentation of a legal theory that is offered to offset or defeat a claim or demand.

Deposition   A pretrial discovery device consisting of a question-and-answer session involving a party or witness designed to assist the other party prepare for trial. The person who is questioned is called the *deponent.*

Depo Summarizer   An employee whose main job is digesting discovery documents.

Digesting   Summarizing discovery documents. *See also* Depo Summarizer.

Digests   (1) Volumes that contain summaries of court opinions. These summaries are sometimes called *abstracts* or *squibs.* (2) Volumes that contain summaries of annotations in A.L.R., A.L.R.2d, etc.

Directed Question   *See* Closed-Ended Question.

Direct Examination   The first questioning of a witness you have called.

Discovery   Pretrial devices designed to assist a party prepare for trial. *See* Deposition, Interrogatories.

District Court   *See* United States District Court.

Diversity of Citizenship   The parties to the litigation are from different states, and the amount in controversy exceeds the amount specified by federal statute.

Docket Number   The number assigned to a case by the court.

Document Clerk   An individual whose main responsibility is to organize, file, code, or digest litigation or other client documents.

Draft   Write.

Enrolled Agent   An individual authorized to represent taxpayers at all administrative proceedings within the Internal Revenue Service—this person does not have to be an attorney.

Entry-Level Certification   Certification of individuals who have just begun their careers.

Estate   All the property left by a decedent from which his or her debts can be paid.

Ethics   Rules embodying standards of behavior to which members of an organization are expected to conform.

Evidence   That which is offered to help establish or disprove a factual position. A separate determination must be made on whether a particular item of evidence is relevant or irrelevant, admissible or inadmissible, etc.

Execution   Carrying out or enforcing a judgment.

Executive Branch   The branch of government that carries out, executes, or administers the law.

Exhibit   An item of physical or tangible evidence offered in court for inspection.

Ex Parte Hearing   A hearing at which only one party is present. A court order issued at such a hearing is an *ex parte order.*

Federal Question   A legal question that arises from the application of the United States Constitution, a statute of Congress, or a federal administrative regulation.

Fee-Generating Case   The case of a client who can pay a fee out of the damages awarded or from his or her independent resources.

Felony   A crime punishable by a sentence of one year or more.

Filed   Formally presented to a court.

First Instance, Court of A trial court; a court with original jurisdiction.

Formbook A manual that contains forms, checklists, practice techniques, etc. Also called a *practice manual* or *handbook*.

Forum The court where the case is to be tried.

Freelance Paralegal A self-employed paralegal who works for several different attorneys, or a self-employed paralegal who works directly for the public. Also referred to as an *independent paralegal*.

Functional Resume A resume that clusters skills and talents together regardless of when they were developed.

General Counsel The chief attorney in a corporate law department.

General Practitioner An attorney who handles any kind of case.

General Schedule (GS) The pay-scale system used in the federal government.

GOD The "Great Overtime Debate." *See* Exempt Employee.

Grand Jury A special jury whose duty is to hear evidence of felonies presented by the prosecutor to determine whether there is sufficient evidence to return an indictment against the defendant and cause him or her to stand trial on the charges.

Grounds Reasons.

Group Legal Services A form of legal insurance in which members of a group pay a set amount on a regular basis, for which they receive designated legal services. Also called *prepaid legal services*.

GS *See* General Schedule.

Handbook *See* Formbook.

Hearing Examiner One who presides over an administrative hearing.

Hearing Memorandum A memorandum of law submitted to a hearing officer.

Hearsay Testimony in court, or written evidence, of a statement made out of court when the statement is offered to show the truth of matters asserted therein, and thus resting for its value on the credibility of the out-of-court asserter.

Holding A court's answer to one of the legal issues in the case. Also called a *ruling*.

Hornbook A treatise that summarizes an area of the law.

Impeach To challenge; to attack the credibility of.

Independent Contractor One who operates his or her own business and contracts to do work for others who do not control the details of how that work is performed.

Independent Paralegal *See* Freelance Paralegal.

Indictment A formal document issued by a grand jury accusing the defendant of a crime. *See also* Grand Jury.

Indigent Poor, unable to pay for needed services.

Inferior Court A lower court.

Information A document accusing the defendant of a crime (used in states without a grand jury system).

Informational Interview An interview in which you find out about a particular kind of employment. It is *not* a job interview.

In-house Attorney An attorney who is an employee of a business corporation. *See* Corporate Legal Department.

Initial Appearance A court apperance during which the accused is told of the charges, a decision on bail is made, and arrangements for the next court proceeding are specified.

In Issue In dispute or question.

Instrument A formal document that gives expression to a legal act or agreement, e.g., a mortgage.

Intellectual Property Law The law governing patents, copyrights, trademarks, and trade names.

Interlocutory Appeal An appeal of a trial court ruling before the trial court reaches its final judgment.

Intermediate Appellate Court A court with appellate jurisdiction to which parties can appeal before they appeal to the highest court in the judicial system.

Internal-Interoffice Memorandum of Law A memorandum written for members of one's own office. *See also* Memorandum of Law.

Interrogatories A pretrial discovery device consisting of written questions sent by one party to another to assist the sender of the questions to prepare for trial.

Jargon Technical language; language that does not have an everyday meaning.

Job Bank A service that lists available jobs, usually available only to members of an organization.

Judgment The decision of the court on the controversy before it.

Judicare A system of paying private attorneys to provide legal services to the poor on a case-by-case basis.

Judicial Branch The branch of government with primary responsibility for interpreting laws and resolving disputes that arise under them.

Jurisdiction The power of a court. *See also* Geographic Jurisdiction, Subject-Matter Jurisdiction.

LAMA Legal Assistant Management Association.

Landmen Paralegals who work in the area of oil and gas law. Also called *land technicians*.

Lateral Hire An attorney, paralegal, or secretary who has been hired from another law office.

Law Clerk An employee of an attorney who is in law school studying to become an attorney or who has graduated from law school and is waiting to pass the bar examination. In Ontario, Canada, a law clerk is a trained professional doing independent legal work, which may include managerial duties, under the direction and guidance of a lawyer, and whose function is to relieve a lawyer of routine and administrative matters and to assist a lawyer in the more complex ones.

Law Directory A list of attorneys.

Law Review A legal periodical published by a law school. Sometimes called a *law journal*.

Legal Administrator An individual, usually a nonattorney, with broad management responsibility for a law office.

Legal Analysis The process of connecting a rule of law to a set of facts in order to determine how that rule might apply to a particular situation. The goal of the process is to solve a legal dispute or to prevent one from arising.

Legal Assistant *See* Paralegal.

Legal Assistant Clerk A person who assists a legal assistant in clerical tasks such as document numbering, alphabetizing, filing, and any other project that does not require substantive knowledge of litigation or of a particular transaction. *See also* Document Clerk.

Legal Assistant Division A few state bar associations, e.g., Texas, have established special divisions which paralegals can join as associate members.

Legal Assistant Manager A person responsible for recruiting, interviewing, and hiring legal assistants who spends little or no time working on client cases as a legal assistant. He or she may also be substantially involved in other matters pertaining to legal assistants, e.g., training, monitoring work assignments, designing budgets, and overseeing the billing of paralegal time. Also known as a *paralegal manager*.

Legal Executive A trained and certified employee of a solicitor in England; the equivalent of an American paralegal but with more training and credentials.

Legal Insurance *See* Group Legal Services.

Legal Issue A question of law; a question of what the law is, or what the law means, or how the law applies to a set of facts. If the dispute is over the truth or falsity of the facts, it is referred to as a *question of fact* or a *factual dispute.*

Legalman A nonattorney in the Navy who assists attorneys in the practice of law.

Legal Technician A self-employed paralegal who works for several different attorneys, or a self-employed paralegal who works directly for the public. Sometimes called an *independent paralegal* or a *freelance paralegal.*

Legislation (1) The process of making statutory law. (2) A statute.

Legislative Branch The branch of government with primary responsibility for making or enacting the law.

Legislative History All of the events that occur in the legislature before a bill is enacted into a statute.

Liable Legally responsible.

Licensed Independent Paralegal A paralegal who holds a limited license. *See* Limited Licensure.

Licensure The process by which an agency of government grants permission to persons meeting specified qualifications to engage in an occupation and to use a particular title.

Limited Licensure The process by which an agency of government grants permission to persons meeting specified qualifications to engage in designated activities that are now customarily (although not always exclusively) performed by another license holder, i.e., that are part of someone else's monopoly.

Limited Practice Officer A nonattorney in Washington state who has the authority to select and prepare designated legal documents pertaining to real estate closings.

Litigation The formal process of resolving legal controversies through special tribunals established for this purpose. The major tribunal is a court.

Magistrate A judicial officer having some but not all the powers of a judge.

Majority Opinion The opinion whose result and reasoning is supported by at least half plus one of the judges on the court.

Malpractice Serious wrongful conduct committed by an individual, usually a member of a profession.

Maritime Law *See* Admiralty Law.

Market Rate The prevailing rate in the area.

Martindale–Hubbell A national directory of attorneys.

Mediation In lieu of litigation, a neutral third party (the mediator) tries to encourage the parties to a dispute to reach a compromise.

Memorandum of Law A memorandum is simply a note, a comment, or a report. A legal memorandum is a written explanation of what the law is and how it might apply to a fact situation.

Misdemeanor A crime punishable by a sentence of less than a year.

Model Code of Professional Responsibility An earlier edition of the ethical rules governing attorneys recommended by the American Bar Association. The Model Code consisted of Ethical Considerations (ECs), which represented the objectives toward which each attorney should strive, and Disciplinary Rules (DRs), which were mandatory statements of the minimum conduct below which no attorney could fall without being subject to discipline.

Model Rules of Professional Conduct The current set of ethical rules governing attorneys recommended by the American Bar Association. These rules revised the ABA's earlier rules found in the Model Code of Professional Responsibility.

Model Standards and Guidelines for Utilization of Legal Assistants A statement of ethical and related guidelines of the National Association of Legal Assistants.

NALA National Association of Legal Assistants.

NALS National Association of Legal Secretaries. *See also* Certified PLS.

Neighborhood Legal Service Office A law office that serves the legal needs of the poor, often publicly funded.

Networking Establishing contacts with a relatively large number of people who might be helpful to you later. Similarly, you become such a contact for others.

NFPA National Federation of Paralegal Associations.

NJC Neighborhood Justice Center.

Nolle Prosequi A statement by the prosecutor that he or she is unwilling to prosecute the case.

Nonadversarial Proceeding Only one party appears in the proceeding, or both parties appear but they have no real controversy between them.

Nonbillable task A task for which an office cannot bill a client.

Notary Public A person who witnesses (i.e., attests to the authenticity of) signatures, administers oaths, and performs related tasks. In Europe, a notary often has more extensive authority.

Oath A sworn statement that what you say is true.

Of Counsel An attorney with a special status in the firm, e.g., a semiretired partner.

Office Sharing Attorneys with their own independent practices who share the use and cost of administration such as rent, copy machine, etc.

OJT On-the-job training.

Open-Ended Question A relatively broad question or request (e.g., "tell me about yourself") that forces the interviewee to organize his or her thoughts and to exert a relatively large measure of control over the kind and quantity of information provided.

Opinion A court's written explanation of how and why it applied the law to the specific facts before it to reach its decision. Also called a *case*. Opinions are printed in volumes called *reporters*.

Ordinance A law passed by the local legislative branch of government (e.g., city council).

Overhead The operating expenses of a business, e.g., cost of office space, furniture, equipment, insurance, clerical staff.

Paralegal A person with legal skills who works under the supervision of an attorney or who is otherwise authorized to use those skills; this person performs tasks that do not require all the skills of an attorney and that most secretaries are not trained to perform. Synonymous with *legal assistant*.

Paralegal Manager *See* Legal Assistant Manager.

Paralegal Specialist A job classification in the federal government.

Partner, Full An attorney who contributes the capital to create the firm and to expand it, who shares the profits and losses of the firm, who controls the management of the firm, and who decides whether the firm will go out of existence.

Partnership A group of individuals who practice law jointly and who share in the profits and losses of the venture.

People The state or government.

Percentage Fee The fee is a percentage of the amount involved in the transaction or award.

PI Cases Personal injury (tort) cases.

Plaintiff The party initiating the lawsuit.

Plea Bargaining An attempt to avoid a criminal trial by negotiating a plea, e.g., the defendant agrees to plead guilty to a lesser charge than initially brought.

Plead To deliver a formal statement or response.

Pleading A paper or document filed in court stating the position of one of the parties on the cause(s) of action or on the defense(s).

PLS Professional Legal Secretary. *See also* Certified PLS.

Practice of Law Engaging in any of the following activities on behalf of another: representation in court, representation in an agency proceeding, preparation of legal documents, or providing legal advice.

Preliminary Hearing A hearing during which the state is required to produce sufficient evidence to establish that there is probable cause to believe the defendant committed the crimes charged.

Prepaid Legal Services *See* Group Legal Services.

Pretrial Conference A meeting between the judge (or magistrate) and the attorneys to prepare the case for trial, and perhaps to make one last effort to settle the case.

Prima Facie On the face of it; that which would be legally sufficient, if believed, to support a verdict.

Private Law Firm A law firm that generates its income from the fees of individual clients.

Private Sector An office where the funds come from client fees or the corporate treasury.

Pro Bono Work Services that one volunteers to provide another at no charge.

Procedural Law The rules that govern the mechanics of resolving a dispute in court or in an administrative agency, e.g., a rule on the time a party has to respond to a complaint.

Professional Corporation The organization of a law practice as a corporation.

Project Attorney An attorney who works either part-time or full time over a relatively short period. Also referred to as a *contract attorney*.

Prosecution (1) Bringing a criminal case. (2) The attorney representing the government in a criminal case. (3) Going through the steps to litigate a civil case.

Prosecutor The attorney representing the government in a criminal case.

Public Benefits Government benefits.

Public Defender An attorney who is paid by the government to represent low-income people charged with crimes.

Public Sector An office where the funds come from charity or the government.

Rainmaker A person who brings fee-generating cases into the office.

RE Concerning

Record (1) The official collection of all the trial pleadings, exhibits, orders, and word-for-word testimony that took place during the trial. (2) A collection of data fields that constitute a single unit, e.g., employee record.

Redirect Examination Questioning your own witness (i.e., one you called) after cross-examination by the other side of that witness.

Referral Fee A fee received by an attorney from another attorney to whom the first attorney referred a client. Also called a *forwarding fee*.

Registered Agent An individual authorized to practice before the United States Patent Office. He or she does not have to be an attorney.

Registration The process by which individuals or institutions list their names on a roster kept by an agency of government or by a nongovernmental organization. The agency or organization will often establish qualifications for the right to register, and determine whether applicants meet these qualifications. Also called *enrollment*.

Regulation Any governmental or nongovernmental method of controlling conduct. *See also* Administrative Regulation.

Reporters Volumes containing the full text of court opinions.

Respondent *See* Appellee.

Retainer (1) The contract of employment between attorney and client. (2) An amount of money paid by a client to make certain that an attorney will be available to work for him or her. (3) The amount of money or other assets paid by the client as a form of deposit or advance payment against future fees and costs.

Review To examine in order to determine whether any errors of law were made. *See also* Appellate Jurisdiction.

Rule of Three Gross revenue generated through paralegal billing should equal three times a paralegal's salary.

Rules of Court Rules of procedure that govern the conduct of litigation before a particular court.

Satisfy To comply with a legal obligation.

Second-Tiered Attorney *See* Staff Attorney.

Senior Legal Assistant An experienced legal assistant with the ability to supervise or train other legal assistants. He or she may have developed a specialty in a practice area.

Service Company A business that sells particular services, usually to other businesses.

Service of Process The delivery of a formal notice to a defendant ordering him or her to appear in court to answer the allegations of the plaintiff.

Sole Practice A single attorney owns and manages the law firm.

Solicitor (1) A lawyer in England who handles day-to-day legal problems of clients with only limited rights to represent clients in certain lower courts. *See also* Barrister. (2) In the United States, some high government attorneys are called solicitors, e.g., the Solicitor-General of the United States who argues cases before the United States Supreme Court for the federal government.

Special Interest Group An organization that serves a particular group of people, e.g., a union.

Specialty Certification Official recognition of competency in a particular area of law. The National Association of Legal Assistants, for example, has a specialty certification program to recognize a person as a Certified Legal Assistant Specialist (CLAS). A paralegal must first become a Certified Legal Assistant (CLA), and then pass one of NALA's specialty exams. *See also* Certified Legal Assistant.

Staff Attorney A full-time attorney who has no expectation of becoming a full partner. Sometimes called a *second-tiered* attorney.

Staffing Agency An employment agency providing part-time employees for businesses. Often the business pays the agency, which in turn pays the employee.

Standard Form A preprinted form used frequently for various kinds of transactions or proceedings.

Statute A law passed by the legislature declaring, commanding, or prohibiting something. The statute is contained in a document called an *act*. If the statute applies to the general public or to a segment of the public, it is called a *public law* or *public statute*. If the statute applies to specifically named individuals or to groups—and has little or no permanence or general interest—it is called a *private law* or *private statute*.

Statutory Code A collection of statutes organized by subject matter.

Stay To delay the enforcement or the execution of a judgment.

Stipulated Agreed to.

Substantive Law The nonprocedural rules that govern rights and duties.

Summary Quick, expedited, without going through a full adversarial hearing.

Summary Judgment, Motion for A request for a party that a decision be reached on the basis of the pleadings alone, without going through an entire trial, because there is no dispute on any material facts.

Summons A formal notice from the court ordering the defendant to appear.

Superior Court Usually a trial court.

Supervising Legal Assistant Someone who spends about fifty percent of his or her time supervising other legal assistants and about fifty percent on client cases as a legal assistant.

Supra Above, mentioned or referred to earlier in the document.

Supreme Court The highest court in a judicial system. (In New York, however, the supreme court is a trial court.)

Surrogate Courts A special court with subject-matter jurisdiction over wills, probate, guardianships, etc.

Sustain To affirm the validity of.

Tort A private wrong or injury other than a breach of contract or the commission of a crime, although some breaches of contract and crimes can also constitute torts.

Transcribed Copied or written out word for word.

Transcript A word-for-word account.

Treatise, Legal A book written by a private individual (or by a public official writing as a private citizen) that provides an overview, summary, or commentary of a legal topic.

Treaty An international agreement between two or more countries.

Trial Book *See* Trial Brief.

Trial Brief An attorney's set of notes on how to conduct a trial, often placed in a *trial notebook*. Sometimes called a *trial manual* or *trial book.*

Trial de Novo A totally new fact-finding hearing.

Trial Manual *See* Trial Brief.

Trial Notebook A collection of documents, arguments, and strategies that an attorney plans to use during a trial. Some-times referred to as the *trial brief.* (It can mean the notebook in which the trial brief is placed.)

Unauthorized Practice of Law Services that constitute the practice of law, which a nonattorney has no authorization to provide. *See also* Practice of Law, Professional Judgment.

United States Court of Appeals The main federal appellate court just below the United States Supreme Court.

United States District Court The main federal trial court.

United States Supreme Court The highest court in the federal judicial system.

Venue The place of the trial.

Verdict The final conclusion of the jury.

Verification An affidavit stating that a party has read the complaint and swears that it is true to the best of his or her knowledge.

Veto A rejection by the chief executive of a bill passed by the legislature.

Voir Dire The oral examination of prospective jurors for purposes of selecting a jury.

Waiver The loss of a right or privilege because of an explicit rejection of it or because of a failure to claim it at the appropriate time.

Warrant An order from a judicial officer authorizing an act, e.g., the arrest of an individual, the search of property.

WESTLAW The legal research computer service of West Publishing Co.

Writ of Certiorari An order by an appellate court requiring a lower court to certify the record of a lower court proceeding and to send it up to the appellate court which had decided to accept the appeal.

Index

A

▪ D

■ E

■ F

▪ G

▪ T

■ U

■ V

■ W

▪ Y

▪ Z